BIG SEX LITTLE DEATH

SUSIE BRIGHT

SEAL PRESS

OTHER TITLES BY SUSIE BRIGHT

"Lusty. Outspoken. Unapologetic. Susie Bright's life is a Molotov cocktail wrapped in leopard print, a star-spangled call to political action, and a rousing paean to the pleasures of the body. Her riveting chronicle urges us to seize life by the balls, and to savor our freedom. Bright's voice is necessary and galvanizing."

—Rachel Resnick, author of *Love Junkie*

"I have always admired Susie for inspiring others to take control of their sex lives, and in her memoir, you'll get to read about how a sexual revolutionist is made. *Big Sex Little Death* makes me want to dust off my peace symbols and have a virtual march online, chanting, 'MAKE LOVE NOT WAR!'"

—Betty Dodson, PhD, author of *My Sexual Revolution*

"Inspiring and prophetic. Bright balances her way along the tightrope between Big Sex and Little Death with considerable honesty, wit, and empathy."

—Paul Krassner, author of *Confessions of a Raving, Unconfined Nut*

"Susie Bright's life story truly is stranger than fiction. From Catholic Girl Scout to revolutionist young woman to respected journalist, sexual politics pioneer, and mother, she spares no detail as she recounts the adventure, sacrifice, and controversy that comprise her life story."

—Harriet Lerner, PhD, author of *The Dance of Anger*

"Susie's memoir grabbed me and brought me way close up to a period of time that's only been covered from the outside—perhaps explained by a man or two—but not written from the deep-pink inside of an awesome giant girl brain like hers."

—Jill Soloway, playwright, screenwriter, "Six Feet Under," "United States of Tara"

Big Sex Little Death
A Memoir

Copyright © 2011 by Susie Bright

Published by
Seal Press
A Member of the Perseus Books Group
1700 Fourth Street
Berkeley, California

Library of Congress Cataloging-in-Publication Data

Bright, Susie, 1958-
  Big sex, little death : a memoir / Susie Bright.
    p. cm.
  ISBN 978-1-58005-264-1
  1. Bright, Susie, 1958- 2. Bright, Susie, 1958—Sexual behavior. 3. Feminists—United States—Biography. 4. Women radicals—United States—Biography. 5. Women socialists—United States—Biography. 6. Women adventurers—United States—Biography. 7. Lesbians—United States—Biography. 8. Sex—Political aspects—United States—History—20th century. 9. On our backs. 10. Socialist International (1951-)—Biography. I. Title.
  CT275.B6824A3 2011
  305.42092—dc22
  [B]
                              2010030224

Cover design by Natalya Balnova
Cover photo: Becky With White Veil © Jessica Tanzer Conroy
Interior design by Tabitha Lahr
Printed in the United States of America
Distributed by Publishers Group West

In order to respect the privacy of individuals mentioned in the book, the author has changed some of their names.

This book is dedicated to:

Elizabeth Joanne Halloran Bright
1925–2004

&

William Oliver Bright
1927–2006

CONTENTS

ALL ALONG THE GIRLTOWER

PREFACE

"At the risk of making a dozen devoted enemies for life, I can only say that the whiffs I get from the ink of [women writers] are fey, old-hat, Quaintsy Goysy, tiny, too dykily psychotic, crippled, creepish, fashionable, frigid, outer-Baroque, maquillé in mannequin's whimsy, or else bright and stillborn."

—Norman Mailer, *Advertisements for Myself*

HOW DOES A WOMAN, an American woman born in midcentury, write a memoir? The chutzpah and the *femmechismo* needed to undertake the project go against the apron. I was raised with "Don't think you're so big." Yet to be a writer at all, you have to inflict your ego on a page and stake your reputation. To be a poet, the effect should be transcendent, and disarming.

I already knew the best result of my memoir before I finished it. The days of my writing—a couple years in earnest—inspired many of the family and friends around me to write their story, to put a bit of their legacy in ink. Reading what *they* had to say was a revelation. If more of us knew the story of our tribe—and carried it from one generation to the next—it seems like the interest would pay off.

I know so little of my own family history that, when I was young, I often read memoirs in search of blood relation. I wanted to be Emma Goldman. I wanted to digest Doris Lessing's *Golden Notebooks* like biscuits. I felt like Harriet the Spy, looking for a dumbwaiter to hide in, scribbling down all I witnessed.

At the onset of my memoir, I thought I would bring myself up to date on the autobiography racket. I researched the current bestsellers among women authors who had contemplated their life's journey. The results were so dispiriting: diet books. The weighty befores and afters. You look up men's memoirs and find some guy climbing a mountain with his bare teeth—the parallel view for women are the mountains of cookies they rejected or succumbed to.

The next tier of best-selling female memoirs, often overlapping with the diet tales, is the tell-all by a movie star, athlete, or political figure. The first two subjects are designed to exploit gossip—the last are so boring and circumspect you wonder if they're funded by government cheese.

The last group of popular memoirs—and this goes across the gender divide—are the ones in which the author unloads a great deal of weight in the form of psychic burdens from childhood. The subject is nearly driven mad by lunatic or intoxicated parenting, sidetracked by years of self-destruction bred into her family line, only to be redeemed at the end by a clean break from addiction and pathology.

I'm as vulnerable as anyone to the toxicity of the American nuclear family. But I wouldn't call it disease or moral failure as much as I would point the finger at a system that grinds people down like a metal file. Who doesn't need a drink? Who isn't going to crack and lash out at the people they love? I have a lot of sympathy for the dark places in my family history, while at the same time repeating my mantra, "This can't go on."

I came of age and became a sexual adult at the moment that women—in jeans and no bras, of course—were taking to the streets. Sexual liberation and feminism were inseparable topics to my best friends in high school. As I entered my twenties and feminists began to disown one another over sexual expression, it reminded me all too well of what I went though in the labor movement, civil rights, the Left—"let the weak fight among themselves." Radical feminists didn't need FBI infiltration—the mechanism for sisterly cannibalization was already well under way.

When I was first involved in politics, it was part of our group ethos not to proclaim our names and so-called talent all over the map—it went against our sense of the collective. When people ask me how I became a professional writer, I couldn't give them a "climb the ladder" scenario, because I went out my way to be part of a group. Everyone was supposed to know how to write, talk, run a web press, unclog a toilet, stage a demonstration.

I saw a news article today by a corporate headhunter who said he liked to get under his applicants' skin by asking them how, exactly, they were most misunderstood. What an endearing literary question!

It was a good interrogation to ask myself, midmemoir. What do people think about me that is off base? And how do I gauge this misperception?

Most people unfamiliar with my work imagine that anyone with the youthful nickname of Susie Sexpert must be an adolescent airhead, a happy but too-dim nympho, someone who set out to shock her strict parents—or, alternatively, was raised in a den of hedonists.

They also think, along the "dumb blond" trajectory, that I just haven't thought things through, about where sexual liberation might lead—how a female Narcissus could drown in a pool of clitoral self-absorption and drag unfortunate others with her.

I would say, for one, I haven't broken any records in sexual adventure, but I have always been curious—and empathetic. I haven't set any records in sexual feats or numbers—far from it. I was motivated, always, from the sting of social injustice—the cry of "That isn't fair!" gets a lot more impulsive behavior from me than "I want to get off."

My parents were far more radical than I am, because of basic changes in their generation: My mother didn't die in childbirth. She went to college. My parents married even though they weren't of the same religion. They divorced—before that became the American way of life. My father's ashes can be found in a Native burial ground instead of a WASP family plot. They strayed so much further than I did from their immediate ancestors. They were better educated than I, but I have had a bigger mouth. I don't know who to blame for that.

The other side of my character, the one that isn't the "*Sí, se puede*" version of Auntie Mame, is exemplified by loss, constant and too-early. I'm more preoccupied with people dying than with people coming.

In the world of sexual risk and revolutionary politics, a lot of voyagers die before their time. Evangelist Jerry Falwell famously preached at feminists, queers, and integrationists that all their fatal problems—their assassinations and plagues—were retribution from an angry God, who wanted people to keep their legs crossed and drink at the "colored fountain."

I don't believe in God or retribution, but I accept that there are consequences from pushing, *hard*. Pioneers don't look good on an actuarial table. Sex radicals tend to be excellent at hospice care, at the rites of the dying, at memories that leave legacies. Perhaps because we are blunt about sex, we're not so afraid of death's taboo, either.

Every loss uncovers an edge about why we persevere in spite of the empty space. Sex—its quixotic vitality, not its banal marketability—is one of those things that makes you feel like *I'm not done yet.*

This memoir is a progress, not a final deliverance. You'll see some of the flowers that pressed themselves into my scrapbook. Using Mr. Mailer's criteria, I'm going for "dykily psychotic," definitely "bright," and, hopefully, crowning.

Had I the heavens' embroidered cloths,
Enwrought with golden and silver light,
The blue and the dim and the dark cloths
Of night and light and the half-light,

I would spread the cloths under your feet:
But I, being poor, have only my dreams;
I have spread my dreams under your feet;
Tread softly because you tread on my dreams.

—W. B. Yeats

FIRST
BITES

BABY TEETH

I COULDN'T SLEEP LAST NIGHT. Every drunk yelling under the window finally slipped away by 4:00 AM and left the street silent. My beloved was deep in slumber. I curled up against his back and woke him up.

"Jon, tell me a story," I said. "You know, a really personal story."

It's a little joke between us that if he talks to me in intimate, sonorous tones, I will fall into a dead sleep. The more secret the story, the sooner I'll drift off.

I thought of a question to get him started. "When you were a little boy, what was the first time you can remember getting hurt?"

Jon remembered a spill. He took a fall in the public commons of a housing project in State College, Pennsylvania. He was running—tripped and scraped his knee on the edge of a slate staircase. He remembered the blood pouring out of his knee, the shock of all that red ink. His mother came running out, bundled him up, wiped his tears. I've always wanted to be bundled like that.

I fell asleep dreaming of a mommy's blanket.

I remember the first time I got hurt. I was bit by a little girl, hard enough to bleed. I was in a daycare, the first daycare I can remember. My mother was working as a secretary, and we were living in Berkeley after her divorce from my father.

I hated this daycare. The rooms were large, cold—even in my memories it looks like a set from *One Flew Over the Cuckoo's Nest*. When the teachers got impatient with you, they rolled out dark, narrow wooden panels, seven feet high, that they could wheel into position and use to effectively trap you in a box, anywhere on the floor.

You could see light at the top—the panels did not reach the ceiling—but otherwise it was like being stuck in a refrigerator. You lay on the floor inside your "box," and they told you not to make a sound or it would get worse.

Outside the classroom area, there was an asphalt yard. One afternoon a little girl with raven curls and blue eyes—I remember being struck by how pretty she was, even at two—came right up to me, grabbed my forearm, and sank her teeth in.

I have no idea why. I yelled bloody murder; I saw the marks and red holes welt up on my skin. Someone—not our mothers—rushed over and punished both of us. We were walled up in separate boxes.

I had complained about the box to my mother, with no effect, before. But this time, there was no hiding the injury. I remember her outrage—and her impulse. Elizabeth jumped into the car and I sat at home watching the kitchen clock, imagining the tongue thrashing she was going to give them. I never had to go back there again. When she came home, she was grim, but I could tell it was over.

There's never any misunderstanding about broken skin. No "What if?" or "Should I care?" We yell or cry out, hit or block; there's no wondering how we feel.

When I first started teaching about sex, in my thirties, I tried to whittle down what it was that people viscerally react to when sex horrifies them. I kept coming back to our openings, the expected and unexpected openings to the body. We don't like invasions we didn't ask for.

I did an exercise with a classroom of mine, students analyzing sexual representation. I said, "Let's try to get to the nitty-gritty of what is called 'offensive.' Let's stop talking about it." I gave them all crayons and butcher paper, reminiscent of a daycare.

I set the mood. "I want you to quickly sketch the most disgusting, abhorrent thing you can think of, the thing you are utterly repelled by, the thing that you cannot endure for one second."

I told them I didn't care if it was phobic, or irrational, or if everyone would probably agree with their choice. Just to go for it.

I asked them to draw two pictures. One that depicted an "offensive" situation that was not about sex. Another one that was pointedly sexual.

We pinned the drawings to the wall. It was a parade of horrors and sillies. It was hard to stop laughing or gasping. Of course, most of the students were not adept renderers, and their pictures were crude. I had given them only a few minutes.

The nonsexual themes of offense evoked brutal violence, the monster versus the mouse. Images of people hurting children, or animals, or each other in a vast war. The red crayon was used to draw the cuts, the explosions, the cruelty. The world split open. Faces with blue tears pouring out of the eyes. Anyone can draw that.

The sexual offenses were sometimes fetishistic, other times universal. Many students went to shit. One student drew an ice cube tray of "shit-sicles"—god, how did he ever think of that? There were the bugaboos of the sexually inexperienced: anal sex, *ew*. Oral sex, ugh. One young man drew a dripping snatch, the horror. But others drew a penis that wouldn't stop ejaculating, choking its recipient. Gang rape was represented. One young woman drew the aftermath line of a violent abortion. Her belly and vagina cut open. Someone drew a penis forced in another's ear.

The themes of bullying and powerlessness unified us. But sexual confessions were more surreal. They were unusual . . . or symbolic. The students knew that their fears were unlikely to come true, or were exaggerated—but the horror persisted nevertheless.

I kept saying, "Look at the openings." The place where we say, "I can push out, but you can't push in."

We take tremendous pleasure in those same places, but there's no ignoring their perilous entry. We don't want to be caught off guard; we don't want to be preempted and struck.

Our nose, ears. Eyes, mouths, vaginas. Anuses. Our tender flesh. We arrive bundled up, and we don't want any poking. We work up the courage to invite another's hands, tongue, a soft or persistent pleasure.

It's the opposite of automatic. When you're born, you don't know you're separate from your mother. As your baby-self grows, it starts to dawn on you: The umbilical cord is gone. You become conscious of where you begin and where your mother ends. You realize you have to protect your own tender openings.

I didn't want to get bit by that pretty little girl at the evil day-care. She reminded me of Rose Red. I was Snow White. I was smitten with her perfect face and piercing eyes. I thought she was coming to me with a wreath of flowers, instead of incisors.

So my early desire was nipped. I wanted to smell, to listen, to taste, to be felt and achingly fondled . . . with discrimination. I wanted to speak my mind and be understood. That bite proved something I wasn't able to get across any other way.

Would I have learned anything without being hurt? I was hurt too much, like most of us . . . and not by incoherent, dazzling two-year-olds. More by the wall-boxers. There were way too many of them.

I was bullied as a kid because I was intellectually precocious but socially inappropriate. I read constantly, but I had my thumb in my mouth half the time. My moral universe was populated with fairytales my mother read me, opera librettos and folk songs she'd sing to me—I had no idea what kids were talking about down the street. I wore thick glasses at a time when you didn't see many children with prescription lenses. My shoes were funny and the hems of my hand-sewn dresses fell below my knees. I attended ten schools before I was seventeen and had a vocabulary that didn't sound as if it had come from anywhere nearby, because we never had.

My mother and I moved every year or two, all our belongings stuffed into a 1963 VW Bug. When Elizabeth got fed up with something, she cleared out. There was no doubting the injustice that propelled her.

One time she was teaching English and German at a local high school in Contra Costa County, the barren eastern side of the San Francisco Bay Area. It was Christmastime, and she decorated her classroom with a few UNICEF cards, *National Geographic*–style photographs of people celebrating seasonal holidays all over the world. I remember urging her to put the Diwali card in the best-lit corner, because I loved the photograph of the little Indian girls surrounded by candles, bangles sparkling on their arms.

Elizabeth had costume jewelry pins to wear for all the holidays; I loved helping her clasp them to her Jackie Kennedy shifts. She was so slim, she could carry them off like a model—and would wear every bright color, including fuchsia lipstick, especially on drab days. For Diwali, she wore some of her blue and gold glass bangles from the early days of her marriage when she had lived in Bangalore with my father.

The vice principal came into the classroom the first afternoon of Diwali—you had to wonder, who'd tipped him off about a Hindi holiday?

"He told me to take the cards down," Elizabeth said, "*this instant*—that UNICEF was a front for the Communist Party and would *not* be tolerated at Amador High." She laughed, as if CP members would take an interest in a rural spur of California that was about to change from walnut groves to suburban tract homes.

"What did you say, Mommy? What does that mean?"

Elizabeth dragged in some empty milk cartons from the car to load our records and books. She had already made the decision to move. "I told him he was an idiot."

I didn't get explicit political rhetoric in our house. It was all implied. I had no idea what communism was, or what its opposite might be. Hating winter solstice?

What I understood was that there were bigots and bullies everywhere, and you coped with them by giving them a piece of your mind and then turning your back on them forever. Did the silent treatment teach them a lesson? I was never there long enough to find out.

After 1965, I knew the drill. I lifted my most beloved possession, our fifteen-inch black-and-white Zenith, into the front seat, tucked under my feet. I couldn't wait to get to our next destination and plug it in. From Contra Costa County, we moved to Riverside County, in the tumbleweeds. Then the San Gabriel Valley Mountains. Up to the Bay Area, back down to Los Angeles. There was a tiny hole in the VW's running boards where you could see the road rushing underneath us, like water. I daydreamed that if I were small enough, I could slip right through.

I was thrilled when my mother turned her sword of indignation on others—but I was afraid to be alone with her. She'd get in these moods. I didn't see them coming when I was small, but by the time I was six, I was adept at avoiding her. Just not adept enough. Sometimes she'd ambush me in the night, storming out into the living room, where I slept on the sofa, and throwing a bucket of dishwater on my snoring body. An excellent cure for snoring. Or she'd turn on me in the kitchen with a wooden spoon or her hand across my face. I was "an idiot," too. Then she'd cry and say she was sorry. She wanted me to hold her tight. She couldn't help that she wished me dead, along with everyone else who was tormenting her.

The boys' dean at Amador High School got off light, in my estimation.

As I grew older, I wished Elizabeth would leave me and go away forever. Finally, she did. The bite is quite lasting, isn't it? Only now can I look at some of my memories, the ones I don't have a photograph to prompt, and see how all the little marks come together.

INDIA

PRETEND I WAS BORN IN INDIA. I'll wind your worn sari around my shoulders and waist. I'll take your bright pink lipstick and put a mark on my forehead. We'll pretend that all the freckles are gone. I'll bathe in lemon juice, and they'll disappear. My hair will be so black, glossy, and long that I'll be able to sit on it, or twist it up on top of my head like Sita.

I know where all my mom's Ravi Shankar records are. I can put the needle down on the vinyl without scratching. I know the location of the jam jar where she keeps her sandalwood.

My mom didn't make jam, and her mom . . . I don't know. Agnes Williams Halloran, my maternal grandmother, died from pneumonia in 1932, shortly after giving birth to her fifth child. I do know she had a lively life before she married and started having babies—she was the first Nickelodeon piano player in Fargo, North Dakota. She got beautiful autographed photographs and letters from all the early stars, and judging from her collection of dark-eyed femme fatales, like Theda Bara and Pola Negri, I think she would have understood why I wanted to pretend I was born in India, somewhere very far away from milquetoast and freckles.

My first memories are of this game: "Pretend I Was Born in India." I would beg my mom to play with me in our apartment in Berkeley, on McGee Street, shortly after my parents' divorce. They had lived in Bangalore in the fifties, as linguists and travelers, and my mom had gotten pregnant on their voyage home. The things they had brought home in their suitcases were the furnishings I lived with as long as I stayed with my mother. It had nothing to do with the hippie embrace of all things Indian that emerged in the sixties. It was mythological. It was proto-beat Berkeley.

When we moved to a new apartment, we'd turn one of the moving boxes upside down and put the red-and-white Indian tablecloth on it, and that was the coffee table. The prayer statue of Krishna dancing with his flute might go in one corner of sunlight, and the one where he is a baby, playing with his ball of butter, might go next to him.

My mom had a set of twenty-some cloth dolls representing all the castes in India, every sort of person, perfectly dressed and bejeweled. The pale-skinned raja has a sword and red satin jacket with gold braid and pearls, while the untouchable mother is barefoot, her baby tied to her back and a brass pot sewn at the top of her soft, kinky braids.

She told me all the stories of what each caste meant—and I was beside myself over the inequity. I foisted my Cinderella fantasies on the entire doll collection, making the Brahmins leave their castles in disgrace while the teachers and carpenters and slaves got to take all their jewelry.

I was actually born in Arlington, Virginia, as my parents stopped in nearby D.C. when they reentered the country, looking for English as a second language jobs. I have some photos of them lying on a blanket on the banks of the Potomac with me, an infant, in April, and they look very hot but blissful. My mom said they were in brick government housing that was like an oven. She hated it there.

When I would ask her later what it was like "having a baby," she said that as they wheeled her into the hospital, she was so mad that it had turned out to be the "Confederate" Virginia location, instead of D.C., that her last words were "I don't want my baby born in the South!" Then they gave her a shot and she didn't remember anything else.

At my christening, in a Catholic church, the witnesses—other linguists—were also recent arrivals to the United States. The women were dressed in saris; my mom's long hair was in a bun, and her gold bangles cascaded down her arms.

My dad, who had been studying every writing system and language in India, writing books on Tamil, essays on Sanskrit, was finishing his PhD in a different kind of "Indian" language, with the Karuk Native American tribe in Northern California, on the Klamath River. My mother had published her field notes, songs, and stories on other California tribes, such as the Patwin, Hoopa, and Yurok. Even after their divorce, they would still go to brush dances, sometimes to hand me off for a weekend or school-break visit.

To say that I didn't really get the difference between "Indian" and "Indian" for a very long time is an understatement. I gathered only that there was this sensual, spiritually omnipresent world, a "gone" world that was under attack, and then there was a white, square world, pinched and plastic, away from which parents couldn't distance themselves enough.

My parents found that world, their India and Indians, through their education in Berkeley. In my young childhood, I had no idea how far they'd come.

THE IRISH SIDE

Irish are Spaniards who got lost in the mist . . .
—Bob Callahan

THE FIRST PERSON IN MY mother's family to come to California was my great-aunt Tessie Halloran, who went to make her living as a governess in a Hollywood home.

She came home to Minnesota one Christmas "a great success," loaded down with navel oranges and wearing a two-piece suit the color of a peach. No one in my family had ever worn any other color than blue or black or brown. The children didn't know that peach-colored fabric existed, and when they touched Tessie's outfit, they worried that it would melt away like ice cream.

In St. Paul at the time, there were signs on respectable establishments that said NO DOGS, NO INDIANS, NO IRISH. There was no work in the ghetto, and Tessie's good fortune out west was intoxicating. Soon one Halloran after another was either joining the service or moving out to San Francisco to work in the Hunters Point shipyard.

My mom stopped speaking to and corresponding with her blood relatives when I was seven, after several years of brinkmanship. It started out, from what I could see, as a solitary silent treatment against her father, to whom she never introduced me. Nor did I ever see her turn to him for a look or a word. Not once—his eldest daughter. That was Jack Halloran.

Then there was her brother, Patrick James, or Bud. I never met him, the oldest of the five, and my mom would offer his name only reluctantly, spilling out a few tearful words: "I worshipped Bud when we were kids."

My dad, the "leak" for every fact of my maternal history, told me that Uncle Bud had joined the army, had been a sergeant of a division in the CCC, and was a regular war hero . . . but that he'd come back a regular drunk. He had abandoned his wife and eight children, just like his father had done to him and the girls in the Depression.

My mom would sob, as if marked for damnation, "And I introduced him to Georgia"—Bud's wife. I never met her, either. At nineteen years old, she looked so pretty in her Red Cross outfit in a portrait I discovered in my mother's hatboxes. My family threw themselves into the war effort. But my mother could never face Georgia again, either, for the sin of her matchmaking.

The shame of all the history, the errors, the regrets. A river you could drown a city in. No Dogs, No Indians, No Irish. There was something about being the last group on that sign that was the last nail in the coffin.

Why were the Irish so despised? They were dirty, they were drunk, they were hungry, and they were liars—the final two being somewhat related. And their religion was full of smoke and powders and infinite chambers of ghosts—mysteries for the sake of mysteries.

My mom didn't drink; I rarely saw her with a beer. She was obsessive about cleaning up one side and down another. If I never scrub another floor again, it will be one too many.

One time when I was just little, she put two yardsticks like a giant X on the bare floor, and taught me an Irish jig. She laughed and threw her head back, the sweat making her flat hair curly. Her feet never tripped or hesitated. She could sing or recite epics that went on for verse after verse, as if she were inventing them on the spot. Maybe she was.

But if we were around other Irish Catholics who did the same things, the corners of her mouth drew tight. She was thinking something vicious, and her parting words would pinch as hard as her hand on my shoulder, to steer me away from "that awful clan."

She'd take me to church, refuse Communion for herself, and after all that trouble to get dressed up in our patent leather shoes, she'd leave at the end of the service, furious that they'd given up the Latin and provoked by the priest's banality. "Those bastards!" she'd say.

When I was in my thirties, I got an invitation from a gay group in Belfast who invited me to speak at an exhibition. I was flattered and thought, *Here's something I can tell Mama, and she'll be proud.*

She was ticked off. "Who's paying for it, Susie?" she asked, as if she'd just caught their hand in her pocket.

"Don't trust a word they say," she said, when I told her the hosts were still fundraising. "Don't you forward them one penny, because you'll never see it again."

My mouth dropped. My mother, who wouldn't tolerate a single cliché related to any racial stereotype, was a bigot when it came to our cousins across the way.

My mother was born in Fargo, North Dakota, christened Elizabeth Joanne and nicknamed Betty Jo. Then just Jo. She was the first of the first generation to break away. Patrick James, Betty Jo, Molly, Frannie, and Pid—but she was the "smart" one. People who've wondered what my parents had to say about my path have no idea that my parents were the ones who broke the cardinal rules, not me. My mom was the first in her family to go to college. The nuns told her she would burn in hell if she attended the public University of Minnesota in Dinkytown. She cackled every time she relived the story, proclaiming, "I couldn't wait."

She was the first in the family to marry outside the faith, to divorce, to bear only one child. More important, she didn't die bearing children—the number one cause of death among Halloran women.

She played footsie with my father in Greek class. She was the first girl he ever kissed. She and he agreed, in separate conversations with me, that he was the only straight man studying classical languages and anthropology at the University of California. When I "came out" to my parents, it was anticlimactic—together, they'd had far more of a gay social life and witnessed more emerging queer history after World War II than I'd seen in my lifetime. They preferred gay life, intellectually and socially, but were really relieved to find each other, an erotic and intimate connection in an otherwise lavender universe. My dad would say,

"I wondered if I was gay. But I dreamed about Rita Hayworth, Esther Williams, and your mom."

My mom would never have described herself as a fag hag: first of all, because she would never, ever use an epithet, no matter how good-natured; and second, because she thought of herself as Lucy Van Pelt, completely fed up with virtually everyone.

When my aunt Molly died, the one sister who didn't let my mother disappear altogether, I found out that Molly had collected what was left of the family scrapbooks. I was amazed to find a "baby book" for my mom and her brother, which their mother, Agnes, had kept until the first two kids were toddlers. I was shocked at the prosperity the little book implied. How could they have kept a lovely illustrated diary like this when a few years later my mom was on the street, collecting rice from relief wagons with her head hanging down?

My grandmother Agnes died in my twelve-year-old mother's arms while the little ones screamed with hunger in the same one-room apartment. Her family's farm had been foreclosed on, and her husband had abandoned her.

But in her teens, my grandmother had had another life. She was the glamorous Nickelodeon piano player, Fargo's one and only. When Agnes was first married, things were . . . okay. She had the time and good health to make a baby book. Her husband, Jack's, writing was beautiful and filled some of the pages with their first two children's accomplishments. Jack was selling tractors for John Deere, and he would send perfectly fountain-penned post-cards from the road: "Wish you were here; kiss the babies."

"Yes, he was famous for his hand," my mom admitted when I showed her the evidence that her father had once been something more than a complete basket case.

She looked at the postcard I showed her as if it were a museum piece, not connected to her. How could this be the same guy who hid out and let the orphanage come pick up the children when his wife died, the man whose hands shook in photographs, the one who looked like Ichabod Crane in his black duster?

The baby book was composed before the crash, in the mid-twenties, before the banks took Grandmother Halloran's farm, before skid row claimed my grandfather's allegiance. The baby books were full of promise. On the page where the doting parents record Baby's First Word, instead of "Da" or Mama," Elizabeth first word was "Bud." Written in that beautiful cursive pen.

When my mom was dying a few years ago, she was on a lot of morphine, and she gaily told stories I'd been waiting to hear all my life. I wasn't ready for it; I'd given up so long ago ever hearing anything from her lips.

When I was a child in Berkeley, I would make the mistake of asking, "What was it like when you were my age?" She'd cry as if I'd stuck her with a pin, her face accusing me, as if she were the little one and I was too cruel. I didn't ask her again after I started to read.

When my mother died, cancer protruding all over her body in giant lumps and bumps, she wasn't grieving. She could recite a chapter of her life without blinking, even laughing at it. She didn't cry at all, except when she was looking for her grandmother, in bouts of sleepwalking.

I realized after one of her nocturnal walks that my mom could barely remember her birth mother, because her only childhood memories were of a sick and dying woman who kept getting pregnant. "Mama" was a saint, not a person.

Instead, my mom looked to her real mother figure, her grandmother. "My grandma," she told me, during one of her loquacious Fentanyl-patch moments, "was the only person in my family who ever praised me or told me I was good. She told me I was smart and I could do anything."

Forty-plus years it took to hear that.

My mother was a star; when I meet people who still remember her, they shake their heads and remember an incandescent anecdote where she burned hot, in either temper or passion or blistering empathy. She felt things so deeply, and she could bury them just as long.

Elizabeth told me a story one morning, when we were meditating on the plum blossom outside her window. "When Grandma still had the farm," she said, "there was a fence at the edge of the property right on the highway, where the Greyhound bus passed every day on its way west.

"There was a song on the radio I liked then—it was Jules Verne Allen, that Texas cowboy—'The Red River Valley.'"

> *I've been thinking a long time, my darling*
> *Of the sweet words you never would say*
> *Now, alas, must my fond hopes all vanish*
> *For they say you are going away*

"I would sit on that fence post every afternoon!" She laughed as if the memory of her legs swinging on the fence were a comic newsreel. "I was waiting for the bus to come by, bawling out 'The Red River Valley' at the top of my lungs—because I knew that one day, the bus driver would hear me, and everyone on the bus would clap their hands and they'd stop the bus and pick me up and take me out to Hollywood, where I would be a big star!"

I can see the plow behind her, and our California destiny—way, way out, in front of those wheels.

WAY OUT WEST

WHEN I WAS A LITTLE GIRL and asked Grandma Bright, my dad's mother, where the Brights came from, she said one word: "Kansas."

I was hoping for a thrilling immigrant experience, like my mother's—but no, it was the Bright story, an undramatic yawn.

I appreciate my grandmother Ethel now. I'd give anything to sit next to her at my sewing machine or eat one of her egg salad sandwiches. But as a child, although I didn't see her very often, I thought the lives she and my grandfather Ollie led were dull. My dad, Bill, had me for school vacation visits a couple times a year, and we would always visit Oxnard to see his folks. Oxnard, at the time, was like the Wichita of California.

We had cottage cheese and peaches for lunch. Grandma wouldn't eat spaghetti because it was a "foreign" food. She made enormous quilts and braided rugs from scraps, all day, every day, plus dozens of aprons and potholders perfectly stitched with rick-rack. No store-bought clothes, ever. She canned everything, and since most of the Brights were farmers, there was a lot to can. She let me put on her big smock and go out and pick berries, or take a hoe and make rows in the garden beds. It was the same thing, every day, every visit. Her peanut butter and jelly sandwiches were mitered as neat and perfect as every square on one of her quilts.

My grandpa was a butcher and ran a chicken ranch. They had meat on the table every day during the Depression. Ollie was the one who gleefully called me "Susie," first thing from the hospital, ruining my parents' intentions to call me "Susannah" in all its three-syllable glory. "Susie" stuck. You can see photos of him lifting me in the air, under the big willow tree in their back yard, his dirty suspenders and dungarees fit to burst, a huge smile on his face.

I would love to remember that smile, and I do feel it when I look at the old snapshots. But by the time I could remember visiting my grandparents, my grandpa didn't say a word—he had been rendered mute by Parkinson's disease—and he sat in a living room La-Z-Boy, his mouth a thin tight line. I was afraid of him. His hands shook all the time, and when Grandma helped him to the kitchen to eat, the sound of them clattering on the Formica table-top scared me half to death. My grandma would heat paraffin wax every morning and evening for him to soak his fingers and feet in.

He spent a decade in this condition before his death, which was my introduction to the cruelty of "being kept alive whether you like it or not." Why would no one talk about it? I knew that my grandpa—who loved life so much, who'd sing "Golden River" and drive a plow, who couldn't wait to get a Model T and drive to the seashore—had never wanted to be in a chair watching Lawrence Welk reruns. But that's how everyone acted in Oxnard—you kept going because you had to keep going, and you did not question the rules.

My stepmother Lise said to me once that she had never met anyone who had as much enthusiasm for life as my dad.

I think he got that from Ollie. There're pictures of my grandpa as a young soldier during World War I in Paris, grinning from ear to ear and feeding a flock of birds in the plaza. He always wanted to travel, be on the move. Bill said that when he went into grad school and stored all his college books back at his folks' home in Oxnard, his father read every single one and would call him at night, peppering him with questions.

My dad didn't have the nerve to admit he hadn't read every page of every book in his collection. After all, Ollie had bought the family a red-leather forty-volume set of the *Encyclopedia Britannica* and actually read it—the whole thing. He couldn't imagine buying a book without devouring it. And besides, it would be a waste of money.

My grandpa was the oldest living son in a clan of eight surviving kids, the valedictorian of his high school. But he wasn't able to look forward to college. His parents were ill and he went to work, along with his other siblings, until he was drafted.

Oliver was determined that his son Bill become a scholar, a traveler—and that he never, ever be involved in the family trade. My dad didn't know a steak from a chop—he was never allowed behind the counter of the butcher store. "Go do your homework, Billy," they'd say, leaving him to his books and the radio and the Nickelodeon and the record player.

At the time, he had no complaints because he loved those things. Every nickel went to the movies; every recording and magazine was treasured. But when I was a teenager and Bill talked to me about his life, he said he regretted feeling so physically inept in a family of big men, powerful men, who used their hands for everything.

He told me the worst mistake his parents made, unwittingly, was skipping him a grade, putting his prepubescent self among the older and more jaded upperclassmen.

"I didn't fit in at all with the older kids—it was a disaster. I was beat up every day in gym. It was torment. I couldn't play their games or hold my own—my only friend was your godfather, Bob Thiel, who grew up from me across the street. We would listen to opera and classical music and swear we were going to *get out* of Oxnard . . . someday."

Two generations later, my daughter had the same assignment in third grade that I'd received at her age: "How did your family come to California?" I was determined to pierce the "Kansas" cul-de-sac, and so I encouraged her to press my dad for more information on his side of the family.

Bill told Aretha a different story, all right, the oldest story I'd ever heard of our ancestors. Just think: All those Bright people, all those dusty photographs of characters whose names I don't know, so much life in them, and this is the one story that survived, passed only in the oral telling.

Aretha's great-great-great-grandfather William Riley Bright took his family to California from Kentucky in the 1800s by wagon train. They faced every peril and deprivation along the trail.

William Riley was a tough old bird, and he almost met his match. One day on their travels, as they climbed the Rockies, an eagle swooped out of the sky and *plucked* Bill Riley's right eyeball clean out of his head!

Did that stop him? Of course not. He arrived with his family, one-eyed, on the central California coast, in Ventura County.

I think a lot about that toughness. My dad regretted losing a piece of it, although he treasured the soft intellectual fields he was let loose in. He got to do everything his father ever dreamed of, and more. And he kept more of his connection to California than he even recognized. Sometimes we'd go backpacking in the Sierras, and he knew how to do everything in the mountains, it seemed to me. He knew how to live in the desert. There wasn't a patch of California he hadn't explored, often first with his dad. He wasn't a city person like my mother, who had grown up in an urban ghetto.

I'd say, "You're a mountain man; you know every plant and animal here—you did fall closer to the tree than you think." It pleased him to hear that.

When I first settled with my daughter and partner in Santa Cruz in 1994, where I live now, I took my dad to the boardwalk. It's like a small, West Coast version of Coney Island: games of chance, a huge wooden roller coaster. Bill told me he had been on this same roller coaster in the 1930s, that his whole family had jumped in an Edsel and tooled up to Santa Cruz, a two-day journey from Oxnard. "I loved it here," he said.

"What was your favorite game?" I asked, since we were walking past the carnies.

"The water balloons! The wall of water balloons that you pop with a dart," he said, grabbing my hand to show me the exact marquee he was talking about.

"Why those?" I never would have picked that one.

"I won all the time!" he said. "You throw the dart like this— *pfft!*—high and limp-wristed through the air! The less macho, the better! That's why I was so good at it."

D-I-V-O-R-C-E

THERE IS MORE THAN ONE WAY to unpack a breakup. I've hosted a score of explanations for my parents' dissolution, only to grab my kit and run for higher ground.

My mother and father had an old-fashioned divorce—the kind where you have to sue each other and assign blame. The rhetoric of "extreme mental cruelty" appeared in their court documents. There was a court-appointed psychiatrist. Though they separated in 1960, it was still the morality of another century when they dissolved their partnership—a scarlet "D" etched on their permanent record. My mother's complete estrangement from the Catholic Church was concluded when she was informed that her divorce meant she could never receive the sacramental host again.

By the time I hit puberty, the marriage climate had turned upside down. In 1973, I was in a Los Angeles high school, where I was dressed down by an English teacher who informed the entire class that I was "out of line" because I was "from a broken home." My classmates looked blankly at Miss Baltheir. One of the cheerleaders, who wouldn't have ordinarily crossed the street on my behalf, spoke up: "But Miss B., everyone's parents are divorced." I could see our teacher's lip quiver—she just didn't know what to say to this hell-bent mob.

But in 1960, a female's saying she was divorced was a little like whispering "I'm a lesbian" into your pillow. You'd obviously failed as a woman, although it was almost compulsory that the woman got full custody of the kids. Men were considered incompetent as caretakers. The disgraced couple were then presumed to be adversaries for the rest of their lives.

In the years since my parents died—and death was the card that had to be turned—more truth has arrived, the kind of surprises I'd never have expected while they both were alive.

After my mom passed away in 2004, I got a letter from the woman who inspired my middle name, Ellen. Ellen Eicke was my mother's best friend when my dad was in the army, a German neighbor of theirs in Kassel. Bill was in military intelligence ("the greatest oxymoron every made," he said) during the Korean War, listening to Soviet Czech radio traffic. He hated the army, but he and my mother loved living in Europe. They consumed opera like it was buttered toast. They were befriended by dear Ellen. And she and my mother wrote to each other at Christmas and Easter every year until my mom passed away, even though they never saw each other again after 1956.

Upon her death, I realized how odd it was that my mom had once had a best friend, a bosom buddy, because I never saw her enjoy another woman's company. She never had anyone over to the house; I never saw her on a date, not platonic, not anything. It was as if there were two of us, plus the specter of my father, and no one else.

My father had many relationships in his life—was widowed twice, divorced twice, and, in the end, happy in his last marriage. He went from someone who had a secret book about "the problems of being shy," which I once found in his closet—he never thought he'd be able to have a social life, let alone a love life—to becoming a man who loved to meet new people, thrived at parties, couldn't wait to get to know someone. In a way, the fact that Bill knew so many languages and could make small talk with virtually anyone in the world was a product of his enthusiasm for making new friends.

My mother and father seemed to transform between young adulthood and maturity. My dad went from shut-in to social butterfly, my mother went from the Most Popular Girl on Campus to a wary woman whose very skin seemed to flinch from getting close to anyone.

I look at Elizabeth's high school and early college scrapbooks and see a beautiful, tall ringleader, laughing her head off with a bunch of other curly-haired girls. Where did they all go?

After her divorce, she stayed close with only one pen pal, Ellen.

I wrote to my namesake after my mom died and explained why her yearly Christmas letter had gone missing for the first time. I cried as I scribbled it all down; I had never before communicated directly with this woman my mother had held so kindly in her memories.

Ellen wrote her condolences and asked if I would like to have the correspondence Bill and Elizabeth sent to her when they left

Germany and went to live in India, and then when they returned to the United States.

She added, "Of all the lovers in the world, I never thought Bill and Jo would break up; they seemed like the perfect couple, so well suited to each other."

Perfect couple! I howled.

I can remember my parents together in the same room only once. It was so frightening that even decades later, when I got pregnant, one of my first thoughts was *I can't have Bill and Elizabeth visit the baby and me at the same time.* I once considered that even if I were the marrying kind, I could never walk down the aisle because my parents couldn't possibly control their fighting.

Such a picture makes them sound evenly matched. It wasn't like that. My dad would say something low that I could barely hear. My mom would explode. Then he'd leave and she would go berserk, swearing that I favored him, in looks as well as personality flaws. One thing I figured out early on: Whatever divorced parents tell their children about their arguments, it is surely misleading.

Ellen's innocent observation that my parents were such lovebirds gave me pause. Even before I received the letters, which she sent wrapped in a satin ribbon, I gleaned that, in some respects, my parents were each other's fond companion. My dad told me that until he met his last wife, Lise—thirty years after he and Libby divorced—he never thought he'd meet a woman who was his intellectual match again. They were brainiacs; they were language, poetry, and music fiends; they took enormous pleasure in big ideas and the power of word. They were literary sensualists.

My mother could say things like, "Your father is a cruel, oblivious, selfish pig," giving me examples about how he once made her, his wife, go to the back of the college cafeteria line because it wouldn't be fair to let her cut in with him. He humiliated her in front of all his male friends, who didn't think a woman should even be at the university. Then, a few hours later, she'd sit down at her desk and gaily prepare him a news clipping about a personal dispute she'd read in the *Hindustan Times* that had made her laugh. She said Bill would be the only one who would "get it."

They were both idealistic and cynical at the same time. My mother told my dad she was moving us to Canada after the fourth political assassination in five years (JFK, Malcolm X, Robert Kennedy, Dr. King). She said she "couldn't take this country anymore," and Bill told me he was devastated to contemplate my departure, but impressed at her guts. She said he was the smartest person she knew. But then it was back to daggers and swords.

When I was little, my mother, if she could steady herself, would tell a couple stories about why my father was beyond redemption. She said that his mother had done everything for him, that he couldn't even make himself a sandwich. I had a mental image of my dad staring at a slice of bologna and white bread, uncertain how to stack the slices.

Later, at fourteen, when I moved in with my dad, I did take over most of the cooking; I enjoyed it. Bill explained to me that my mother's complaint was true, that he had been waited on hand and foot in every domestic respect by his mother, who believed a genius needed to be left alone with his books, undisturbed by housekeeping, farming, or "making things." He wished very much that hadn't been the case, that he felt retarded by it.

But by the time Bill married Marcia, his third wife, he was waking up to feminism, if not domestic self-reliance. He was no longer oblivious to the inequality. Even if he couldn't make meat loaf, he could at least do the dishes. He asked me if I would like that trade: He'd do all the dishes and I'd do the cooking, unless we went out. And he loved to eat out! I was ecstatic.

My mom always snorted when she launched into her legends of my dad's crimes against humanity. That breath of utter disgust. She'd blow out her cigarette smoke, contemplating one of his marriages, before she added that she "wasn't cut out to be a faculty wife"—an epithet she used the way most people would say "pathetic loser."

Well, she never got her chance to be a faculty wife and hate it, since she was with my dad only when they were penniless grad students and she worked as a secretary. But she had a vivid imagination. It's true—she would've been bored. I remember one of my dad's mentors, Murray Emeneau, had a wife who truly loved being the domestic arm of their relationship. One time a student said, "Mrs. Emeneau, do you collaborate with her husband?"

"Oh no, dear," Mary replied, in full drag-queen trill. "I'm only for his leisure hours!"

My mom was the opposite of that. She reported that when they were grad students, people would talk in hushed tones around my father but would act like she was a potted plant. The university people assumed Elizabeth's academic credentials consisted of typing his dissertation. (In fact, they were both the fastest, most competent typists I've ever seen. I would be hard-pressed to say which one was better.) She said that in private Bill talked to her about their work as an equal, but among his male peers, it was as if she vanished.

Bill would've argued that she refused to be seen; although, as the years went by, he became discouraged with academic sexism himself.

I do know my dad never doubted his academic prowess; he was so relaxed about it. He was like one of those big dogs that never have to bark or go nuts.

My mom was on the defensive. She had the opposite of his family protection—she was lucky to be alive, or, as she put it, *damned* to be alive. She got so mad about the way her academic elders condescended to her that she insisted on returning all the fellowship funds she had received as a backhanded way of returning the insult. "You don't think I'm worth it. Fine. Take all your money back." Bill told her she was nuts, that her work was outstanding and the Regents of the University of California were indifferent to her protest. She didn't care.

I got that from her. It's the technique of hurting yourself in front of people who are being shits, to see if they even notice. They don't. Other people who love you do, though.

I see Halloran self-immolation in every Irish martyr. Look at the Republican hunger strikers, with their "monomaniacal willpower," as journalist Andrew O'Hehir puts it. They resist Goliath to the point of sacrificing their dignity and, finally, their lives. "Their resistance," Andrew says, "by its very nature, is morally unstable."

After my mother's death came a revealing coda. She did a lot of linguistic work on the Patwin language, from a tribe in Northern California, parallel to my father's work in Karuk. Members of the Patwin tribe—some of their librarians and language people—contacted me six months after she died and said, "Your mom did so much for us; could you tell us more about her?" They wrote me over and over. They were ready to name a plaque after her, and she never even knew.

These kinds of stories led to my teenage explanations to myself about why Elizabeth sued for divorce and then acted as if she was the one who'd been abandoned. I'd think, *My mom is crazy!* or, *My mom is a proto-feminist!* or, *My mom is a crazy proto-feminist!*

But the more I learned about my parents' childhoods, the better I understood their estrangement. They had gaps between their childhood views of the world that neither of them could put words to for years.

One of the causes of my mother's death was a weak heart due to scars from rheumatic fever. In her seventies, she told me of her doctor's discovery, and that this would likely be the cause of her death, slowly but surely.

I asked her what "rheumatic fever" was, and she brushed me off. That made me suspicious. I looked it up in the medical dictionary, which indicated it was a disease of poverty, not seen in modern American lives.

My mother's doctor asked her if she could remember being sick in her youth, and she said, "Oh yes, when I was thirteen years old, I was sick for a long time. I used to be the fastest girl on the block—I could outrun everyone, even the boys—but after I was sick I couldn't run anymore."

She didn't tell them, "My mom died when I was almost thirteen, and we were home alone without food." It was then that she became so ill and unable to run anymore.

So yes, I think my mother was affected by poverty, domestic violence, hunger, grave illness, the Catholic Church—the whole *Angela Ashes* cocktail. She got her second chance at life because of her defiance and extreme intelligence.

My father was from a different class background, modest but well fed, appearing on the outside to be stable, even though he had his share of family secrets, too. They were the secrets of the well fed, of the Protestant veil, of small-town, conservative, rural California. He functioned like someone who had been encouraged and reassured from babyhood. He had a youthful sense of entitlement and good health. His folks were behind him no matter what. The Brights owned their own homes, their ranches, their farms. They were frugal and thrifty, and although there was nothing fancy, everyone ate meat and had shoes for every occasion. My grandparents were thrilled that my dad got a Pepsi-Cola scholarship to go to Cal at age sixteen.

Grandpa said to Daddy when he was in grad school, "If it doesn't work out, you can always come back and work on the chicken farm." Many a linguist friend would later tease Bill that he should have chosen the birds! But it was a sweet reminder because there was *something* there for him, a home somewhere that he could return to. For my mom, there was no home plate.

I started eating—and living—well, too, when I moved in with my dad. Steak and ice cream! Allowances! A bicycle! A record player! My first week there, my dad gave me my allowance and a Schwinn. I learned how to ride the thing just to get to Thrifty's drugstore, falling down a dozen times on a ten-block ride. Once there, I spent every cent on eye makeup and emerged elated, with pink, blue, and green powder all over my lids.

My aunt Molly, my mother's sister, had another theory about my parents' divorce. It wasn't about religion, class, sexism, mental health: It was all my fault.

"You wouldn't stop crying; you thought about nothing but yourself!" she said.

"Molly, I was only two years old!" I tried.

"What, that's your excuse? That's you, full of explanations!"

Even now, it makes me laugh, her reproach. My aunt Molly loved me dearly, but she wanted me to know my burdens. My mother's relatives weren't interested in Dr. Spock or any other child development psychologies. If you were "bad," you did your parents a grave disservice; it was your fault that they beat you or got drunk. . . . If only you'd been good, if only you had done the right thing, things wouldn't have gone awry. Children are an obligation and a curse. It didn't matter whether you were six or sixteen, you were full of sin. If you were abandoned, it was because you deserved it, and maybe it'd be a lesson to you.

I took this a couple ways. On one hand, when I came to my father's house in 1972, he was alarmed that the most common expression that came out of my mouth was "I'm sorry, I'm sorry." I wasn't being sarcastic; I was genuinely flinching. I was an expert at walking on eggshells—yet, inevitably, some would always get cracked. I never thought I'd be able to work myself out of the yolks.

A lot of people look back on their parents' generation—the pre–Baby Boomers, the Depression babies—and say, "Well, they were all too young; they got married too soon. Everyone took one look at their draft notices and got married in a panic." My dad said more than once, "We were both so immature."

So yes, young and stupid. The question is, how long does that last? Maybe no one should get hitched until they're well into their dotage.

My mom gave me a glimpse of what could've been, on her deathbed.

She was in hospice in a nursing home on the Iron Range, which is the mining area of Minnesota just south of the Canadian boundary waters. It's where Bob Dylan grew up—and if you think he's an enigma, you simply haven't met anyone else from the Range. They are all the same. Bobby Zimmerman is a Ranger through and through.

The nursing home in Hibbing, the main town, is filled with children and young adults visiting every day; it's not a lonely place. Family is everything up there.

Elizabeth had just a month or two left before she died. She had some lucid moments, and for a period, she could operate the phone by herself.

She called my dad. For the first time in forty years.

Bill told me this, of course—he always blabbed. He was at his desk when she rang, and this voice, one that he hadn't heard for decades, was on the line.

When he said, "Hello, Libby?" she said, "Oh no, no, I thought I'd get your answering machine—hang up! Hang up! I can't say this to you in person."

He said, "Okay, I'll hang up, and if you ring again, the machine will get it."

She phoned right back. She spoke into the tape recorder like she was in the confession booth:

"Bill, I want you to know that I know how I treated you when we were together. I was really cruel; all those things I said—none of them were true. The truth is, you were the kindest man I've ever known."

I could hear her breath as Bill repeated her message to me. When my mom talked about their marriage, it was as if it had happened yesterday, instead of in 1950.

"So, what did you do?" I said. I felt dizzy.

"I was really touched," he said. "I wrote her a note. I said that neither of us was perfect, that we were both haunted by our own demons. I said that we made an incredibly wonderful child, so it must have been worth it, and we could be proud of that no matter what."

I could hardly respond. Indeed, I eventually found that letter in my mom's apartment in Hibbing, exactly as he described. My mom kept it in a very special place; I know she treasured it.

I was happy for her, for him. But the two-year-old inside me quaked. I had to bite my lip to keep from being a spoiler. How could they enjoy this private makeup that I had nothing to do with?

My dad got a second chance to father a little girl. He bent over backward to help me when I had my daughter, Aretha. He couldn't wait to see us, visiting every few months even when he lived far away. He was a bigger part of Aretha's growing up than he was of mine, and every time I'd see him sing with her, hold her little hand, play Russian Bank with two stacks of cards, I'd think, *This is the do-over; this is the mending.* The greatest myth of divorce is that you never, ever think you're going to see the day.

RUNS THROUGH IT

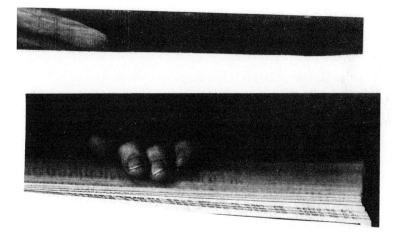

Suicide not only runs "in" families, it runs through them.

—Laura Miller

THE REASONS FOR SUICIDE ARE always distracting. But the reasons don't seem to predict *who's* really going to do it and *who's* only taking you to the brink.

A terrible tragedy can befall three different people: One will insist on moving forward, another will snuff herself out, and yet another will threaten death so convincingly that you don't know the difference anymore.

The first time I heard the phrase "suicidal gesture," I was outraged. What do you mean, "gesture"? I believed each one, every time!

My mom set the suicide clock in motion so frequently that by the time I hit puberty, I just wanted her to get it over with. I knew it was probably my fault; she'd clarified that a million times. So be it. Call the devil, tell him to save my seat, kill yourself—at least the suspense will be over.

I imagined, a thousand times, the quiet of sitting in our apartment—an apartment we'd just moved into—after her suicide death. I would imagine it all being over. So still, so absolutely silent, for a period of time before I called the police to come to our apartment. I wouldn't want the peaceful moment to end. I would imagine this silent aftermath over and over again; it was such a comfort.

The last time my mom tried to kill the two of us was a few days after she got a letter in the mail from a lawyer. The attorney had been trying to find her for a year, which I found impressive—that she had "disappeared" us so effectively that no one in her immediate family had a clue what our address was. The attorney had finally contacted my father, who, postdivorce, spent twelve years at the University of California at Los Angeles. I guess my mom trusted my dad with our whereabouts more than anyone she was related to. Thus, the lawyer discovered our location in Edmonton, Alberta, Canada.

The attorney's letter informed my mother of her father's death, as well as her sister's. Frannie had died first. Her father was buried in the Veterans Cemetery and had left each of his children $200. That shocked me, because I was under the impression that he had nothing to offer anyone, least of all his eldest daughter. I didn't even know he was alive—I'd never heard her mention him, except to say, "My father abandoned us when our mother died, and then our aunt Tessie came to get us from the orphanage and keep the older kids together."

But my adorable aunt Frances—there was no further information about her in the letter, no burial information. I still don't know where my aunt lies. She was so young—in her thirties—and she'd had three sons. What had happened?

I didn't know, but whatever was missing, or whatever was well understood, my mother tore the letter in two. She was gunning for something right then. I crawled under the bed for a while, suspecting a blowup, but then decided getting myself to school was even safer.

I remembered my favorite photograph of my aunt Frannie, which my mom had also torn up, a long time ago, before I was born. Some time later she had painstakingly Scotch-taped it back together.

Frannie was the "pretty one," my mom said—and that was impressive, because my mother was beautiful. In high school, Frannie had snuck out of the house wearing my mother's favorite sweater to pose for her annual class photo. She looked great in it; her smile was like a movie star's.

When my mom found out about the borrowing, discovering the yearbook picture, she was so enraged she tore every copy she could find into little pieces.

"It was the only nice thing I had," she said—referring to the sweater. Another one of those "reasons" that always seemed to end a discussion. I examined the photo as best I could. The sweater was gray wool, store-bought, and utterly undistinguished to my eye was except that a pretty, slender girl was wearing it like it belonged to her.

I found the photo in my mother's old shoe box. My aunt's warm smile and the lights in her eyes were frightening to look at with all the rips and tears so clearly visible, the yellowing tape barely holding it all together.

A couple nights after the lawyer's letter arrived, I was lying awake on my sofa bed. I couldn't get to sleep; I kept thinking about our white Persian cat we'd left back in the States. His name was Swithin—we'd named him after mischievous Uncle Swithin in *The Forsyte Saga*.

Swithy was pure white, deaf, and had blue eyes. He was completely enchanting. I'd never had a pet before, nor did we ever stick around long enough anywhere for me to enjoy anyone else's animals. My mom said we could feed him, if he didn't eat too much and stayed outside. I would give him my canned peas from supper if I could sneak them into a napkin.

When Mom told me we were moving to Canada in 1970, it came as such a surprise. She said it was because of the assassinations, because of the war, because this country made her sick. But she said those things all the time—why Canada now?

I saw a letter on her sewing table from the University of Alberta offering her a position as a librarian. She had been substitute teaching in high school for years. I knew she wouldn't change her mind.

We had just "adopted" this little cat. I was on the swim team, and the coach had given me a red, white, and blue American flag swimsuit to compete in in the summer races at the public pool. That very month, my mom had acknowledged that I had $75 in the bank, from all the $5 bills that had accumulated in my name from birth to First Communion. She'd suggested that I buy a bike—I'd never even bought a candy bar before. I was twelve and didn't know how to ride a bicycle. It was so exciting.

And then it was all over. One memorable afternoon, she said that we were moving to Edmonton, that this country was abominable, that there were no jobs. She said that she'd sold my bike to help with the moving expenses, and the cat couldn't come.

My first bouts of insomnia were in Edmonton, Alberta, a week into our new living situation. We lived in a tall apartment building on Eighty-seventh Avenue, the main street bordering the college library where she now worked.

I really missed holding our kitten and hearing him purr, wondering if he could feel himself purr even if he couldn't hear it. I worried that he was hungry, that no one was taking care of him.

It's odd that I remember that part so clearly: missing the cat. I have a detailed memory of the minutes before I crept into my mom's room, into her bed, and told her tearfully that I missed Swithy so much.

"That's it, that's enough!" she said. "You make me sick." She pushed me off the mattress and shoved on her shoes while I wheezed and apologized.

She pinched the top of my arm and dragged me out the door.

I remember her grip on my arm—and her disgust at my blubbering. I was pathetic, I knew it, but I couldn't stop. I could see in her eyes how loathsome I'd become. If only I hadn't said anything about the cat, or crawled into her bed like a baby.

I told her I needed my glasses; I was blind. I couldn't see the stairs we were taking to the parking garage, and I kept tripping.

"You won't need them in the bottom of the river," she said.

Maybe I was tripping because I was trying to stop. I could remember only the gray cement of the stairwell and the underground garage where all the tenants' cars were parked. Gray cement, the same hard color of her eyes.

My mom pushed me into the front seat of the VW. I popped out, protesting. She pushed me in again. It was like playing jack-in-the-box. Of course she won, or I gave up too soon. Was she really stronger than me?

I yelled, "But where are we going?"

She replied with the kind of satisfaction you imagine only in perfect victory, "I'm driving us into the river."

The Saskatchewan River in Edmonton is frozen in parts most of the year. Really, everything is frozen from September to May.

You wouldn't even have to crack the ice to die in the river—it's so cold—and I was wearing too-small pajamas.

I didn't know what my mother's drowning plan was, but she seemed to be soaring.

When I stopped pushing the door back open, I said, "I don't want to die."

"Too bad!" Elizabeth's laugh echoed through the garage. She said it was too late.

The car started out slow, but then she hit the gas. She ran a string of lights on Eighty-seventh. I was afraid to grab the wheel or whatever it is that movie heroes do when someone evil needs to be pushed out of the driver's seat. My own thoughts got very small and slow. Was this the relief I'd imagined so many times? Was the aftermath beginning now?

It was glacial. I had all the time in the world to think. I had regrets, and complaints. I wished Mom had just taken pills this time, like before, or had used a razor in the tub, where it was warm. I felt so sorry for myself because I was going to die *cold*, but it was like feeling sorry for someone else—I couldn't sense my limbs anymore. No more tears. I didn't have a private conversation with God, because we all know how those had gone before: He had never shown up. The windshield wipers were pushing the snowflakes this way and that, like little cards being shuffled from one part of a deck to another.

The car screeched and spun—we plowed into a curb, and my head hit the dash. It wasn't the river, but blood poured out of my nose. It was wonderfully warm.

I heard a door slam. The car was stuck half cocked in a snowbank. She was walking away—my mother was walking fast on a dark street that fronted the river. I saw her step right up to one of the first doorways with a porch light. Then she disappeared. I couldn't see much without my glasses, but I was glad they hadn't broken in the crash.

I don't know how long I sat there by myself. No one walked by—it can be very lonely in Windsor Park. It was that January when it was forty below zero for forty days, and afterward everyone wore a button to brag about it. Coming so recently from California, I was still fascinated by snowflakes, the way I'd once been thrilled with four-leaf clovers. I liked to watch the way each one pasted itself to a windowpane before it was subsumed by another, and then another.

Was it hours or minutes that went by? I became curious and impatient again, two signs of life. I got out, walked to the door I guessed she had gone to, and rang the bell. It was a dark wood house. I remember the Beatles lyric passing through my mind as I pushed the button: "Isn't it good . . . ?" A middle-aged Japanese woman came to door, reminding me of our old landlady, Mrs. Koyamatsu, in Pasadena.

"I'm looking for my mother," I said, and Mom appeared at the door, on cue, as if she'd summoned a taxi and it had just arrived.

"Oh yes, Susie, there you are. What are you doing in your pajamas?" My mom laughed as if I needed a fashion remedial.

I have never seen anyone carry on as if *nothing* had happened, but then, I'll never be fourteen again in Edmonton with blood on my flannel Pjs, a black eye, a busted lip, and my mouth hanging open.

BLEEDING

AFTER THE SASKATCHEWAN RIVER incident, I wasn't Mommy's little girl anymore. I watched her at a distance—and I didn't tell her things. It was like being in a lion's cage with a chair between the two of us.

She didn't know that I came home from Garneau Junior High at lunchtime to read and watch *Petticoat Junction* on TV. I made grilled-cheese sandwiches using the iron and ironing board like a sandwich press.

My mother didn't get home until six. She might walk in and crack me across the cheek; she might announce she wanted to curl my hair in cloth rags like Shirley Temple's; she might walk into her room and close the door. But the daytimes were my time at home, and they were quiet. I loved how warm it was inside closed doors in Edmonton. They had figured out the heating thing in Alberta, unlike in the apartments we'd had in California. I could stand in our apartment at the ironing board, warm as a bug, and the sun would pour through the windows, reflecting the snow.

Petticoat Junction was a half-hour sitcom about three silly sisters with sexy pigtails: Billy Jo, Bobby Jo, and Betty Jo. They'd have cute problems with their laundry and with boys.

My mother had left a paperback copy of *The Female Eunuch* on the cardboard boxes she used as a dresser. I was old enough to take an interest in her books. This one had a female nude on the cover, and that caught my attention.

I opened *Eunuch*, and it fell to a page where Ms. Greer dared you to taste your menstrual blood. She was witty. "Freud is the father of psychoanalysis," she wrote. "It has no mother." I could feel myself imitating her voice.

She asked women what they were afraid of. I didn't want Germaine Greer to know that my answer was, "Just about everything." But if I could act like her, talk like her, all my trepidations would fizzle away. I had always been a bookworm mimic; everything I read came out of my mouth, as if I were a living continuation of the script.

Tasting my menstrual blood would surely be a walk in the park. I had been raised to be sensible about bodily functions. I decided I would taste mine as soon as my period appeared.

VOILÀ—MY FOURTEENTH YEAR, before I finished the last chapter of *Eunuch*, my first menstruation began. Conveniently, it was during my private lunchtime.

I found some Kotex in the broom closet and started to arrange a pad in my bell-bottoms. It felt like a loaf of bread in my pants. I couldn't believe my mother would put up with something this uncomfortable. She didn't even wear girdles, and she threatened to throw her bras out daily.

Backward, forward—it felt like a wadded-up diaper, and I could only imagine it looked the same. It was time to clean up the ironing board—I had to get back to fifth period. I thought for a half second of calling my mom and asking her, "Is there a trick?"

I wanted to tell her I was glad things had changed since she was a girl, and that I knew I wasn't dying. But I just didn't want to tell her anything anymore. I sat on the toilet and stared at the floor. I tasted my blood. Okay, done. Unremarkable.

I saw a blue box on the laundry hamper I hadn't paid attention to before. Tampax. Yes! A new box. It had a paper diagram. Annette Laurence, who sat behind me in algebra, had said tampons would ruin your virginity. But I *felt* like ruining something. I slid the tampon into my vagina, and it was like folding a perfect paper crane. I felt nothing—in a good way—and the blood was no longer running down my leg. Now I just had to clean everything up. I was really late for class.

I was never behind in school. Never late, never missed a test, never started a problem in the cloakroom—I found following all those millions of rules at school effortless. The only rule I routinely violated was passing notes, and you couldn't really call them "notes" because we were passing twenty-page scripts back and forth—it was our art.

I walked into debate class five minutes after the hour and slipped a quick missive to my best friend, Jane, to tell her my glorious bloody day had arrived. She gave me a thumbs-up sign.

"Susannah," said Miss MacKenzie—who addressed every pupil by the name on his or her birth certificate, even if it included

"Esquire"—"you will report to Dr. Shalka's office for detention. You will not disrupt our classroom with your tardiness."

The blood rushed to my cheeks now. No Tampax for that.

Mrs. MacKenzie was such a piece of work. "Who has triumphed, class?" she would ask. "Democracy in India . . . or communism in China?" Yeah, the suspense was killing us. This same martinet taught art class, where we were graded on how well we stayed within the lines of a picket fence we drew over and over and over, as endless as Alberta's prairies.

I walked into Dr. Shalka's office like a mad bear. A mad menstruating bear with Germaine Greer on my tongue.

"This is not right," I said, before he could motion me to sit down. "My period just started at noon, and I had to figure out the Tampax all by myself and I am *never* late and you can't discriminate against me just because I am menstruating—"

I probably didn't get that far, actually. I remember the look on his face when I said the "female" word. Was it *period* or the one that started with an *m?* You would've thought I had just sat on his face with my "vagina." He flushed, his giant hands fluttered at his desk, and he coughed repeatedly into his cloth hankie.

"That will be enough!" he gasped, coming up for air. "You will not be kept for detention." He looked at me as if he were begging. "Please go!"

"Okay," I said, "I'm sorry." And I walked out of his office, closing the door quietly, as if I were leaving a patient's room. What was this? A grown man had turned to mush because I had my period? But he had a whole junior high school of girls doing this! On any given day, one of us was probably starting to bleed for the very first time.

Sue, Barbara, Joan, Jane, Molly, Agnes, Corinne, and the French Canadian girls passed notes to me through the next two periods. Mischi invited me outside for a smoke. I was in the club. Susan Johnson, the only other person in school who wore glasses, slipped me a copy of *The Godfather* like she was passing contraband.

"Page twenty-seven," she whispered. "Page twenty-seven!"

I went to the cloakroom before gym and tented my down jacket over my head, to cover whatever Susan had in store for me. The magenta paperback was dog-eared. On page twenty-seven, this guy Sonny is seduced by a woman whose vagina is so big that only a gargantuan penis can satisfy her. You imagine her vagina in Olympian dimensions. Did vaginas come in sizes? Did penises come in such different sizes? I had never even considered this whole *size* thing! The tampon I had just used said "regular" . . . and it was *tiny*. Was the *super* tampon as big as your arm? That's what the book said Sonny's penis was supposed to be like. One of the characters said it would "kill" a normal woman.

The Godfather's prose was purple. I felt secretive and hot; this was the sort of thing you read under blankets. But then the story went on. I was up to page thirty-five when I heard Susan calling my name. . . . I stuffed the book into my satchel and came back out in my navy gym bloomers.

"I'm here!" I said. "Can I borrow the whole thing? I want to read it to the end."

"But there's nothing after page twenty-seven!" she said. Her bloomers were even saggier than mine. Mischi said the school made us wear these in gym so the boys would lose their boners. I suddenly understood what she meant.

"I know; I just want to see what happens," I said.

I got home at four o'clock and started to make supper. I was a big fan of Hamburger Helper. It came in all these flavors, and you could pretend you were eating around the world. The radio was playing Neil Young, Joni Mitchell, Gordon Lightfoot—and then back to Neil Young.

I liked them all, but the DJ was sarcastic. He said the new law was that they had to play 70 percent Canadian artists, but they'd all gotten rich on American dollars.

I picked up the mail. There was a letter from my dad to me—and a letter from my dad to my mother. My chest turned to lead; I wanted to crumple all of the letters in my hand. What were they doing? He never wrote her.

I opened his letter to me. It contained a few elephant jokes, something we'd been trading over the past year.

Q: What's gray and white on the inside and red on the outside?
A: An inside-out elephant.

Every month he would mail me an elephant joke book, or write down extra ones he'd collected, or send me a comic book with Charlie Brown and Snoopy. *Happiness is . . .* I liked that one. I liked the packages that came with letters he wrote himself, so I could see his handwriting. He always wrote on recycled paper from the manuscripts he was editing. I would look on the back of his elephant joke note and there'd be some thesis, or an article he was editing for his linguistics journal, *Language.* I never understood the subject, but I always recognized the proofreading codes he'd taught me. "A slash means lowercase, three lines means uppercase . . . Transpose this, it's like a little snake." It was an international code, so even if someone wrote you in Russian, you could still follow the proofreading marks.

This time his letter to me had a second page, unusual. It said:

Dear Susie,
My wife Marcia has died after a long battle with
breast cancer. I am very sad. I have sold our house

*in Topanga Canyon and moved to an apartment in
Malibu—you will find my address below. I hope I will
see you this summer.*
Daddy

I didn't know Marcia had cancer. Or that she was sick. Or for
how long. I hadn't seen either of them since 1969. *How* long? I put
some water in the teakettle on the stove and steamed open Bill's
letter to my mother.

It said the same thing, except nothing about his emotion. Marcia was dead, and he wanted to see me.

Marcia had a daughter, I thought. Karen—she was a year older than I. What about her? I remembered Karen from when we'd
had a couple of both-kids-at-the-same-time custody visits. Marcia
saw her little girl, and Bill saw me. We shared a bed in the guest
room. I liked her—she was older than I was and knew everything.
Daddy said that Marcia had given birth to Karen when she was
seventeen, with an older guy, and that the guy had taken the kid
because Marcia wanted to go to college and he said she couldn't
do both.

"But wasn't she upset?" I asked. I was eight. "Doesn't she
want her daughter?"

Bill told me that it was better this way for Marcia, and that
she loved her daughter anyway, even if they didn't live together.
Then he told me he loved me very, very much.

When my father died, in 2005, he told me Marcia's story more
completely. My childhood intuition was right. Marcia was not
"fine" about her daughter's absence in her life.

Bill explained, "Her parents were Swedes. They didn't speak
to her when she got pregnant. It was never mentioned. The baby
was supposed to be put up for adoption, but the birth father,
an older fellow, said he'd raise it, with his then-new wife, and

Marcia would have to accept her punishment. It was like she had done something wrong, and he was the savior instead of her impregnator."

When Marcia was diagnosed with cancer, she went to her bed, like *Barbry Allen*, and looked up at Bill one last time. "Karen ... " she said. "Karen. I have failed her completely now."

I was finally old enough for that to sink in.

I had never thought about my dad losing people. He must've been sad—more than that—to lose my mother, or me. Yes, that must be true. And then his second wife, Janie—they had been married barely eighteen months when she'd been killed by a drunk driver who slid over a highway median strip. What had he done after that? I hadn't seen him for a long time after Janie died. He married Marcia a year later, and now she was dead, too.

I'd never heard of someone who lost two wives in a row to untimely deaths. Was he going to kill himself? That's where my mind went. What was my mom going to say when she found out? She wasn't good with letters like this.

I rubbed my cheek. She would probably have a fit. She would be jealous and say that Bill loved Marcia more. Loved all of them more. She might start hitting. And then cry really hard and want me to comfort her.

I could endure Elizabeth's blows, but I could not stand to comfort her. I took Bill's letter and folded it back in the envelope, fastened the seal with a little bit of school-supply paste, and pressed it all back together so it would look like it hadn't been opened. Then I put it with the bills that sat on the table.

I wrote a note on a yellow foolscap pad Momma kept at her desk:

"I am practicing my PE-class routine with Christine Haffke at her house. I will eat there. There is Italian Hamburger Helper and potatoes in the oven." I took my letter from my dad with me.

I bundled up for the snow. I would ask Christine if I could stay the night. Then I wouldn't have to see Elizabeth until the next evening, and by then, she'd either have calmed down—or would have killed herself. I could walk into the apartment and find her body, and it would be calm and I would call the emergency operator and they would be nice to me. I could do that.

Christine's family was Estonian. Her dad was talented at making ice sculptures. He had carved a Santa and eight tiny reindeer on their front lawn. His wife and he slept in narrow twin beds with pink crocheted coverlets, like Ozzie and Harriet. Christine was an only child, just like me.

"What do you want to practice?" Christine asked when I arrived.

We had a modern-dance final coming up. I pulled a Simon and Garfunkel forty-five out of my satchel. "Have you heard this song?" I asked. "It's really good."

She looked at the label. "'The Sound of Silence,'" she read. "That sounds a lot better than 'Puppy Love'—that's what Betty Buggers is doing!"

The most unpopular girl in our school was nicknamed Buggers, and nothing made me happier than laughing at her snotty nose. In Canada, I was no longer the pariah. I was bleeding, and I was part of the elite.

Christine had me in stitches, crooning, "And they CALL IT [pause, huge breath] PUPPY LUH-UH-UH-UVE. . . . "

"My tampon is going to come out," I begged her. "Stop it!"

Christine looked impressed. I could tell she had never used one. "My Oma won't allow it," she said. "It will ruin you for marriage."

"We are never going to get married, Christine," I said, putting the needle on Simon and Garfunkel. "Married people just die and get sad, and that is never going to happen to us."

We reached up with our hands in a ballet flourish and then caught each other, leaning back until we could spin, faster and faster, pivoting on our toes, until we fell into a heap on the floor.

THE TIME HAS COME,
THE WALRUS SAID

ELIZABETH DIDN'T SAY ANYTHING for a few weeks after my father's letter. Then she made an announcement: "I'm going to send you to your father's this summer; it's time he did something for a change."

I was careful not to show any expression. If I was happy, she might take it back. I just said, "Okay."

So in June, I took a plane by myself to Vancouver to meet my dad. That way, I didn't have to cross the border by myself. I hadn't seen him in two and a half years.

I didn't know what to call my father when I saw him . . . was I too old to say "Daddy"? But nothing else seemed to fit. When he picked up my suitcase, I asked, "When we're in a big place and I have to call you across a room, could I call you Bill?"

He held me very tight. We went to Denny's Coffeeshop for pancakes, which I thought was the height of luxury. Bill said I could order whatever I wanted. There was a customer feedback form on the bill, and they asked what you thought of their eggs. He wrote "execrable," and that made me laugh so hard tears rolled down my face.

Bill didn't get mad at me about anything. His eyes crinkled when I apologized, as I did about everything, every five minutes. But I wasn't feeling sorry most of the time, I was . . . happy. If you were to ask me what the happiest days of my life were, I would say the day that my daughter was born . . . and the first week I spent reunited with my dad. We went to the Empress Hotel for high tea. We went to smell the roses in Butchart Gardens. We took a ferry, and then a small boat, to a little island where we picked clams and blueberries and made a huge fire at night. We stayed with Marcia's brother, who looked just like my dad, with his long hair and beard. Everyone talked to me like I was the most interesting person, and pretty soon I couldn't stop talking myself.

At the end of a week, I told Bill about the attorney's letters my mother had received. I didn't tell him about what had happened in the car. I just wanted to know what he knew. What had happened to my aunt Frannie?

Bill's face crumpled. "She hanged herself. She lost her kids to your uncle, because of alcohol and pills, and she'd been very sick." He stopped. "I know your mom tried, a long time ago, to help her—your aunt Frannie was the sweetest kid, the nicest one in your mom's family. She'd give anyone the shirt off her back."

He came over to hug me. "I'm so sorry, honey. I don't know what happened."

Many years later, when my mom was dying, I finally asked her one little question about Frances. I took a chance because she was high on pain meds.

It came up because my mom was talking about how fast she used to be, how she could outrun everyone when she was a girl.

I asked her, "Mom, you ran, Molly ran, Bud ran, why didn't Frannie run?"

Ordinarily, Elizabeth would've looked daggers at me. No questions allowed. Was I trying to make her cry? But she was hospitable on her morphine.

"Frannie got the worst of it. Dada beat her over and over with an electric cord. She hanged herself in his apartment on Third Street. Her son, your cousin Brian, he found her."

She looked at me, cross. "Why can't you get me some butter for my bread?"

That's morphine for you. We needed these little interruptions.

"Make it snappy!" she called out after me, and laughed, like we used to laugh at Uncle Swithin.

That summer, my dad told me everything he knew about my mom's family, as well as his own. It was like a blank book suddenly ablaze with story after story. We'd take a long walk, to pick those berries or to hunt for clams, and the whole family tree would come to life.

At the end of the British Columbia visit, he asked me if I wanted to come to California with him. Of course. I didn't ask to talk to my mom—I didn't wish her any bad fortune, but I was scared that if I heard her voice, I'd be put magically back on a plane, that the spool would reel back. I never wanted to return.

My dad was like heaven. All the groceries I ever wanted, and I could talk about anything with him. He was never scared about the things I was scared of. He said I was an inspiration.

The first year we lived together, Bill started going to group therapy, an exercise I found fascinating. I asked him every night he came home about what each person said.

One night he came home stunned. He said the group's leader and all the participants had encouraged—insisted—that he pick up one of those soft foam "encounter bats" and bop one of the other big men in the group as hard as he could, that he give him a good wallop!

My dad was big as well . . . six feet, two inches. It was surprising even to find another man in this small group who was his size.

But he didn't want to do it. He felt like crying. "I don't have any quarrel with this man!" he said.

"Of course you don't!" the others replied. "That's the whole point!"

"But I'm weak! I'm small," he protested. Of course, everyone laughed and said, "You really need to learn how wrong you are. You need to know it in your body."

He gave in to their cajoling and whomped his fellow mountain man a good one, which made them all laugh—except for my father, who laughed first but then cried. The discovery that he was not a "weakling" was potent, to be sure. But he felt something swinging that bat, feelings that had nothing to do with anyone in the room.

"In my family, you never get angry," he said. "You never show anything you feel, especially anger."

"Well, what did you do with my mom?" I asked. "She lets loose all the time!"

"I know," he said. "I always thought I'd done something terribly wrong, I'd screwed up, and that if only I fixed it, she would never get angry with me again. But I just kept screwing it up, and so there was no respite."

"And now you know."

"Yes, now I do. But I knew even back then that she was depressed, and that was not so different from my mom, that yearning to make her happy, the fear that she would go away."

"When did your mom ever leave you? Grandma Ethel?" I couldn't imagine Grandma going more than two blocks down the street.

"She had what they would call a 'nervous breakdown' today," Bill said, "but I was just a toddler, and no one called it anything to me. I don't know where she went; she didn't say goodbye, and when she returned, there was nothing said then, either. My aunts folded me into their care while my dad was working, and some months later, Mother came home as if nothing had happened. They told me she couldn't have any more children."

In 1990, when I became a mommy myself, my dad explained to me that that year I'd moved in with him, 1972, Elizabeth had asked him to take custody of me permanently, before she made arrangements for me to leave Edmonton. It wasn't just a "visit" in her mind; it was a custody transfer.

When my own daughter turned twelve, I remembered that revelation. My mother's mother had died when Elizabeth was thirteen. She had let me go at fourteen. So no one in our maternal line had mothered her daughter through adolescence for at least a couple of generations. What made me think I could do it?

THE

RED

TIDE

THE BUNNY TRIP

JANE FONDA (left) and ROBERT K. DORNAN (right) during their controversial speeches here at University High School last week.

THE UNIVERSITY HIGH SCHOOL
WARRIOR

Vol. 53   Friday, March 2, 1973   No. 9

I WAS A SWIM TEAM "SCORE GIRL" before I was a Commie. I'm glad things ended up that way, because otherwise I never would've been able to touch the Playboy Bunny and carry on my sensual, if guilty, disposition.

The high school swim team was my ticket to an almost-prom; to halcyon school days; to a bartended, dress-up affair. The Trotskyists, the yippies, the lavender pinkos—they came along later and gave me guns and a good deal to think about, but they provided nothing soft or fluffy.

I went to a school called University High—Uni—a white, mostly Jewish school filled with the children of UCLA staff and the diaspora of the Hollywood colony. Marilyn Monroe went there before she dropped out.

In the seventies, there was no truly integrated school in the L.A. district. A discreet number of black students from South-Central L.A. (with neighborhood-school names like Manual Arts) were bused into white schools from the time they were in kindergarten. It was not a two-way street; it was a cradle-to-cap affair. The neighborhood Chicano and Japanese American students at Uni were tracked, without exception, into blue- and pink-collar trades. They were all but banned from athletics.

Schools like Manual Arts beat Uni in every team sport. Only boys competed, and the girls were either cheerleaders or "score girls." When tenth-graders like me entered the school—and trailed the halls like lost lambs—a clever opportunist from the guidance office asked us if we'd like to "get involved." I was signed up to keep stats for the boys' lightest-weight basketball teams and for the swim team.

I was apprehensive about reentering the American public school system. Edmonton's classrooms had been a relief, because I hadn't gotten bullied for being a bookish girl with glasses. My vocabulary was considered "normal." My wardrobe was as provincial as that of all the other girls. Everyone read books in Canada, even kids who were flunking out. There was no basketball team. You could swim outside maybe two months of the year. I never saw anyone take stats for the hockey coach—would that include how many teeth the players knocked out per period?

But in 1974, living with my father for the first time in West Los Angeles, I was entering a new school that observed Jewish holidays and major film debuts.

I had been so sheltered from anything but my mother's Irish Catholic fatalism that I didn't know a thing about Jewish stereotypes. My knowledge of bar mitzvahs came from reading *All-of-a-Kind Family* storybooks. The kids around me at Uni would rail about "JAPS," and I would blush because I thought they were making anti-Asian slurs. I'd never heard of anyone's getting a nose job—I thought they did so because they couldn't breathe properly.

For my first score girl assignment, I was given printed sheets with diagrams of the basketball court or the swim lanes, and a clutch of pencils to write down times and errors. It was a job where I remained invisible, with not one person speaking to me during an entire game.

I eavesdropped on the basketball cheerleaders. I learned what a Jewish American princess was, who the "fat Mexican sluts" were (which I thought meant girls who had just deplaned from Mexico), and how Kelly Kitano had gotten thrown out of school for her skirt being too short—she was not a nice quiet Japanese girl like the "others." The cheerleaders never talked about the game. Their erotic and racial fantasies ran like diarrhea.

From the boys, I learned that to be a young black man bused in from Watts and expected to play well on the University High "C" team was to be immersed in the depths of personal misery. Every boy on the "B" and "C" teams was called a "fag" by the JV and varsity crowd.

None of the boys who played ever asked to see my stats, either. Coach Lundgrem took my sheaf of papers and slammed them into an ankle-level file drawer at the end of the week. *Bang!*

One time, he caught his fingers in the file drawer hinge and screamed, "You motherfucking cunt!" I stayed in the room with my mouth hanging open just long enough to make him even madder. I'd never heard anyone say that word before, and the sound of his rage made me shiver with envy. One day, I wanted to let loose with something like that.

I had a private left-wing conscience—private because I hated being laughed at. I asked Lily Davidson, one of the other score girls, "Why would you call a girl a JAP if you're Jewish? Isn't that like turning something against yourself that you'd only expect an enemy to say?"

I had to sputter to get even that far. Lily just shook her head at me: "Because some girls are JAPs—what're you supposed to call 'em?"

I learned that my outrage about "wrong words" was something only older people talked about. Like, how could someone be "Mexican" if his family had been in California longer than a single white cowboy? My Spanish teacher, Mr. Gomez, liked to rant about such things. We had plenty of radical teachers; the instructors were on the brink of revolt. They wanted to teach women's history, black history, labor history; they wanted to come out with their gay lovers; they wanted the Equal Rights Amendment passed. Even my typing teacher, who looked like Marilyn Monroe in *Some Like It Hot,* supported the ERA. But most of the students? Not there yet.

One thing I liked about being a score girl was that I got to see the whole city on away games. The night we went to play Crenshaw High, I climbed onto the school bus and there wasn't a single other score girl or cheerleader on board.

"Where is everybody?" I asked Darryl, one of the prominent "faggots."

He rolled his eyes. "Crenshaw's tough . . . they're scared." "Tough" was a euphemism for "black"; I'd picked that up by then.

Wiley, another "C" team member sitting next to him, sang, "Their parents won't let them go." And he looked at me like, *What about yours?*

Crenshaw cheerleaders weren't scared of us; they were a wall of sound. Every girl was a baritone, and when they opened their mouths, they hit the first syllable, "CREN," like an anvil splitting open the sun—and then the "SHAW!" blasted what was left of you against the earth.

They did military cadence with their feet and their voices. Scary? It was exhilarating. My dad would be glad I was seeing and hearing every corner of the city.

So I took the bus to Crenshaw. Not only did no one beat me up, but I sat with the team for the first time. It was like getting a sex change—the boys talked to me like I was . . . *there*. It wasn't bitchy. I got a slice of pizza and a Coke. I had the best time of my meager American high school social life.

Darryl turned to me and said, "Are you going to the swim team banquet at the end of the season?"

"What's that?"

"It's at the Playboy Club, in Century City. Dan and Jimmy need dates." He tipped his head back, nodding to them on the bench, like they needed socks.

"The Playboy Club? Don't you have to be twenty-one?"

Plus, I was thinking, *And a guy? And . . . old?*

"I guess they're desperate; my dad says they'll do banquets for anyone." He looked at me a little closer, like he was searching for something. "You know who Dan and Jimmy are, right?"

"I know Jimmy." Jimmy was fine; he wasn't rude. He was passing as a "not-Mexican" because his mom's last name was Irish.

"Dan Margolis is his friend, right?" I asked, one eyebrow going up. That was how everyone said Dan's name, as if dubiousness were in order. Dan Margolis thought he was a player, but he looked like he was going to shit in his pants most of the time.

Darryl laughed. "Yeah, Dan says he's going to nail a Bunny."

I cracked up, too. I was getting comfortable. "Does that mean that his date doesn't have to touch him?"

"Aw, c'mon, you gotta know someone. Everyone's gotta have a date."

"Did you ask Tracey?" I thought of her because she was a score girl like me—filling out stat forms no one read, very quiet. I had never heard her call anyone a bad name.

The next day, Tracey spotted me standing in the snack-counter line at recess. I thought she was going to walk up and say, "You hooked me up with Dan Margolis; now I'm going to kill you."

But instead, she handed me a flyer. A petition, actually. It read: "We . . . want to bring . . . lesbians and birth control . . . on campus. . . . We demand the administration allow them on campus."

That wasn't exactly what it said, but that was the important part. Lesbians and birth control! They sounded like a couple of armies that could take on Crenshaw. Of course I wanted them to come. I was bored out of my mind.

"This sounds cool," I said, signing it. "You're not going to believe this, but I was going to ask you if you wanna go to the swim team banquet."

"The Bunnies!" she said. That was the first time I'd heard her get loud.

"Yeah, if we're lucky, they'll be lesbians." I had to act smart now, because I realized she was so hip I could not, would not, sell her out to Dan Margolis.

"Dan's already asked me," she said. She started braiding her long silky hair behind her back, like it was nothing.

"Great! I mean, you'll be the only person there I know."

"It's not till June; you'll know everyone by then," she said, as if I were charm itself.

She slipped before me at the snack-line window and lowered her head so her voice could be heard through the wire screen. "Does the burrito have union lettuce in it?"

The lady back there in the hairnet glared back at us, like she'd like to cram union lettuce up our butts.

THE CHURNING MIST

TRACEY TOOK ME TO MY FIRST *Red Tide* meeting. *The Red Tide* was the organizing force behind the lettuce boycott/ farmworker drive, the lesbians/birth-control-ladies-are-coming plan, and a support caravan to the Wounded Knee occupation in South Dakota, which had already been stopped on the Nevada border by the state police. *The Red Tide* was the name of the newspaper that a couple dozen high school students, most of them at Uni, produced and published, much to the distress of the boys' dean and the principal.

The paper's masthead featured the following preamble:

It came—flooding the schools, crushing everything that stood in its way, leaving in its wake a trail of destruction, havoc, rebellion. It razed classrooms, flinging textbooks to the winds, screaming out of turn, leaving foul stains on the desks, ripping the flags from their poles. It caught scores of students, sweeping them onward in its headlong course, trapping them in the whirlpool of its frenzy. Administrators reeled, choking on its noxious reek as it tore their offices asunder. Cut slips, tardy slips, suspension notices, bad conduct notices, report cards—all were swept away in its churning mist. It was . . . The Red Tide.

The first issue of the newspaper that I saw had something about the PLO on the cover, condemning Israel. The varsity team's star forward, David Berry, found me alone, reading it on Coach Lundgrem's desk before a Friday game. Why was David in there? He was part of the athletic elite; I never got within ten feet of people like him.

"DB"—that's what I heard his friends call him—was sweating. He'd come to find Coach but instead found me, reading something that made him lose whatever fragile composure he'd come in with.

The headline set him off.

"Anyone who reads this crap is a fascist and an anti-Semite!" he said, like he was quoting from the playbook.

"It's not fasc—" I started to say. "It says here that the people who wrote it are Jewish; they're socialists," I tried again. "How can it be anti-Semitic and fascist?"

I couldn't believe this was my first conversation with the most popular guy at school. He had wavy hair with a blond streak; he surfed when he wasn't playing ball.

"What are you, a fucking communist?" he asked, snatching *The Red Tide* off Coach's desk in front of me and ripping it in half. "If I ever catch you reading this again, I'll kick your cunt in."

I got out of my chair and realized I was taller than DB. I'm sure I was redder in the face. I grabbed the basketball stat reports for the past week and ripped them in half. Of course, they weren't varsity stats. Now the floor was covered in paper. There was a torn photograph of a dead Vietcong person lying on top of the shreds of the "C" team's pathetic performance the previous night.

"Is that fucking *communist* enough for you?" I had never used either of those big words aloud. But DB had already slammed the door, and I was alone.

That was my last time in Coach Lundgrem's office. I couldn't explain what happened. I started to panic. There was only one thing I really cared about. I ran five blocks and called Tracey from the pay phone at the A&W stand. "Do you think I can still go to the swim team banquet at the Playboy Club? I've just eighty-sixed myself from the basketball team."

She cracked up. "I can't believe you're still thinking about that."

"I've never seen a Bunny; I really want to."

She reassured me, and on we went into March Madness. I did not tell anyone at *The Red Tide,* whose meetings I now attended weekly, that I was still a surreptitious swim team score girl. I picketed liquor stores selling nonunion Gallo wine; I marched to impeach Nixon; I listened to every word the lesbians and the birth control women from Planned Parenthood had to say—and I talked to "Marilyn Monroe" in typing class about why the ERA didn't go nearly far enough.

I read Marx's *Wage Labour and Capital* on assignment to make a presentation to *The Red Tide*'s Thursday-night study group—it was by far the most difficult "pamphlet" I'd ever read in my life. I had to read whole sentences more than once. Our high school classes didn't teach this level of critique.

Midstruggle, I walked into my after-school job at McDonald's on Santa Monica Boulevard, and it hit me like a brick. Why did people put up with this exploitation? Why was everyone falling for it? Capitalism was a con job beyond anything P. T. Barnum had ever dreamed of. Why had people formulated revolution so long ago, yet nothing, *nothing* had changed?

That night I got off work and took the bus home. I smelled bad, and my feet were killing me. There was an old lady in the next seat playing her transistor radio, oblivious to my french fry stench. It was the news hour:

> *"And in the market today, U.S. productivity has dipped three percent since the first of the year. . . . Productivity is how Americans work more efficiently, and when workers are more productive, their bosses are able to give them raises."*

"HOW CAN THEY SAY THAT?" I pounded my seat like Khrushchev with a shoe. The radio lady darted her eyes at me. I had tears in my mine. "THEY'RE LYING, AND EVERYONE JUST KEEPS SLEEPING!"

I stood up, even though it wasn't my stop, and hailed the bus driver: "When was the last time *you* got a raise?"

He pointed at the red plastic sign dangling by his mirror: FAVOR DE NO ESTAR CHINGANDO.

"Exactly my point," I said, and got off a mile early to walk the rest of the way. That was the day I became a devoted socialist.

I ABANDONED MOST OF HIGH SCHOOL—other than protesting its petty nuisances and attending swim meets. My life was *The Red Tide*—or hiking with my dad, driving everywhere with him on weekends from Mexico to Mojave to the Sierras. He told me about a gifted student he had named Carlos Castaneda, who was writing a dissertation my dad couldn't put down.

I told him everything that went on in my *Red Tide* meetings. I asked him what he thought about "picking up the gun," and he told me how much his stint in the army had deepened his pacifism. He was like a rock about it.

"But what if someone was pointing a rifle right at you?" I asked, waving my arms as only a fifteen-year-old girl can do to emphasize her point.

"I would not shoot back," Bill said, implacable, bending down to look at some coyote scat on the mountain we'd been climbing.

"Okay, what if they were going to shoot *me?*" I spit back.

Bill stood up slowly and looked at me. His eyes filled up. "I would defend you," he said.

I felt like a murderer. I had to stop talking like this. Did the others in *The Red Tide* have these debates with their parents? How did anyone win at these questions?

My duties as the swim team score girl were a cool, dull relief. Everything just stopped, except the *splash-splash* rhythm of laps up and down the pool. And yet swimming was not as square as basketball. I was sure the swim coach, Dale Swensen, smoked pot—he was under thirty, a substitute teacher, and seemed to be doing something progressive at UCLA that he cared about more than high school sports. He was not an overt racist; that alone made him unique.

Plus, there were no cheerleaders in swimming. Those girls were harpies with pom-poms.

I also started having sex. Not with anyone at school, but with the socialists, the ones with all the ideas in their heads. Some of them were married. Some of them were hookers. Some of them drank all the time. But lucky for me, some of them were really, really good in bed—and since everyone was down with women's liberation and nonmonogamy, that made things extra good for me.

I was in no one's debt; I was no one's property. What little I thought about school anymore involved feeling bad about how scared everyone was: scared of having sex, scared of leaving their gilded cage, scared of dreaming about anything that hadn't been premeditated by their parents.

I decided to drop out of school in June and take one of those instant-diploma tests that the state was starting to offer. I saw a preview of the exam that asked you to figure out the best deal on toothpaste in a given supermarket comparison. I could do that. I'd been doing all the shopping and cooking for both my parents for years.

Tracey, Jimmy, and Darryl found me sorting a box of flyers after we swam in an intercity conference Memorial Day weekend. I had to hurry; I was on my way to a labor solidarity picnic. My double life!

"We have to plan this Playboy thing," Jimmy said. He'd grown his curly brown hair all the way down his back and kept it tied in a navy bandanna when he rode his Honda. Tracey looked like his sister—they were both in pin-striped overalls covered with patches.

"What's to plan?" I asked. "I'm not wearing a dress."

Darryl explained: "Everyone wants 'ludes, but no one seems to be able to score."

"You should ask Coach," I said. "He's probably wrapping them up in 'Mr. Natural' cellophane at Royce Hall."

Tracey said we could call a dealer named Bruce, but that I had better connections with him, 'cause Bruce's old man was a burned-out Maoist. I, on the other hand, baby-sat for people in the canyons who paid me good money to clean a kilo for them after their kids were put to bed.

Tracey was in such a good mood, I had to ask her about Dan Margolis. Dan was now seen on campus in gold chains, shiny polyester shirts, and a cloud of cigarette smoke. He looked like a pornographer from Studio City. But now that I was actually fucking, I had the strangest feeling Dan was still a virgin.

"Oh Susie, it doesn't matter about Dan. I'm only seeing women," Tracey said. She had a little smile like a halo over her head.

So there really were going to be lesbians at the Playboy Club.

Jimmy interrupted. "I promise you I'll keep Dan ten feet away. He'll be mesmerized, anyway, by the—"

"BUNNIES." We all said it.

SWIM BANQUET

THE FOLLOWING IS THE UNITED STUDENTS FOR DEMOCRATIC EDUCATION PLAT-
FORM.

I. FULL DEMOCRATIC RIGHTS IN THE SCHOOLS.
    A. Right to hear any speaker on campus without administration
     interference.
    B. Right to distribute and sell any material on campus without
     censorship.
    C. Right to peacefully assemble without administration inter-
     ference.
    D. Right to privacy--freedom from search and seizure.
    D. Right to have all police, security aids, etc., off campus.
    F. Open campus for all, at all times.
II. JOINT CONTROL WITH TEACHERS OF OUR SCHOOLS.
    A. Formation of school government.
    B. Control of Curriculum.
    C. Freedom to form any class.
    D. Right to review class materials.
    E. Right to hire and fire teachers.
    F. End to mandatory classes.
III. END TO RACISM AND SEXISM IN THE EDUCATIONAL SYSTEM.
    A. Womens and minorities study classes.
    B. Role of women and minorities taught in history classes and
     textbooks.
    C. V.D., Birth control and abortion information centers on
     campus, controlled by students.
    D. End to discrimination and harrassment of gays.
    E. Bi-lingual education for Chicano students.
IV. END TO THE TRACKING SYSTEM;the placing of students in classes
against their will according to race, class and sex.
    A. The right of students to take any classes desired.
    B. Equal opportunity in atheltics for women.
    C. An end to the present grading system.
SCHOOL IS NOT IN ISOLATION FROM THE REST OF SOCIETY, AND WE THEREFORE
DEMAND THAT AMERICA'S WEALTH SERVE THE NEEDS OF THOSE WHO PRODUCE IT.
V.   A. The right of all people to have a decent standard of living.
    B. Full employment opportunity for all.
    C. Free 24 hr. child care centers for all.
    D. Free health care.
    E. The right of all workers to strike and to form their own
     unions.
    F. Free public transportation.
VI. AN END TO ALL U.S. AND FOREIGN IMPERIALISM IN ALL OTHER NATIONS.
e.g. A. U.S. out of Indo-China.
    B. U.S. out of Founded Free.
    C. England out of Ireland.
    D. Portugal out of Africa.

THE MORNING OF THE SWIM BANQUET, I had my first
hangover. My stomach felt like a garbage pail.

I'd spend the whole day before target shooting with Comrade
Munk's guns out in Simi Valley, beyond Magic Mountain, in the
scrub off of Highway 5. Munk and five other comrades, all the
boys, brought several twelve-packs, a fifth of whiskey, two shotguns, three rifles, a .45 automatic, and a .357 magnum. I had no
idea they had such a kick.

"I'm scared," I admitted to Munk.

He gave me a little pep talk. "You haven't learned gun safety; that's why you're scared. A firearm isn't a wild animal; it's a tool. After today, you won't be afraid of guns anymore, but you'll have learned to be wary of people who don't know how to use them."

Munk's pedagogy was impeccable—I learned all the safety basics, plus I experienced the thrill of beginner's luck and the "female aim" advantage, according to him. I blew the stuffing out of those beer cans, which the rest of our party drained in quick succession.

I'd never tasted hard liquor before, and the aftertaste in my mouth was, as Daddy would say, "execrable."

I went into my little bathroom, with the mirror above the sink, and saw that I didn't look like myself anymore. I had something stuck in my teeth from the night before. Besides the beer yesterday, I'd had only a burrito. I was sixteen; I couldn't really be old, but it was the first time I'd noticed I wasn't a child. I didn't have my mother's choice of bowl haircut; I had visible breasts; I'd picked out the glasses I was wearing; I had calluses on my hands.

When I sat down on the toilet, I could see my stomach slightly curving out, instead of in. *I'm fat,* I thought. *I can't go anywhere, it's the end.* Then I was ashamed of myself for caring. I felt like I was six, sixteen, sixty.

After our target practice ended, we'd driven all the way back to Lynwood for a Teamster organizer meeting. One of my lovers, Joe, who'd skipped the firearms training, passed me a note during an agenda item. He scrawled, "As Marx said to his Jenny, 'I care more for your sweet thighs than anything else.'"

"Really?" I wrote back. I was so enamored of Marxism now. After the meeting, when we rendezvoused in the bathroom, he kissed me and said, "I hate to tell you I made that up. . . . I love you."

I loved him, too; I loved all these guys. But if we shot guns in Simi Valley again, I wasn't going to drink anything just to make empty targets. I went to sleep on my sloshy waterbed, and when I woke up, it was Tracey calling to ask me what I was going to wear to the Playboy Club that night.

I had a halter-top leotard I really liked at the time. It was a baby-blue, frosty stretch velvet. It snapped at the crotch and was skintight. I had to wrestle on my jeans, which had two zippers on each side of my belly, like sailor pants with zips instead of buttons.

I hoisted them on lying down, for maximum tummy flatness. Then I slipped on the silver labrys earrings that Tracey had gotten me. Finally, my hippie sandals and my mother's ring—as much as I dreaded hearing from her, I wore that ring every day.

Jimmy picked me up in his Chevy Nova. I realized it was a real date, and that I'd never been on a date . . . I just went to meetings and demos and ended up in bed with my friends.

We went to pick up Darryl, then Tracey, who jumped in the car, wearing the same jeans as me, maybe tighter.

"Bunny!" she said, sliding in.

"Bunny-Bunny!" I echoed back.

"You guys are embarrassing me," said Jimmy, who had a nifty technique of rolling a joint with his hands and driving with his knees. I finally zeroed in on what he was wearing.

"Your blue tuxedo matches Sue's leotard!" Darryl noted.

Tracey was nicer. "I've never seen you boys look so good out of Speedos."

I thought that when we got to the Playboy Club, it was going to be organized the way Uni planned our movements for games, where the coach herded us into a group and we marched around like summer campers.

But this scene was as if we had graduated. Jimmy drove his car up to a valet and pulled a wad of money out of his blue trousers. "I've got it."

Valet parking jobs looked much better than my shifts at McDonald's. We saw some other kids we knew, all decked out in glitter and rainbow colors. We all were walking into the Playboy Club as if it were our usual routine on a Friday night.

Dan Margolis hadn't made an entrance yet. "Is everything okay with him?" I whispered. This was too good to be true.

"Oh yeah, he hooked up with one of his bloods; I'm sure he'll be here soon," Darryl said. He was resplendent in peach satin.

We walked down a long red-carpet-style foyer. A maître d' greeted us like old friends, and we could see Coach Swensen waving his hand—gaily, no less—from a table near the dance floor. He had on a shirt with at least five buttons undone, and a silver and turquoise peace pendant hung around his neck.

Finally, everywhere, like pixie dust, were the Playboy Bunnies. They were more magnificent than the magazine had ever showcased. Their figures were unbelievable—packed into satin bathing-beauty suits like pastel cupcakes: periwinkle, coral, and lavender hourglasses. Their breasts spilled out almost to the nipple, poured in like cake batter. You couldn't help but stare. Their faces were heavily madeup—every one of them with false eyelashes—and their hair was teased high and long, like Nashville's Loretta Lynn. At the tippy-top were their fuzzy rabbit ears.

Coach Swensen handed me a glass of champagne, as if I were free, white, and twenty-one. I couldn't thank him, though, because our Bunny waitress had just turned her back to me.

Her satin cupcake suit was cut up on the sides, so her legs looked unstoppable to the waist. Satin princess seams in the back of the suit cleaved her butt cheeks. Right where the outfit disappeared into a thong, where "X" marked the spot, where all donkey tails must be fixed, was a giant, cotton-candy puff of a bunny tail.

When I was a little girl, my mother had a talcum box from Nina Ricci that had a powder puff under its lid. I wasn't supposed to touch it, but I loved the smell and I longed to take that soft cloud out of its box and dust myself like I saw my mother do. The puff was soft as a kitten's ears. When she was at work, I took baths that lasted two hours, and I let myself take the plunge.

That Bunny's tail took me right back to those moments. I had to touch it. *Had to.* Nasty Dan Margolis was a perfect gentleman, wherever he was, compared with my single-minded perversion.

I peeked around the table to see if anyone had noticed my drool, but the others were in a similar hypnotic state. No one was being ID'd. Dan Margolis, "The Man" himself, came right up to me and crowed, "Hey there, baby. Poppa's got a brand-new bag!" Reeking of Hai Karate, he kissed me wetly on the cheek. He clasped my hands together as he slipped something small and hard, like a bead, into my palm. It had to be the quaalude.

I saw Darryl across the table drop his pill into a flute of champagne and hold it aloft, making a toast. God, these swim banquets were a gas! Was this what Mark Spitz got to do every weekend?

The disco ball lit up and swept the floor next to our table with iridescent sparkles. The DJ, with a voice as low as the hottest Crenshaw girl's, said, "And now, ladies and gentlemen . . . let's . . . get . . . it . . . onnnnn!"

The bass guitar hook began:

Money money money money
MON-ey
Some people got to have it
Some people really need it

I jumped up in my baby-blue leotard and joined the whole Uni High, very high swim team undulating in one booty-dipping, shimmering wave of grind.

A Bunny caught my bump and gave me the eye. She was brown, with a towering Roman ponytail. The pink soles of her feet were firmly planted in four-inch mules.

"How old are you, anyway, baby?" she asked, one hand on her hip, the other holding two martinis perched on a tray.

I breathed out. "Really, really close to you."

It took so long to say that. Would she wait for me? I had to get one more thing out before she disappeared like a genie into a bunny bottle.

"Could . . . could I touch it?" She *had* to know what I meant; I couldn't get my mouth to form any more words.

"Oh, for you, baby, anything," she said, taking a perfumed step closer to my reach. Not spilling one drop, she turned around and bent, just slightly, at the waist.

GEORGE PUTNAM'S SHOW

FOR ALL MY *RED TIDE* ACTIVITIES, I felt like we were swimming against a tide of apathy. From listening to my dad, I felt like nothing cool had happened in L.A. since the sixties—nothing. My dad said that in '67, when *Sergeant Pepper* came out, everyone in the whole city took the day off, went to Griffith Park, sang "All You Need Is Love," and dropped acid. He told me the story of how his colleague Peter Ladefoged lost his hearing in one ear because of the police beating he endured while protesting the war, along with ten thousand others, in front of the Century City Hotel when president Lyndon B. Johnson came to town.

But by 1973, we were lucky to get four people to stand in a picket line in front of a store carrying Gallo wine, and we were even luckier if Hells Angels hired by the store owner didn't come along and stomp us. One goon threw Tracey into the gutter and smacked her in the face. He spit a wad of green mucus in mine.

"Is there anything you'd believe in if you weren't paid off?" We wouldn't shut up.

I asked my dad, "Where did all the people go who give a damn?" and Bill said, "San Francisco. Or they died trying."

People always imagine there is something *happening* in Los Angeles because of the celebrities. They think that because they see a movie star buy a bag of marshmallows, it must be an event. They think wiping their ass with the same toilet paper that a movie star's maid wiped her ass with is an accomplishment. This is a company town, and Hollywood is just as crushing as a Carnegie Steel mill. The vast majority of Angelenos have so much nothing in their lives that "celebrity nothing" makes them feel like they have something.

I could hardly wait to get out of school, to get someplace real as soon as possible. I could not take one more minute of trying to convince the people of Los Angeles that a workers' revolution and a complete overhaul of society were a tiny bit more exciting than getting a bit role in a Burger King commercial.

I'd had it with chanting in the rain, invisible to the passing crowd. I was already bitter over their indifference, and I was only fifteen. My sole activist feedback at high school consisted of Jewish Defense League–member cheerleaders putting notes in my locker that said, "Our campus does not need bitches like you tearing down Israel" As if I even had time to tear down Israel. I was too busy tearing down Westwood.

And then something happened.

The Red Tide got on the news. Not just any news, but the newscast of George Putnam, the most right-wing broadcaster in all of Southern California, the fellow who tried to stop a black man, Tom Bradley, from becoming mayor of Los Angeles, because he said that it would "start a Negro revolution from which white citizens would never recover."

Putnam, like all popular conservative broadcasters, had a gift for articulating the fears of his paranoid "John Bircher" tribe that was a radical's propaganda dream come true. I secretly wanted everything Georgie prophesied to come to pass. I *wanted* to be overrun by communists, potheads, and homosexuals! But the left-wing tsunami never arrived.

I don't know how Putnam got into news, or Cold War politics, but he was obviously a frustrated movie star—a great silent star born at the wrong time. You could turn down the volume on his singsong cadence, yet easily understand the entire monologue from his melodramatic performance. He had the grief of Lillian Gish, the grim sorrow of William S. Hart, the eye-popping intensity of Rudy Valentino. He had everything but the humor of Chaplin—the man did not have one funny bone in his body.

We heard through the grapevine of Tracey's dad, whose sister worked at the KTLA television station, that Putnam had gotten ahold of a copy of *The Red Tide* and was eager to expose us on the air, Friday night.

We scrutinized our latest issue to see what topic he would target. The lead story was about Nixon invading Cambodia, and all his lies and cover-ups.

But we didn't think the Tricky Dick story would be Putnam's favorite—he considered Nixon a liberal. Maybe he would go for our story about undercover narcs on high school campuses. Our intrepid photographer Joel had taken surreptitious photos of the fake "high school seniors"—from the LAPD—who posed as perfectly groomed beach boys trying to score.

Another suspect in our latest issue was our history of the FBI's infiltration of the Black Panthers—but we thought that might strain Putnam's reading level. He would face the same challenge with our exposé on sexism in driver's ed class. I loved our driver's ed story, because we'd found an illustration from the student driving manual that showed a blond who couldn't figure out how to get the key into the ignition.

Which story would Georgie pick to illustrate our depravity? At six o'clock, we gathered at our clubhouse—the Letwin brothers' garage—and Darryl twisted the TV antenna to make Putnam's show appear without floating horizontal lines.

Tracey and my other favorite *Red Tide* girl, Tammy, argued about whether we should be down in front of KTLA's offices protesting this very evening or should wait till the next morning. Michael, whose parents were hosting our vigil, told them if they didn't shut up he would stuff them in the trunk and George would never hear from either of them again. Darryl popped a Bud and turned the volume up. Showtime!

George Putnam held a copy of the latest *Red Tide* in front of his cameras so the viewers could see the cover and back page on half the screen.

"I have here before me," he said, his eyebrows and hair moving with great feeling, "a picture of the most *disgusting* thing I have ever seen."

We looked at one another, bewildered.

"I cannot," he warned, "show this obscenity on television." He paused. The suspense was unbearable.

"It is an illustration"—his voice dropped to a baritone—"of a woman's . . . private parts."

I grabbed the issue out of Tammy's hands and ripped it open to the last pages. "Oh my god, it's the IUD birth control story!" The picture he was referring to was a *Grey's Anatomy*–style cross-section of a woman's vagina and uterus.

"Why?" Putnam raised his eyes to the heavens for an answer. "Why are our children subjected to this kind of filth, this kind of promiscuity, in the schoolroom?"

"Oh man, Principal Dornacker is going to have a fit," Tammy predicted—and it was true, because Georgie was making it look like Uni itself was funding our birth control campaign.

"This rag, if you can call it that," George said, lowering the paper, "claims to be the work of high school students—yet we know this *pornography* is the work of a cynical group of so-called adults who fund and exploit their communistic, atheist ideologies on our precious children."

"Why isn't he saying *feminist?*" Tammy demanded.

"Because he doesn't know that word," Tracey said.

"Where's our fucking cynics to fund us, that's what I want to know," Darryl said, and opened another Budweiser.

"Our daughters," George continued, "our daughters cannot defend their virtue when godless putridity is flaunted in their faces!"

"Okay, I've got the headline," Tammy interrupted: "'George Putnam Claims Women's Vagina Is Most Disgusting Thing He's Ever Seen.'"

"It's the *only* one he's ever seen!" Michael said. I looked at a couple other faces in the room, and I wondered if that described a few of our members as well. I knew George Putnam wasn't a virgin, but some *Red Tiders* were.

"I think," Tammy said, "it was the fallopian tubes that did him in."

"I know George is shocked," I said, "but this story didn't even do its job. If we want birth control access for high school students, these stories can't be so boring and technical, like sex is a valve job. No one we know even reads these."

I reminded everyone of a short piece I'd written about the essentials of lubrication, the benefits of coconut oil, and how even saliva was better than nothing.

Michael gave me a look. Last time he'd seen my lube story, he'd told me he was going to throw up. People were dying in Vietnam, and I wanted to talk about vaginas—how could I?

School went like a slow drip the next day. The same ten people who always watched the news had seen our big "exposé," but it was like we were in a bomb shelter while everyone else was whistling Dixie.

I was annoyed. I'd rather be on my picket line in the rain, arguing with company goons. After lunch I went to the gym office, where for some reason I was allowed to use the phone with impunity. Ms. Larsen, the only teacher using "Ms." on campus so far, was lifting boxes of something onto a rolling cart.

"Here, I'll help you," I said, taking one of the loads out of her arms.

"I am not giving you a note for PE today, Susannah."

"Ms. Larsen, you don't need to. I'm doing independent-study PE now, remember? I'll never need a note again."

She took two boxes to my one and kept stacking. "Hmpf!" And then, "What do you want, then?"

"Did you see you see the George Putnam show last night?"

"I don't watch that fat bastard."

I tried again. "Well, I still want to know if you're going to sign our petition for the self-defense workshops we want to do during girls' gym. I put the paper on your desk last week, and you said you'd think about it."

The petition had been written up by *Red Tide* women, but we'd given ourselves a liberal name, High School Women Against

Violence Against Women. Tracey said that name made her dizzy—
but I argued it would work.

"That's the shit they like. We can't say, 'Pinko Dykes Who
Want to Get Their Hands on Your Daughters.'"

"Susannah, how many rapes, exactly, do you think are happening on this campus?"

"I can't believe you're asking me that!" I dropped a box at her
feet. "You, of all people, know that those girls crying in the locker
room are not telling anyone what goes on, and that's the whole
problem. No one around here reports rape; it would 'ruin' their
reputation."

"What do you mean, me, 'of all people'?" Ms. Larsen's face
turned beety.

"You're a feminist—"

"I'm a *what?*"

"You're *not* a feminist? Oh, c'mon!"

"You don't even know what you're talking about."

Everyone else acted like Ms. Larsen was some gray-haired
stoic, but I felt like I'd been in a bar brawl with her every time we
were alone for five minutes.

"Do you know what people think you're saying when you say
'feminist'?" she whispered. Her blue eyes darted at mine.

"I don't know—what do you mean? Who are you talking
about?"

She stared at me, and we both stopped picking up boxes. I felt
tears coming up. Why did she always have to break my balls?

I tried again: "Are you trying to get me to say something like,
they think I'm a lesbian?" I was hot now, too.

Ms. Larsen's head trembled back and forth.

"I don't care what they think!" I said. "They're in the dustbin
of history; they're not what's going on! What does their prejudice
have to do with anything?"

"It has to do with how you are perceived by this administration, the faculty, and the rest of the community." She barely moved her lips.

"Well, if they 'perceive' me as a dyke, I don't care," I said. "I don't care! I mean, I *am* bisexual."

Larsen took a step back and held up her hand in front of her eyes. "You can't talk to me like this, Susannah," she said, and moved closer to her desk.

"Ms. Larsen, you know things are changing. You don't have to be ashamed anymore." I leaned against her desk, then hoisted myself up to sit on it.

It was too much. She grabbed my wrist and pinched me until it hurt.

"Jesus!"

"You have no bloody idea what shame is." She didn't let go. I could count every dark line on her face.

"Ms. Larsen," I yanked, but she had me in a vise. "Shame is a fifteen-year-old girl in the locker room next to me who's bleeding from her vagina and won't tell anyone but me that a varsity player just raped her and told her he'd kill her if she ever told anyone."

She let go of my arm. "Where's your fucking piece of paper?"

"You're standing on it." It had fallen off her desk, but I could recognize my handwriting on the floor. I picked it up and handed it to her, half-torn. Her eyes were watery. My heart was ready to burst out of my chest.

"You can fix it with some Scotch tape," she said, and pulled a red pen from behind her ear, signing the bottom of it. Her phone rang, like a stage cue, and she turned to answer it, steely as ever: "Coach Larson, what do you want?"

I tried to read her first name on my self-defense petition. Her signature was unreadable, like a little scarlet scar.

SEX EDUCATION

MY FIRST PARTNERED SEX WAS a group of three. My best friend, Danielle, and I seduced and conquered an "older man" of twenty-seven from down the street. Gary was an unemployed soap opera actor, hustling for commercials, going to auditions every day. I was almost sixteen, Danielle a year younger. She'd been in the States only six months, from Belgium, coming to stay with her father, just like me.

I found out that Gary's soap career consisted of playing "teenagers"—no wonder he cried about his aging process. We thought he was ridiculous—but pretty. He envied our lack of concern about growing up.

Kissing Danielle is what I remember the most. We were all on the futon, watching the World Series after we'd finished doing Gary's laundry. Danielle and I had a housecleaning/-sitting service, and every other Thursday we went to Gary's apartment to hose down his man cave. We pestered him with nosy questions about sex; we found his driver's license and taunted him about his real age; we skinny-dipped in the pool. Danielle delighted in being rude, and I was one of her few calming influences.

The Orioles got the lead. Danielle and I were lying down, telling Gary how boring baseball was and how he should get a life. Dannie started to pass me a joint she'd rolled, and our cheeks brushed each other. How could a tough girl be so soft?

My lips touched hers. It was a shock; it almost hurt. I thought, *Am I trembling because it's Danielle, or because it's a girl, or because it's my first time?*

I had never kissed anyone before. Never held hands, never played Post Office or Doctor. I had read every page of *The Hite Report* and the Kinsey research, but I had never kissed anything but my pillow.

We kissed Gary next. We triumphed over baseball. I don't know what made him surrender that day—we had told him so many times before that we wanted to lose our virginity and that he should oblige us by being the guinea pig.

"It's so weird," he said afterward. "Sue, you have a better figure, but Danielle, she has something that I just can't put my finger on. It just compels you."

"Jesus, Gary," I said, "it's not an audition."

"You just insulted both of us," Danielle added. It's true—it should have hurt to hear his crude appraisals. But when I was with Dani, his words bounced off like rubber arrows.

I felt safe and bold with Danielle—I'd do things with her I'd never do by myself. We could seduce anyone; we could get out of—or into—any situation we wished. When we were alone, she told me that my kissing was terrible, that Americans didn't know how to kiss. She ran a bath for us, and when we got into the tub to practice, we turned on the shower, too, the water pouring down our heads.

Men were intimidated by us, which we thought was funny. Funny, but great leverage. For the first couple months of my sex life, I was too intimidated to do anything alone with a guy—Danielle was my big dog, my fearless leader, the one I could temper and reason with. I loved her. Sex with her, alone, made me shiver. We never talked about it.

At the same time, Danielle had no interest in the women's consciousness-raising (CR) groups that were sprouting all over Los Angeles. She was her own Amazon. She didn't join groups. Maybe it wasn't a Belgian thing to do.

I was in two or three CR groups simultaneously. The first one, a formal session, was all older women, except me. I think I gave them the first taste of teenage impulsivity they'd had since they'd been in high school themselves. A couple of them were ready to turn me in to the police, because they imagined I was the type to steal their boyfriends without a second thought.

I argued with them, in my fawnlike attempts at sexual liberation. "First of all, I don't even *know* your boyfriend," I said to one mad hen named Marcie. "And second of all, why does it bother you that *if* I fucked him, theoretically, it wouldn't 'mean' anything to me? What is it supposed to *mean?* Why can't I be your friend, have sex with your old man, and then have dinner with both of you the next night? Why is that so hard to imagine?" I saw this as a direct line from Engels's *Origins of the Family.*

Marcie hissed at me and used the parental language that I didn't experience at home with Bill. "You are an *infant* who has *no* idea what you're dealing with," she spat.

I never knew how to reply to that. Marcie and the other over-thirties didn't get that I was so much closer to my girlfriends than I was to any man. I barely understood men at all. The older women's approval and affection were critical to me. I could, and sometimes did, have one-night stands with their men, but I never felt with these men the intimacy I had with the women in the CR group. And I didn't understand the women's investment in these relationships.

The second women's group I was in, which was the most influential in the long run, was the Speculum Club, as I called it. We were a self-help group modeled on the famous Feminist Women's Health Centers. The aim was not to talk about feelings, but rather to take down our pants every session and look at our cervixes.

We monitored our cycles, detailed our sexual response, learned our fertility symptoms inside and out, performed vacuum aspirations on our uteruses, and seized control of the birth control process when necessary. My written diary from that group was extraordinary in its detail and observation. It was the first science class I'd ever paid attention to.

I went from being a teenage girl who took the Pill without giving a hoot about its hormonal consequences to being a rabble-rouser who would preach, "When you're not afraid to touch your vagina, you can use birth control that doesn't screw up your body every day."

The Pill was ideal for marketing to women who had never taken a mirror and looked at their genitals. They never had to deal with their cunt; they just popped a colored tablet in their mouths—"Barbie Birth Control."

When you use diaphragms, cervical caps, condoms, it's a hands-on experience—and hands are so good for everything sexual. The girls in my locker room at high school, who were always trying to "borrow" a Pill for a special occasion, didn't take to my exhortations. Well, maybe some who were eavesdropping did.

I remember Julie, the girl with the locker next to mine, who, aside from thinking that the Pill only had to be popped within a couple days of "doing it," was particularly disdainful of my approach to letting boys know what was going on.

"I'd rather die than have my boyfriend see me sticking my hand down there!" she said. "What a turnoff! How do you expect to get a date?"

We were talking different languages. "Dates" were for morons and squares.

"Why, are you trying to convince him that you're infertile?" I asked. "That you have a magic pussy that can't get knocked up?"

"STOP SAYING *PUSSY!*" Julie screamed, loud enough for the guys in the boys' locker room to hear her.

As much as I lectured Julie on her backwardness, I wasn't so liberated myself beyond the birth control basics. I was timid about bringing my orgasm out of my secret masturbation life and into bed with someone else. I knew, technically, that vaginal poking was unlikely to make me come without more direct clitoral stimulation, but I was too shy to "lead the way." I wished someone would just look into my eyes and *know.* I couldn't believe that so many older guys I met with Danielle seemed neither to know nor to notice whether a girl came or not.

The third women's group I belonged to was the broader group of women at high school my own age. We were all devoted to the women's movement, especially the music. It was a happy lesbian-bi launching pad—everyone was so game, so open to "what *could* happen if you just tried it," unlike my older CR comrades or the nerd of my Speculum Cub. My high school girlfriends were the ones who schooled me about what it looked like to get turned on enough to just follow your clit to its natural conclusion.

Sure, they were shy sometimes; we were all shy. But when your arousal level exceeds your timidity, you don't need an instruction manual. Like Danielle—she just went for it.

My girlfriends' bedroom conversations were deeper than anything I ever said in a circle with chairs and tortilla chips. We talked about our sex with other people—with boys and men of all types, and with other women, both inexperienced, like we were and committed dykes.

When Danielle said no, she meant it, and when she said yes, it was without duress. I wanted to have the nerve to touch my clit when I was fucking, just like she did. Dani didn't apologize or explain.

"I want to be like you," I murmured under my breath more than once my first year of fucking. "I don't want to be trying to prove anything."

YOU ARE NOW A CADRE

AFTER MY SIXTEENTH BIRTHDAY, I wanted to get more serious about politics. *The Red Tide* was aging—what were we all going to do when we got out of the playpen? Many of us joined the "grown-up" socialist group we were most attracted to at the time, a small sect called the International Socialists, the IS.

Why them? In some ways, it was probably chance—there were a lot of leftist groups that salivated at the idea of recruiting a bunch of fearless teenagers who never slept. The IS was attractive because its members weren't doctrinaire about many things the rest of the Left was hysterical about. They were all in favor of independent feminist groups, gay organizing, black power, whatever—you didn't seem to have to choose between causes. You just brought your class consciousness to every potluck, and that was easy enough to do. They also—and this spoke directly to our generation—didn't believe in a socialist paradise that might be thriving a plane ride away. I got so embarrassed listening to other Reds talk about China or Russia, like they were some kind of Shangri-la.

The IS, at that time, had two branch organizers, a mom and dad with two kids. They were normal. They were not Hollywood; they were not ascetics. Geri and Ambrose could talk Marxism or labor history all night, but they'd feed you macaroni and cheese and watch *Star Trek* reruns.

I knew I'd have to ask their permission to join the IS. They thought of me as a baby, a slightly older baby who could diaper their youngest. I knew they cared about me, but they were protective. Plus, as they were always pointing out, I didn't even have a driver's license.

I kept bugging them; I didn't want to keep being treated like a kid. They fretted and fretted—and finally told me to meet them at Betty's Lamplighter coffee shop to talk about "possibly joining."

I made a face: "Gee, should I get a note from my dad?"

"Yes," Geri said, "this isn't going to happen at all if you don't have his permission."

Betty's Lamplighter coffee shop was in the Valley, next to a nursing home, and there were no bus stops for miles around. I'd need a ride. My idea of a cool place to meet to talk about my entrée into full-time revolutionary knighthood would've been one of the cooler joints down by the beach, someplace where you might smoke a joint outside and order a cream-cheese veggie roll with a smoothie on the side. Close to the bus lines.

But Geri and Ambrose, like bobble dolls on a dashboard, just shook their heads at me. No, no, no. Workers went to the

Lamplighter. Petty bourgeois wankers went to smoothie bars. Wankers were hippies.

But we were hippies, weren't we? Geri knew the wacky version of every folk song in the Pete Seeger songbook:

Oh, they always have to ask her if she comes . . .
Oh, they always have to ask her if she comes . . .
Oh, they wouldn't have to mention if they'd only pay
attention,
Oh, they always have to ask her when she comes.

I'd seen Ambrose tie-dye socks for his oldest son. They couldn't fool me. Lots of workers were hippies, too.

I waited for them in the Lamplighter like an unrepentant flower child in my catsuit, granny glasses, and cutoffs—which I'd embroidered with a version of *Whistler's Mother,* holding a machine gun, stitched on my ass.

I couldn't have imagined a duller word than *worker* before I was initiated into the IS's inner sanctum. Before, if I'd said "that worker over there," it would have meant someone of an indeterminate profession, hanging out in a field or on a sidewalk. The guys who waited to be picked up in front of the hardware store were "workers." Miserable fucks standing in line at the unemployment office were "workers." The white-collar version would be drones squeezing into a subway. Who knows where they *worked?* We knew only that they must hate whatever it is they did and they ground away at it like a stone. Work away, you suckers—I didn't ever want to be like that.

Sometimes I'd hear an old Woody Guthrie song, or see Henry Fonda wiping his brow in *The Grapes of Wrath,* and I'd think about my grandma and grandpa during their dust bowl days, about the farm the bank took away from Grandma Halloran. Then

I'd think *worker* with a little compassion and guilt. A Dorothea Lange black-and-white photograph. Now I got up every morning, spoiled rotten, and ate sugar-frosted flakes.

But at this point *worker* meant something else to me. I'd been educated. *Worker* had Studs Terkel written all over it. It meant turning everything you knew upside down. The untapped potential, the General Strike, the lie exposed. Workers controlled the means of production, and I thought that was the most brilliant idea anyone had ever come up with.

Ambrose didn't wear anything colorful to the Lamplighter. Neither did Geri. But who needed color when we sat in bench seats of fluorescent orange and gold, while red cuckoo clocks chimed five different times on a fake rock wall?

Our waitress and our food were more impressive than our opening conversation. Geri and Ambrose seemed fidgety, but the hash browns were perfect. The lady serving us could kick fifty smoothie-stand operators on their butts. She had a red beehive and a lot of wrinkles, but she moved like a lightweight artillery unit.

I watched her handle ten tables while Geri and Ambrose rattled on about how the IS had five industrial priorities that each member needed to get involved in. Like a quiz-show kid, I quoted them back before they could finish their sentences: auto, trucking, steel, coal, phone. The idea was to build a rank-and-file movement in the most critical areas of American industry, and then, you know, "strike," like a Commie cobra.

I twisted my menu in my hands, looking at "Flo" in her gingham uniform. "It's too bad 'food service' isn't one of our priorities." We needed forces of nature like her. People do have to eat.

Geri followed my eyes. "I waitressed for fifteen years, Sue. I was working in a place like this when I had my first baby . . . and you're right, these women deserve pearls instead of the swine they serve. But they're not unionized; they are frozen in these jobs, and they're never going to get out of them until the strongest people in labor start taking the lead."

"Yeah, like him?" I asked sarcastically, rolling my eyes toward a hungover trucker the next booth over, whose breath was so bad I had to wave my hash brown steam in his direction to cover it up.

"Exactly like him!" Ambrose pounced on me. "That guy drives for Roadway. He's in Local 208, and they're about to vote on a national master freight contract that, if contested, will lead to a strike in which the whole over-the-road trucking system will be paralyzed."

"Which means this restaurant won't get its hash browns delivery," Geri added, taking the ketchup bottle out of my hands.

"If this waitress demands a raise or bitches too much, she's going to be fired, and you'll never hear from her again," Ambrose went on. "You have to look at the material conditions, Sue, not your emotions." His face looked like an unmade bed. They were pregnant with their second kid.

"But what about the garment workers in Texas who're in the news today?" I asked. "They're not our priorities; they just unionized, and people are flying in from all over to congratulate them." Mexican women making blue jeans in this little border factory where no one cared whether they lived or died—now the whole labor movement was carrying them on their shoulders.

"They should be congratulated," Geri said. Her eyes were red, too.

"A century ago, they would have been up there with coal—" Ambrose started.

"But the garment unions are being wiped out by overseas factories" Geri finished. Ambrose and Geri traded sentences without even noticing it.

"Oh Christ, don't tell me, they're the exception that proves the rule!" I raised my hands in surrender.

"What does your dad have to say about all this?" Ambrose asked.

"About me being a trucker? Or working in a coal mine?"

"Don't be a smart-ass."

"I'm not! I told him that I didn't want to go to college, that it was my idea of the bourgeois nightmare."

"And he said?"

"That he felt the same way!"

Ambrose cracked up. "When's your dad retiring from UCLA?"

"I have no idea," I said. "He's not that old." My dad seemed like a feature at the school, the perennial professor. "All I'm saying is, he doesn't think a college degree is the be-all and end-all. He told me if I wanted to be a gardener, he would have the highest respect for me."

They both shut up at that. Geri finally said, "If our parents had ever said anything like that to us, we probably wouldn't be here today. . . . "

"I would definitely be composting." Ambrose nodded.

"But he just says that because it's like a Zen aspiration," I said. "It's cool, but you know, for him, it's just a wish to be free of all the bureaucracy. He doesn't think working in an auto plant is inspiring, but he understands that I'm not into it for the cars."

"Well, you're fifteen, so the whole thing is a moot point for a good long while," Geri said, comforting herself.

"I'm sixteen."

"Yeah, well, we feel like we're a hundred and sixteen, cutie pie."

"Let's move on to state capitalism versus bureaucratic collectivism," Ambrose suggested. He licked some ketchup off his fingers.

Was I going to be quizzed on the finer points?

"I'll take state capitalism for five hundred!" I brightened up. "Bureaucratic collectivist definitions are for losers!"

"You don't even know the difference, I bet," Geri said.

"Half the people in our branch don't know the difference," I said. "What the fuck does it matter what you call Russia as long as you're not some kook who thinks it's a paradise? They're just like the United States, except there's only one corporation, the Party. Pretty soon they'll do the same thing here, except it'll be Chevron or Bank of America—"

"Oh, hell, you're in," Ambrose said, and laid his fork down.

"What can you pay in dues?" Geri asked, who looked like she was going to make me pay in tomatoes now that I'd emptied the bottle.

"Uh, nothing?" I had no idea there were dues.

"Geri, she's out on the picket lines every day, and no one's paying her for that, either." Duncan passed me the salt.

"I can tell you're going soft," Geri said, "because Sue thinks she's embraced the state capitalist position."

"I can do five dollars a week or something," I said, wondering why I'd picked that number. That was five hours of baby-sitting, and it meant I'd have to forgo pot, blue jeans, and used records.

Geri threw up her hands. "I'll cover you; forget it! Someday you'll get a decent job."

Flo came over with a second bottle of ketchup so things wouldn't get ugly. I didn't want her job, but I sure would have liked to organize with her or, better yet, follow her to wherever she went after work. I wished someone like her were confronting the Master Freight Contract, instead of the lizard muncher behind us.

"Sometimes you just have to get people who have some fight in them," I said, but I was looking at my plate when I said it.

"From the mouths of babes," Geri said.

"Lord help us," Ambrose finished. He took his IS button off his Teamster jacket, and I fastened it to my peasant blouse.

PATTY HEARST

I TOOK THE TRAIN UP TO Paso Robles to see my mom right after I joined the IS. She'd moved three times since Edmonton. She was the city librarian at a little Carnegie-era round edifice in the town square. Almond orchards, cattle ranches. She lived with her white Persian cat, Pussums, in the only apartment complex in town, right near the freeway exit. Pussums had huge yellow eyes and paws as big as bedroom slippers. When I talked to her on the phone, she'd turn and make a remark to him. I hadn't seen her for two years.

Sometimes we'd talk about what she was reading, her *New Yorker* issue. She was as interested in politics and literature as ever.

If she could expatriate us to Canada, surely she would glean why I wanted to move to Detroit, why I wanted to *do* something. But her reaction surprised me.

"What about Patty Hearst?" she asked. She was referring to the famous California newspaper heiress who'd been kidnapped by a self-described "revolutionary" group called the Symbionese Liberation Army (SLA). They proceeded to rob banks and shoot guns, and were eventually wasted down to nothing but ash by the L.A. SWAT team. Patty was one of the few survivors.

"Yeah, what about her? Mom, that has nothing to do with me; I'm not running with a bunch of crazy people."

She raised an eyebrow. My mom never said, "Susie, you're wrong; capitalism is grand." She didn't say I was exaggerating or melodramatic. Why would she? I got my red bleeding Irish Catholic heart from her.

The difference was, she didn't join up with other people who agreed with her. She thought that was just another setup. "Who are these people, Susie?" she asked, her brow digging in. "You don't know them. You *act* like they're family—but they're not your blood."

I had to work on my straight face for that one. I hadn't seen a single one of her blood relatives since 1965.

My mom's voice got higher. "I just don't want to see anything happen to you."

"I'm not blowing anything up," I said. "I'm not robbing banks. That's not our plan. Those people who kidnapped Patty Hearst aren't even for real, they're FBI—"

She turned away and spoke to her kitty. "Little Pussums, Mommy's little Pussums, is hers a little bit thirsty?"

I waited.

"My brother called himself a socialist," my mom said with a snort, putting fresh water in Pussums' bowl.

"Really?" I'd never heard her say anything about her brother except one thing.

"But he was too busy drinking to do anything about that, either," she said.

Yep, that was it.

"I worshipped him when we were young," she whispered.

"But why was Uncle Bud a socialist?" I asked.

"Oh, the CCC camps, during the Depression," she said, like I would know what she was talking about. "They let the Irish in, and so all the young men from our neighborhood went."

"All the Irish were socialists at those camps?" I asked. I loved this kind of stuff.

She thought that was funny. "They were all a bunch of 'social pests,' is what they were," she cackled. "But it was a good thing, what FDR did, or those boys would've starved. Those were the only jobs they could get before the war, the only thing an Irish kid could do."

She started talking to Pussums again. "Little baby, little baby's not going to listen to her mommy, is she? Hers just won't listen!" Pussums had perfected the art of turning her back and ignoring your every word.

I don't know why I even bothered. I mean, Mom didn't know anything about what I was doing; she'd never ask if I didn't bring it up. But sometimes I felt like she ought to know. What if I did end up in jail, or something happened? Was she just going to pretend like it wasn't happening? I wanted Walter Cronkite to come by here, train my mother's eyes on him, and say, "Elizabeth, your daughter needs you to pay attention to what's going on."

I looked at the clock. There were two more hours before I had to be at the bus station for my trip back to L.A. Maybe she would like me to cook something. I could cook; I bet Patty Hearst didn't know how to do that. I bet they ate a lot of cereal in their SLA hideout.

I wonder if they taught Patty to shoot the way Munk had taught me, with the beer can targets in the desert. That would be funny if we went shooting in Simi Valley and met them! They would rise up and shout some overwrought slogan—"*Venceremos!*"—before they pulled the trigger. Drama queens. I was embarrassed to read about their sex lives in the paper, how one man had mesmerized all those women with his cock and his rhetoric.

"What does your father say?" I heard Mom's voice behind me.

Maybe if I had known Grandfather Jack, I would've understood what she was driving at. It was always her prelude to losing control.

I stuttered. I could never think of the right answer to this one. "Oh, he's kinda like you; you know, he's supportive, but he worries about me, too."

"You have to do what your father says, Susie!"

But he didn't say anything. He was more interested in asking *me* what I thought *he* should do.

"You need to listen to him, Susie!"

More advice from someone who had cut her father off when she was twelve.

"Well, he doesn't say anything except, 'Good luck and take it easy!'" I snapped. That was a mistake.

"Well, where *is* he, what is he doing, is he with his new wife?" She didn't wait for my reply; she didn't need it. "I suppose she's very pretty," she said, curling her fingers tight. "But that doesn't mean that he can—"

"Mom, stop, this is going—"

"Well, your father has had everything handed to him, and that's—"

I'd have given anything to talk about Patty Hearst again. But Elizabeth was past talking.

Her hand cracked my cheek and knocked me
hear her last words. She burst into tears and ran
bathroom door slam. I felt my face with my palm a
it was sizzling, but I was okay. I'd better not cry, o
ally mad.

I went to her door and spoke through it: "Mom,
Mom, are you there? Are you okay?"

She didn't answer. I tried the door, but she'd locl
just tell me you're okay. I have to go to the bus, an
to leave you like this. Mommy . . . ?"

Nothing. Goddammit.

"Mom, if you don't open this door, I'm going to
again and they won't be looking for Patty Hearst-
you and me go to the hospital!"

Another one of her faces, the Snow Queen, op
an inch. I was relieved to see her standing up, intac
she said. "Your things are packed; you may go."

"I'm really sorry, Mom. I'm so sorry I made yo

She closed the door in my face. But she didn't lc
She really didn't like the police.

I was relieved to catch the train back early. I
funny blush on one side, but I didn't think anyone
had to pee, but I could wait till I got back to L.A.

I left Elizabeth's apartment and walked across
ring the bell at Apartment 2G. All the older ladie
ment complex knew each other.

"Hi, there, Mrs. Koperski." She recognized wh
exactly like my mother. "Yes, I'm fine; I have to
now, but would you go check in with my mom in a
not feeling well, and I made her some tea. I'm worr
to drink it."

"Oh, yes, sweetheart, of course I will."

My mom's neighbors were good-natured busybodies. I didn't
want them to discover her body, but I had to do something. She'd
probably pull it together to save face. She'd forget what had happened between the two of us. Presto. I wished I could pull that
off. I wished I could just turn around, like Pussums, and show you
that I looked like walking away from every last bit of it.

DAGO ARMOUR'S APARTMENT

I FINALLY GOT PERMISSION FROM my dad to go to "Commie camp" in Detroit the summer of 1975. I was seventeen, and you would have thought I'd been invited on a tour of Europe—I was so excited. As far as I could tell, Motor City was filled with charisma, a 100 percent working-class town with factories on every corner, like pastry shops in Vienna. I could not wait.

But I had no money for my destination, no ticket to ride. I was going to have to baby-sit and hamburger-fry my way to the revolution launch pad.

My father didn't say anything directly about my plans. It was more like, "You earn it, you plan it, go ahead."

But his newest girlfriend, Judy, didn't hold back, and I heard her dramatizing it on the phone to one of her girlfriends. "She wants to go to *Detroit* for the summer. . . .

"Ha! Yeah, I know, why not throw in Newark and Carbondale and make it like a cruise! I told Bill, I told him, you're her father, you . . .

"No, no, I don't think Susie has any idea; she's never really been out of California. She says to me [using a prissy schoolgirl voice], 'I'm sure there are nice places in Detroit, just like anywhere else!' Yes, I know, we're all waiting for the film to be developed!"

More laughing. I didn't think Judy had ever been to Detroit, either, so what did she know? I'd develop the pictures, all right, and I wouldn't show them to her.

Judy was so ignorant—she didn't understand that Commie summer camp was not going to be in the city itself. It was a real camp, the kind of place out in Michigan's forests that gets leased to Girl Scouts and Rotarians. I guess the owner didn't have a problem with Reds, either, at least for a week.

Or maybe the camp managers didn't know who we were. One year we organized a high school anti-apartheid conference, for which I made up phony brochures for the kids' parents that said that the whole thing was being sponsored by the YWCA. It was the only way we could get those permission slips!

I had a couple more months to make the money for my bus ticket. I had applied for a scholarship to the camp itself; that would cover my bunk and meals. I asked Geri and Ambrose to plead on my behalf. Geri called me back with something I didn't expect. "Some of the members of the executive committee think your family is loaded."

"What?"

"I know, I know—they think everyone in California is a millionaire, unless they're industrialized."

"Well, did you set them straight?" I was so embarrassed. I thought the executive committee met in robes to solemnly discuss the future of a Leninist cadre building, not Sue Bright's dad's financial statement.

"Of course I did. I told them that the average feeder driver at UPS makes more than your dad does teaching, and don't you worry, they're going to do it. I told them they were full of shit. But it's just like rubbing salt on a wound to tell the executive committee your dad is a professor; that's what they were supposed to be if they hadn't dropped out and become Teamsters."

"Those guys went to college?" I pulled the phone from my ear and looked at the receiver like it was alive.

"You didn't know that? That's their secret shame—they're all Cal and Columbia dropouts." She told me that Mac Lofton was one quarter away from his PhD in English literature.

"Is it really a secret?" When I saw Mac in public, he wore a blue satin Teamsters' jacket with the American flag embroidered on the chest above LOCAL 5. He married a comrade named Arlene, even though she was a lesbian, and listened to George Jones because "that's what workers do." Every time he saw me or one of the other kids from *The Red Tide,* he'd make a face, like someone had put a hippie hair in his Danish. And every time I saw his wrinkled face, I thought, *My god, you don't know a single "worker" under sixty-five.* I loved the Teamsters Union rank and file, but Mac acted like no one mattered who wasn't over fifty and driving "over the road"—while most Teamsters I knew were young and loading trucks, like at United Parcel Service. We weren't listening to George Jones.

"Everyone knows," Geri said. "It's the story of half this organization—don't let them fool you. They don't want any of you kids to go to college, 'cause they would have to see you graduate, when they didn't."

I'd never heard her talk like that. "Geri, didn't you drop out of school, too?"

"Yes, I hated it, but it had nothing to do with communism—I just got pregnant, and I wanted to live on an organic farm and bake bread with my baby on my back." Geri cracked up at herself. "It's no secret and no shame; I have no regrets. If I ever go back to school, I'll be doing it for me."

I didn't know what she was talking about. Mac and the rest of the IS leadership acted like going to college was the same as turning your back on the whole class struggle; it was like saying you were going to a fiesta while people were starving. I agreed a thousand percent. I was not going to waste the revolution's time by sitting in a classroom with a bunch of dilettantes who thought they were going to get a degree and *be somebody*. Whenever someone said that shit to me, I'd come back with, "Instead of *being somebody*, why don't you *do something* for a change?"

Yet here was Geri, acting like it was no big deal one way or the other.

She had one more question for me. "Sue, I didn't know what to say about this, but can your mom help you out? I don't even know if you talk to her."

"My *mom?*" I acted like it was something you might or might not have, like an extra limb. "Look, I'm baby-sitting and house-cleaning my ass off for the bus ticket, and I can work at camp, too—isn't there something I can do for my room and board?"

Geri called me back the next day and told me that Murray, the International Socialists' head pressman, was going to be running the kitchen, and that I would do supper duty with him each night. Excellent. Murray even sent me a postcard, telling me he'd learned to cook in the Navy brig and now he was going to share all his special recipes with me.

The Greyhound ticket from L.A. to Detroit, round-trip, was $172. The problem was that I was making $1 an hour baby-sitting and $2 for housecleaning. I had a couple weeks left, and aside from bus fare, I still needed cash for everything else before I left: burritos, books, ice cream.

Danielle, my girlfriend who'd turned me on to my first cleaning jobs, advised me, "Raise your prices."

"Oh, yeah, right."

"Whaddaya mean? I did." She slammed her cigar box shut and started tamping down a hand-rolled cigarette. "These assholes can afford it," she said, licking the paper. "Stop cleaning their dope for free. Stop taking record albums instead of money. Start charging them for blow jobs."

"Jesus Christ, Dani, I'm not going to charge *money* for sex!"

"*Jesus*, Sue," she mimicked me with an American drawl, "what *will* you charge money for? *Qu'est-ce que tu fais maintenant?*"

This was why we couldn't keep cleaning together—she knew how to clean, but she also knew how to get on my nerves. I knew she didn't want me to leave, either.

I went to the Dennises' that night to take care of their twins. I wasn't having sex with Mr. Dennis or Mrs. Dennis—ha! They were a middle-class *Ebony* magazine–type family, probably the only people I worked for in the canyon who didn't have giant spider plants in macramé baskets, or a shoe box full of Colombian. I couldn't imagine asking them for more money—they were so nice, and I imagined they had moved to this neighborhood so their kids could go to West L.A. schools without being bused for two hours.

My lover Reggie Johnson came over to pick me up from their house at ten thirty. Mr. Dennis took one look at Reggie at the door—Reg's twelve-inch afro and black leather coat, versus Mr. Dennis in his suit and tie—and made a terrible face.

I could read his mind: *What are you two trying to prove?*

"Don't say anything!" I mouthed to Reggie behind Mr. Dennis's back. Mrs. Dennis came to the door, too, with some homemade macaroons. "Do you want some for you and your friend, honey?" she asked, just like a mommy on a TV show.

"Thank you, Mrs. Dennis," Reggie and I said in a one-two chorus. I was glad Reggie's mom was kind of like Mrs. Dennis, because at least he had good manners with her.

The next day after school, it was time to clean Dago Armour's apartment. He was a self-professed filmmaker whom I had never seen leave his apartment except to go to Odie's Stop 'n' Go for more beer. But Dago was very smart and had stories about every single person in Beverly Glen, from the kids working on *The Partridge Family* to Beatle George Harrison's secret masseuse.

Dago was always bitching about money, so I wouldn't sound out of place talking about my problems. Maybe he would have a scheme, not for getting money, but rather for how to get out of needing it—he was good at that.

I hadn't seen Dago make a normal financial transaction in the five months I'd been cleaning for him. He paid me in windowpane acid, or hash, or peyote buttons, which I could always sell to Danielle, who split whatever she got with me.

Danielle had cleaned for him first, but she'd dumped him because of his no-cash policy. "Besides, he's fucking nasty," she told me. "Bastard. He is responsible for Misty's death, and everyone in this canyon knows it except her fucked-up parents."

Misty—was she the kid who'd fallen off the cliffs of Schweitzer Canyon the year before and everyone had said it wasn't an accident? No one had seen it happen. Even my dad, who knew nothing of neighborhood gossip, had read in the paper that a fourteen-year-old girl named Misty Dawson had fallen right off the ridge, and that her dog's howling in the middle of the night had woken up everyone in Beverly Glen Canyon. Her parents weren't around; they were in Vegas or something. The ridge she rode up that night was now being carved up and leveled for a monster development project, with a whopping five different floor plans that buyers could choose from. But when Misty was alive, it was like the rest of the canyon: coyotes and sage and desert poppies.

I asked Dago about Misty, and he started crying. "Get me a couple Tuinals, darling, or I'll never stop," he said.

"I'm sorry to just be so blunt," I said. "I didn't know—"

"No, no, she was the best, the best," he said. "I want to talk about her all the time, and no one does, goddamn them all!" He sounded like her guardian, not her murderer.

Dago got out some pictures of Misty and him together, standing in front of the corral, where her gelding, Sallyboy, used to be stabled. Misty was in cutoffs and a handkerchief gingham halter top. A little blond stick figure with a huge smile and an oversize baseball cap. A tomboy. She hugged Dago like he was Santa Claus. He looked about twenty years younger than he did now, but I knew Misty had died when she was only fourteen, before I'd moved in with my dad. Fourteen! I was sixteen, but fourteen years old seemed too young to die and too young to be Dago Armour's girlfriend. Maybe it was unfair just to draw the line there, but it made me feel weird. When I was fourteen, I was pressing grilled-cheese sandwiches on an ironing board in Edmonton.

Misty did have a grown-up face in the pictures, with all her black eyeliner—her trademark. Her tiny legs disappeared into turquoise moccasins.

"Dago, don't cry; it's okay," I said, getting him a glass of wine for his pills. "I didn't mean to make you upset. I just don't understand what happened to her; everyone seemed to love her so much."

"They did—she was their fucking ringleader," he shouted. "She and her Sallyboy!"

This was the part I'd heard before: Misty and her pony. Everyone would get together at the corral, get stoned, and play wasted versions of Mother May I? and Red Light, Green Light. They would drop acid and change all the colors and steps. Misty was the only one who could get the child actors to laugh. She got some girl from *All My Children* to show everyone her third nipple, and then she wouldn't let anyone make fun of it, because she said it was a "gift from God." Everyone had to play Ouija with the young actress because Misty said her third nipple made her psychic and she could see the future.

Apparently, when Misty was around, everything was different. The uglies became goddesses. Misty was so charismatic that she didn't have to make herself a deity; she could afford to be generous and give other people a taste of her power.

"You know what happened to her? They fucking killed her! Mum and Dad!" Dago sobbed, with the same accusing tone Danielle had used in talking about him. He starting banging his head on the edge of the coffee table, and it made all his drugs fly into the air.

"Stop it!" If Dago thought I was going to get on my hands and knees to pick up granules of Thai stick and cocaine, he was out of his mind. I'd fucking vacuum it all up and throw it in the trash can.

"I still don't get it," I said, "because her parents weren't even there when she fell, right?"

"Yeah, well, there you go, babe," Dago said. "They weren't there; they weren't ever fucking there, every fucking time, inn't that the way?" When Dago got mad, his English accent got even thicker.

Enough already. I knew that Misty's parents were alcoholics and that after she died they sold Sallyboy ("to the glue factory," Danielle had sobbed). We still played at the old corral, but it wasn't the same. The Ouija board had been launched into a bonfire.

Dago said he had dropped out of the film he was producing and moved into his current basement apartment, where he paid rent in cocaine and charm. The landlady was another former child actress—so pretty, but the kind of woman who needed to hear the compliment ten times a day or she just fell apart.

Dago's barbiturates were taking effect. He sprawled on his "divan," as he called it—an orange-and-brown-plaid sofa. It was covered with his tantrum-flinging remains now, but he let his head drop back like he didn't have a care in the world.

"Don't clean that up, luv. I know it's all my fault; you don't mean any harm. You're such a luv—the most innocent child in this world, such a beauty. Misty would have made you into one of her goddesses."

I knew what was coming, and I'd rather have vacuumed. It wasn't like he was a bad lay or anything; in fact, he was, like, the most experienced man I'd been with—he was at least thirtysomething. But I never would have even done it with him in the first place if I'd known he was such a crybaby. I always felt stupid that I hadn't noticed that in the beginning. How were you supposed to tell? Guys seemed so tough on the outside, and then when they came, they would cry and cry.

The first day I showed up to take over Danielle's usual shift, Dago made me the most incredible Spanish omelet, with potatoes in it, and talked to me about Ingmar Bergman. He said that I must go see *Persona* that very night at the Nuart with him, and I told him that my dad had taken me to see it the previous week, which impressed him to no end. I really didn't get *Persona,* but after Dago finished explaining it all to me, I may not have been sure if Bergman was a genius, but I was certain Dago was.

He ate my pussy till I screamed; he made me come like he was just skipping stones. That didn't make him cry. I'd never seen anything like it. I wondered if it was this fancy with everyone over thirty.

"I am God's gift to unusual," he said to me, pinching my cheeks, "and I love you already."

"I wish high school guys weren't so uptight, because there are three I know who I wish you could give lessons to," I told him in earnest, and he roared.

"You are a delight—bring them on, bring them all on!" he said.

Dago offered me a line of cocaine, which did nothing for me but was served up exquisitely in the bowl of a miniature silver spoon. I didn't wash one dish that afternoon, and he told me to come again in a week, or even sooner if I wanted.

I came over every two weeks out of sheer concern that he was drowning in his own garbage. You never knew if he'd be brilliant, lucid, or unspooling like a frayed cord.

"C'mere, luv, let me lick your . . . cunt." Dago motioned me over. I hated it when he was too high to handle the longer-syllable words. He was not a pretty picture on his plaid divan. I knew from experience that he could perform sexually no matter what he had ingested, but there was only so much I could stand, even with my eyes closed.

Danielle had once used an expression in front of me: "mercy fuck." I didn't ask her what it meant, because I knew I was guilty. But now, looking at Dago in his dirty clothes, unshaven, splayed out on his sofa bed and beckoning to me like Bacchus on a hospital gurney, I thought, *Well, this is it. A mercy fucking nightmare.*

"Dago, I have to talk to you about something; it's not Misty, it's a real emergency," I said, determined to get my problem aired before he passed out or got so crabby he started breaking his last few wineglasses.

"Yes, luv, my beautiful dolly, tell me anything, but sit on top of me, will you?"

I couldn't come while sitting on top, but I could talk that way—I could talk for hours astride anyone; it made me feel very important. I pulled my cutoffs down.

Dago's cock was clean—why was everything about him so dirty except for his cock? It was the one thing I never felt like laundering.

"Sweet Henry," he swore, pushing into me. I put some spit on my finger and traced the top of my clit, like he'd shown me—that felt good. I was starting to get the hang of not being so self-conscious.

"Your fucking cunt is fucking tight; you're fucking killing me, luv," he moaned. I knew that if I closed my eyes now and he kept talking to me like that, maybe I could come; if I let myself fall on top of his chest and pressed my head into the pillow so couldn't see his tobacco-stained teeth and his pinprick black pupils, and just listened to that voice and kept thinking how much he wanted me, all my empathy would reach a pitch where I was lost in sensation, not running commentary anymore. That would make me come, as Dago put it, "like a star-spangled fucking rocket."

My fingers drew the magic diagram on my clit. It was like releasing a valve; everything else got pushed out. If he would only just fuck me—"Just like that," I breathed.

"Yes, luv, just like that," he repeated back, and his cock pushed me open again. This wasn't romance, it wasn't revolution, but it wasn't playing games, either.

"You're an angel, my cunt, my tight, sweet angel cunt," he whispered, never stopping with his cock or his mouth. I followed his cue and pressed down on him with my clit and my sticky fingers and came, just like he said.

I pulled myself off him, the tender ungluing. I was fond of him—but he had to listen.

"I haven't told you about my Detroit thing." So much for afterglow.

"You can tell me anything, darling, anything," Dago said, pulling me back into his lap, sans penetration, and pushing up my top so that he could hold my breasts with his hands.

"My eyes," he moaned again. "You're still on the Pill, aren't you, darling, aren't you?"

I narrowed my eyes. "No, I'm going to have your love child and sing about it like Diana Ross and have a big hit."

"That's what I was hoping, darling; you're right, you're always right—I must never, never condescend to you. . . . Is there any coke left that I haven't spilled on the floor?"

I got off him and found his little spoon nestled behind one of the bolsters. He smiled at me: Mr. Lucky Strikes. Yuck. He could be so nice, but his teeth, how did he stand it?

"Tell me about Detroit, luv. When are you going?"

I forgot about his teeth and just loved him then, because he said *when* are you going, not *if,* or *why*—and I could have just as soon said "the moon," and he would have acted the same.

"You have to see a film before you go, you have to—maybe it's at the library," he said, getting excited as if he were persona non grata at the UCLA film department. It's called *Detroit: I Do Mind Dying.*"

For once, I knew what he was talking about.

"How do you know that?" I asked. "Geri and Ambrose and Michael and Temma, they all say I have to see it, too. It's a documentary—how do you know about anything like that?"

"There are a few Marxist filmmakers who aren't idiots, luv." Dago smirked.

I looked at him harder. He was so stoned, but he could still say things like this. I never heard anyone say words like *Marxist* unless I was in an eponymous meeting of them. It was like a secret language, a code ring—no one said *Marxist* unless he was one, but Dago wasn't *anything.* He just liked movies and young girls and his coffee table holdings.

"Well, anyway," I explained, "I have to get there. I'm going to Commie summer camp, and they're going to let me work in the kitchen for my room and board, but I have to buy my own bus ticket, which I'm still eighty-eight dollars short on, and I have to eat on the bus, too, and I cannot baby-sit the Dennises into bankruptcy in the next month." Saying it out loud made realize how completely hopeless it was.

"You are such a beautiful doll," Dago said, and he reached deep into another sofa cushion hidey spot. The divan was like Mother Goose's skirt. "I'm going to give you a whole book-and-film list before you go, and you have to come and shag me and tell me all about it when you come back, my little Commie camp cunt angel."

I reached out for the reading list he'd dug up, but it wasn't a list in his hand, it was a fistful of twenties. It looked like plenty more than $88. He could have more than paid off his cigarette tab down at Odie's that he'd been running for the past ten years.

I couldn't believe it. I burst into tears. "I don't want you to give me money for fucking you; I never said that!" I felt like Danielle was right next to me, boring her eyes into me. I might tell her everything, but I wasn't going to tell her *this*.

Dago dropped the money on the floor and tried to grab me with his skinny arms. He wasn't weak, but I was already standing, and I could shake him off. Where were the Kleenex? Where were my cutoffs? I ignored whatever he was calling out to me and headed to the bathroom. I was so stupid; I never should have told him.

The bathroom door consisted of a bamboo bead curtain, and half of the beads had fallen off, so you could look anyone in the eye while they were taking a dump. I ignored Dago's gaze when he came to peer in at me.

"Miss Fucking Bolshevik Cunt, I would never dream of paying you to fuck me—it's my assumption that you do it out of pure fucking joy. Isn't that right, darling?"

I looked down into my naked lap and sighed.

"Really?" I said, still not looking at him.

"I don't even *pay* you to clean this apartment; you are fucking unpayable and a lousy housecleaner and a tight cunt, and if you don't pick the money up off the floor, I'm going to make you vacuum it up with your pussy lips."

"You're disgusting!"

"I'm so glad you noticed. And hurry up, too, because my boyfriend's coming over, and I don't want him looking at you and having a heart attack on my divan."

"Boyfriend" was Dago's drinking, Truffaut-watching buddy who was some kind of dirty old man by proxy. He wanted to do everything Dago did, but I don't think he'd been laid in a million years.

"He doesn't have my looks, angel; that's what the young girls demand," Dago said, cackling and lifting his glass. "Here's to all the angels, and to all the communists!"

"I'll never forget this, Dago," I said, grabbing my granny pack and the money and shaking the cocaine dust off of everything. "When I get back, I'll wash your walls and beat your rugs, I promise."

"If you do that, the whole neighborhood will be plastered for a week," he said, and swiped at my thigh as I leaned against the front door to leave.

"You've still got my come dripping down your leg," he said.

"I do not!" I yelped, jumping over his broken porch stair into the garden. "You're such a sick fuck." That's what he would say. I'd never said it before. I hoped he knew I was joking—because after I went to Detroit, I never saw Dago again.

THE NEW BRANCH
ORGANIZER

MICHAEL, JOE, AND I WERE LEAVING for Detroit, maybe for summer camp, maybe forever, each of us scrambling for money and rides. Meanwhile, the Los Angeles IS branch was being "reorganized" by the Detroit Executive Committee. They figured our youthful *Red Tide* energy—a.k.a. 24/7 devotion—would be missed. Our newspaper was moving with us; there would be no more Los Angeles *Red Tide*—instead, the Detroit Unified School

District was about to have its collective student-body mind blown. Yahoo! I had only two months left till school got out, and I was counting the days.

In April, Stan Holmstrom was assigned to Los Angeles from Seattle, to become our new branch organizer. He drove straight from the airport by himself and showed up at one of our Teamster organizer meetings with a six-pack.

Stan wasn't the family type. The IS Executive Committee had the steely resolve to send us someone who wouldn't sing folk songs or make brownies or wipe our noses when they ran.

We got to have someone fresh from Seattle—someone mysterious, single, childless. He told the Teamster comrades that he not only drank beer but knew how to brew it.

He needed a home, so everyone pitched in to set him up in fewer than twenty-four hours. Stan's first gift was *The Red Tide's* old white sofa, from Michael's parents' garage. Stan took one look at our monster, all eight feet of it, and it was as if every semen, weed, and Top Ramen stain were visible to him, illuminated on its ratty gray-white nap.

Joe said someone should've cried. Tracey said someone should've cleaned it.

Ambrose said Stan drove out his first day in Lynwood to play pickup basketball games a couple blocks away, in Compton. "He picked his location because it's right off the freeway and a couple blocks from some courts."

Stan didn't come on like a ton of bricks. He had a loping gait; he moved like he was always on the court. His hair was shaggy, if not exactly long, and it hung in his eyes. He was tall, taller than anyone else in our group. Michael said he was almost thirty. He dressed in a work shirt, blue jeans, a leather belt, and sneakers every day. Dressed like a kid, played ball like a kid, but with those sad, downward-turning eyes like someone older.

I didn't know someone so quiet could be a branch organizer. Geri was charismatic, and Ambrose was always chatty. Michael was an orator, Joe would not stop arguing, and the other half of the branch were loquacious UCLA professors. Even young members like me would argue and make speeches at the drop of a card.

Some of the other women, the "girlfriend" members—women who never said a word but were someone's girlfriend—they were quiet. We'd have these private talks afterward where they'd promise to say something "next time," but then they never did.

Stan sounded sure of himself when he spoke, but he didn't offer a lot of explanation or rah-rah. It was just, "This is what we're going to do."

The idea was that by having a laser focus, we would reform a moribund and corrupt union. Just saying, "I'm going into Teamsters" to anybody else on the Left was outrageous. Everyone thought we were joining an organized-crime syndicate.

"There is no other left sect in the International Brotherhood of Teamsters, because no other group would have them," Joe said.

"Isn't Fitzsimmons like Nixon's lapdog?" I asked. The Teamsters' current president appeared in press photographs with the president all the time.

"Yeah," said Joe. "Drinking buddies, for sure."

"Well, what am *I* supposed to do in Teamsters?" I asked.

Joe pinched my tummy. "You can head up the ladies' auxiliary, Sue." He'd made me come with his mouth the night before, and it had just made my head spin. His teeth were white, and he was young like me. Was that love? But I loved everybody in our branch—sleeping with them just made it a little deeper.

Stan gave everyone an assignment at the next branch meeting, except me. I raised my hand: "What can I do?"

"Yeah, right," he said, not looking up. "You can report here tomorrow, oh six hundred. You can flyer the Gateway yard with me."

Gateway: that meant trespassing and chatting up total strangers. I was good at that.

"I don't get out of school until after three; I could come then—"

Stan scowled. I saw it like a comic bubble over his head: *Haven't we gotten rid of all the bourgie college coeds yet?* What a jerk; he didn't even know who I was.

Geri touched his arm.

"Sue's still in high school, Stan."

He shook his hair out of his eyes for a minute and snorted.

Fuck him. My god, he'd been here only a week, and he was sitting on what had been my bed with Joe and Reggie.

"I'll be here by three," I said. I wasn't going to use military time, either.

Temma, another *Red Tider* who'd dropped out of Uni, passed me in the hall when I got up to use the bathroom. "Oh, he likes you," she laughed.

"Don't bullshit me!" I whispered.

"I fucked him last night."

"What?"

"Yeah, yesterday—he's okay. You should check him out . . . his partner, Shari, you know? She's in Fresno all the time."

I hooked my arm around Temma's belt loops and dragged her into the bathroom with me.

"*What* partner? Are you kidding? Are you going to do it again?" It was like hearing she'd made a statue come alive.

"He's practically married to Shari Z.—that's why he's down here, because she got an offer to teach women's studies at Fresno, and she's going to come visit him when she can on weekends. We don't have any comrades in Fresno, so—"

I cracked up. "Oh, yeah, well, she can build a branch out of the women's studies department, and they can come make cookies for the Teamster meetings!"

I couldn't believe Stan was acting like the Original Mr. Worker, and his old lady was a professor. One of the unrepentant ones who wasn't going to industrialize, apparently.

"His first wife, Marie, she's famous; she's the queen of the Wolf Socialist Party, and she's, like, the biggest dyke in Seattle. Even the local pigs are afraid of touching her . . . she's some kind of wild woman."

"He was *married* to her?" God, he was old.

"Yeah, that's what Geri told me, but I guess she 'expelled' him for being a man at some point." Temma laughed and pushed me off the toilet seat. "It's my turn."

Somebody knocked on the door. "Hey, High School, get off the can."

Temma reached over and pushed in the lock. "Go run the water," she told me. I turned on both spouts.

"Shari's going to be at Ambrose and Geri's tonight for the potluck," Temma said. "Come early, 'cause she's not a night owl. She's this perfectly nice white academic; she comes up to about Stan's elbow. Dresses just like him, but in tighter jeans."

The knocking started up again, warpath-style. I knew Temma would no sooner open the door than surrender at Pearl Harbor, but I had to get out. She'd already lit up a cigarette and opened the window; I opened the door just wide enough to squeeze through.

One of the older women, Xena—a professor's wife—blocked me, looking outraged. She'd been outraged ever since I had fucked someone she'd fucked a hundred years ago. Jesus.

"There's still someone in there," I said, like I'd come out of a train station lavatory.

"Someone!" she spat. I shrugged.

Stan appeared behind her. "Hey, take it easy," he said, and he touched her lower back. She shuddered, then moved up against him, like a kitten that couldn't help it. He didn't take his eyes off me.

I walked into the meeting space again with my arms open wide. "I'll show you a Teamster ladies' auxiliary, gentlemen," I said, bowing to everyone huddled on the floor. "Give me some flyers."

Temma was right about the tight jeans. Shari was petite and curvy. I found myself scrutinizing her body more than I did Stan's. She was one of those women who make a sacrifice by not wearing a bra, because she was narrow-shouldered and her tits were full and . . . *pendulous*. Every time I said that word, I felt like I was sneaking a peek in *Penthouse* magazine. I wished my breasts were on the pendulous side. It was sexy. When I told Geri that, she said, "Oh, you'll get your wish eventually."

But when? I could be really, really old by then.

Shari had a tiny waist. Her hips flared out like a Mexican guitar. Short legs, and, due to her strict feminist costume, flat sandals. It was funny because, sure enough, the UPS women who came to the potluck, including Geri, all wore at least three-inch platforms. So did Temma, who'd permed her hair into an afro and had burned herself a dark red-brown at the beach.

I patted the top of her perm to see what it felt like. "You went to the boardwalk after the meeting."

"You could have gone, too; the Hare Krishnas fed everybody," she said, slapping my hand away. "But I guess the 'ladies' auxiliary' was calling—are any of you holding?"

I tilted my head behind me. "Go ask Joe, or go through his pockets, if you can stand it. He's the new dope dealer of the 208 Teamster hiring hall."

Joe was rarely working a shift, but he wore his blue Teamster jacket all the time. He said he was making more money selling weed and speed to drivers than he'd ever made on campus.

I heard someone take Linda Ronstadt—Ambrose's heart-throb—off the turntable, and Kool & the Gang started up.

I joined some of the girls in the living room, swaying and chanting.

"Watermelons, fresh ripe tomatoes, apples and oranges, Idaho potatoes, yeah . . . Fruitman!"

Geri was ladling out chili, and it smelled so good, but I just wanted to dance.

Stan may not have liked high school, but he was lucky *The Red Tide* was there. He was lucky to see Temma in her high heels, plus all the local girls and all the non-Teamsters, the ex-Panthers and "crazy motherfuckers," as Joe called them. We knew how to have a good time. It was the only way new people, our "contacts," would ever give our politics a chance; those awful meetings would kill them first.

Stan wasn't dancing; I didn't know where he was. I kept picturing the way Xena had shuddered against him. Shari was dancing without him, her arms around Xena's husband's shoulders.

Soon I wanted to lie down, crash in one of the other rooms where there wasn't any dancing. Ambrose and Geri had a room in the back where they kept a plush leather coffee table. I found it, curled up, and dozed off, until Geri came in and put a blanket over me and tucked a little pillow under my head. It must have been a pillow for the baby. I dozed off again.

Shari stumbled in and woke me up. She cursed the stack of books on the floor that she'd tripped over. She didn't know where the bathroom was. She looked excited, or really high, or both. Fresno must be awful.

I wish I could remember what I said first. It was a polite question. I wish I could remember if I was precocious, or awkward, or earnest. I felt all three afterward.

I only remember how she answered: "Go for it . . . he's a great fuck." Her smile was like sunshine itself. Her blond ringlets bobbled as she nodded her head.

I remember thinking, *Wow, this is how it's supposed to be.* You're supposed to be able to approach your sister and say, "Comrade, I'm feeling it for your old man. May I proceed?"

And then she would say, just like Shari did, "Go for it . . . he's a great fuck."

You could say, "Women are more important to me than men." You could blush and stammer, saying, "I wanted to ask you, if you wouldn't mind, and I don't mean to be rude, and this really isn't a big deal . . . " But I don't know what came out of my mouth. I wasn't even sure I wanted Stan; I just kept thinking about Xena's back arching up.

It didn't seem to matter. The Blond Goddess would've cut me off with a warm smile, like a mother to her chick: Go for it. He's a great fuck.

Shari was so low-key, just the way I imagined it would be after a massive sexual revolution. Women wouldn't be catty. No one would bother to be jealous. Who would have the time? Sex would be friendly and kind and fun. You'd get to see what everyone was like in bed. You'd *learn* things in bed, and that would be the whole point. Romances would seem like candy cigarettes. You could have all the sex and friendship you wanted for free. Exclusivity would be for bores and babies.

The way Shari spoke to me, the way her curls bounced everywhere, was the new shine. Like a challenge. I wanted to go back to Fresno with her and drink from the same fountain. I'd negotiated boys with my own girlfriends before, but it had never sounded like this.

I thought I understood women. I never knew what went on in a boy's head before I went to bed with one. I always wanted to see.

See how it was. I liked the whole finding-out part. They were so brainy and vulnerable at the same time.

Shari was different—she was advertising her man. She wanted a tribute! Was I supposed to file a report? Maybe none of my friends had ever bragged about anything, because there was nothing special to brag about. Just what did this Stan do in bed that was so extraordinary? I felt like I should call and make reservations right away, before he got a cramp or something.

But for someone so generous, Shari bowed out a little quickly.

I was saying to her, "Wow, thank you, thanks for letting me know . . . " Maybe I was a little breathless.

She exhaled a short breath out of her nose and turned on her flat heels, away from me, before I finished expressing my gratitude. Maybe I was too much. Maybe she was on her way to fuck someone else.

She left me sitting there, like a kid with the wrong pizza delivery. Her shine had settled on everything around me. The brown carpet twinkled; the purple sofa and love seat were royal. I could feel my wet underarms, and even my head felt damp.

"Hey, Sue, what's the matter? You look soaked!" It was Joe.

Everyone came through this room on the way to a nonexistent toilet.

"I've just been dancing too much; I gotta change," I said, getting up. "I'm so glad it's you."

Geri had told me her grade-school-age son, Billy, went through three T-shirts a day, he was so hard on clothes. I bet he had one I could borrow, and my chest wasn't that much bigger than his. I went down the hall to find his stash.

Joe followed me and saw me staring into the kid's dresser mirror.

"'WHO DAT?'" he said, reading the slogan on my T-shirt.

"Oh, shut up," I said. "Do I look okay?"

"It sure is tight," he said, hooking his thumbs in his jean pockets.

"You wanna go somewhere?" I felt like I could slap him or fuck him, but not much else.

"We can go for it in the john, if you want," he said. "Jesus, you're wound up." He walked over and put his hand on my shoulder.

"I don't want to be wound up!" I hissed. "Close the door— oh, shit."

Little Billy was dead asleep on his bunk bed with a pile of coats stacked up on top of his covers. Only a little neon light from the window leaked into the room.

"He's dead to the world," Joe said. "So, what's up?"

I made him sit with me on the floor on someone's leather trench coat. I held the sleeve up to my face. "God, this smells good." It was like a tonic.

"Shari Z. just said something really trippy to me; I gotta tell you," I began. I quoted her. Joe burst out laughing, but Billy didn't miss a beat of snoring.

"You've gotta be quiet! Do you think she was being sarcastic? Is that why you're laughing?" All my anxiety came back again. I was going to soak this fine House of Wilson leather coat with my sweat.

"I don't know what that chick means, but I know you'll hold her to it, Sue; that's a promise. Man, she is in for it—"

"It sounded like she was giving Stan a guarantee, like he came with a certificate!"

I could feel Joe scowl, even if I couldn't quite see his face in the dark.

"Yeah, call me right afterward and tell me how he ate you out," he said. "I wanna hear if it's a six-point-oh."

"Oh, c'mon, Joe, don't pout; this is serious!"

He started giggling. "Oh, man, serious, yeah—I wanna know, too. If he's that good, I wanna fuck him."

"He's straight, Josephine!"

"Yeah, that's the point. He's straight, white, over thirty, can't dance—what else do you need to know?"

"He's twenty-nine!"

"Right."

"You are so fucking cocky," I said. I was starting to relax.

"You know I'm right. Here—here's my bet. If he eats you out the first time you do it, I'll . . . "

"What?"

"I'll give you my green flake helmet that you want."

"Really?"

"You can count on it," he said, and took my hand and pressed it against his erection.

I squeezed his cock too hard on purpose and rolled over on top of him.

"Hey, mean girl, cut it out," he said, grinding against me. The neon light cut up and down across my WHO DAT? tits. I took off the T-shirt and bent down to his ear.

"You are a *funky worm,* Joey Baloney," I said. We sealed his promise with our tongues all tied up.

THE MASTER FREIGHT AGREEMENT

I CUT MY LAST PERIOD, high school driver's ed with Mr. Burns. He wouldn't understand that the revolution was not going to wait for me to take his stop-signal exam. Instead, I grabbed the bus and showed up at the Gateway Freight yard right before the start of swing shift, as promised.

I'd changed my clothes, too—I looked like a Teamster girl in tight jeans and a T-shirt, standing in mile-high platforms instead of hippie sandals.

Stan pulled into the parking lot right after me in his Valiant. I wondered how many decades he'd had his driver's license. Temma told me he'd dodged the draft in Canada, married and divorced, and lived underground for five years before he popped up and started running the Seattle branch of our little insurgence. That was a lot of driving.

He handed me a pile of flyers and told me to go to one end of the employees' parking lot while he took the other. The leaflets were an invitation to a meeting of rank-and-filers that we called Teamsters for a Decent Contract—people getting together to talk about the upcoming contract and what we thought might go down. Not socialism, just this miserable, corrupt union and shitty job. You had to start somewhere. The expiration of the Master Freight Agreement was a good place to begin—it covered every over-the-road driver in North America.

"Temma said you know how to talk to people," Stan said—apparently my only vote of confidence.

I thought, *Did she tell you that in bed?*

Instead, I was chipper. "Yeah, it'll be fine." I smiled at him like a Girl Scout. "I'm a regular 'Teamster girlfriend,' according to Sister Temma."

"You are?" he asked, picking up a clipboard like he was going to write down my answer.

"Yeah, I'm sorry; what's your excuse for being here?" I said, not wanting to go where he was leading.

"Maybe I'll be a Teamster boyfriend." He flipped his wrists.

That cracked me up. It was going to be okay. Maybe he wasn't such a snob after all.

We walked to opposite corners. The parking lot was enormous; there must've been more than a hundred cars. No one had come out of work yet. I talked to some taco truck guys who were packing up. They liked my leaflet. I had typed, laid out, and printed this thing on the mimeo machine—it didn't look half bad. I'd put a cartoon I liked at the top: Fitzsimmons and Nixon having a toast together in bed, with their feet sticking out from the sheets at the bottom of the bed.

I went up to each vehicle and tucked a flyer underneath the windshield wiper. I got a rhythm going, singing that Ohio Players vamp to myself:

> *Rollercoaster*
> *of love*
> *Say what?*
> *Rollercoaster*
> *Ooo-oooo-ooo-ooo*

Fuck! Something hard, really hard—like a brick—punched me in the lower back. I fell, sprawling onto my hands and knees in the dirt. I couldn't breathe.

"Hey, girlie!"

I pushed up off my belly, my hands on fire. A squat, muscular guy with a worse grin than a junkyard dog's stood above me, a wrench in his hand. I'd been smacked before, but neither my mother nor the nuns had ever smiled at me while they were doing it.

"What's this crap you're sellin', girlie? This is private property. You better get your can outta here."

He grabbed the goldenrod flyers in my satchel, which was still hanging from my shoulder. I scrambled to stand up, spilling most of the papers onto the ground. Blood was dripping on everything, but I didn't know where it was coming from. I couldn't feel anything.

The wind picked up the flyers and started sailing them over the cars. I wished I could sail away, too. My mind was leaving the premises. I had missed driver's ed for this.

My palms—that was where most of the blood was coming from—looked like stigmata. The pitbull man held up his wrench again.

"Now look what you've done!" he shouted, like he was personally offended. "You little whore, you're gonna clean up this fucking lot before I stick my foot up your ass—"

We both heard a loud *click,* and the little man stopped talking.

There was Stan—right between me and the demon. Instead of just his blue work shirt, Stan was wearing a blue work shirt and a holster. He was holding something, too.

He said two things: "Don't talk to the young woman like that—we're leaving now."

And to me: "Get in the car." He threw me his keys. I caught them without a bounce.

I don't know what else he said. I ran with the keys—ran, ran, ran, like the Gingerbread Man—to Stan's white Valiant, climbed into the back seat, locked the doors, and threw his old-dude basketball sweats over my head. I wanted to crawl in the trunk. It was ninety degrees, but I didn't crack the window. I was freezing, shaking; my clothes were like wet rags. I'd never had a man look at me like that, like he was going to enjoy hurting me. He was a head shorter than I was— even if he was twice as wide—and he'd made me pee in my pants.

"Sue!" I could hear Stan jogging up to the car. I lifted my head up to peek out the window. He didn't look hurt.

I unlocked the door and handed him his keys. He took one of my cut-up hands in his like it was a petal. "Are you okay?"

I burst into tears. Finally time for questions, and that was when I fall apart. "Who was that?" I sobbed through my snot. "Was he from the company or the union? What did you do?"

"Hold on . . . " Stan got in the driver's seat, started up the engine, and peeled out. "I'm taking you home; this was bullshit. You never should've been here."

I cried harder. What did that mean? I'd failed at my assignment because I hadn't kicked that bastard in the nuts? I was frozen? I was useless, wasn't good enough to pass out a fucking flyer?

Stan pulled into the circle driveway in front of his duplex and parked at the door. "Don't move," he said.

He came around to the back door and opened it up, crouching down so he could look me in the eye.

"I'm sorry, I'm okay, I can get out," I said, holding my hands up in front of me. But when I glanced down at my chest, I saw my shirt was ripped open, too. Who had done that? I started gulping air again.

Stan put his arms around me. "Hold on to my neck," he said. He coaxed me out of the car, and once he got me to my feet, he picked me up like a new bride—a bride who couldn't stop sobbing—and carried me through the front door. I don't know how he managed the lock.

He laid me down on the white sofa and went to get one of his extra work shirts for me to change into. I heard him take off the .45 and the holster. No more *clicks*. He came back with a bottle of Povidine, the shirt, and a steaming wet towel.

I had some bloody scratches on me, plus snot and sweat—not as bad as it seemed. The warm towel felt so good.

"What do you drink?" Stan asked. I could hear him opening his kitchen cupboards.

"Ginger ale?"

"Yeah, right," he said, and came back with two jam jars and a bottle of Jack Daniel's. "Drink up," he said, handing me the glass like it was medicine.

I took a sip. Worse than medicine! It was almost as bad as NyQuil.

I gagged, and he laughed.

"Don't laugh at me; this is horrible."

"The horrible part is over—we're lucky to be alive. You're going to be okay, baby."

Baby.

"You think I shouldn't have been there," I said, "because I can't handle it, because I'm not part of the new macho Teamster campaign and I don't have a six-shooter to wave around, like I'm some freak girlfriend diaper baby."

The Jack was giving me something to talk about.

Stan said no. He said it was his fault. He said Ambrose and Geri and Joe and Michael all thought the world of me; he said he'd been a bastard. Temma was right: I was sweet as pie.

He tucked me in, found more blankets and a couple of pillows. I slipped on his shirt and kicked off my pants. Was he watching? I didn't care. I passed out on his sofa like it was the middle of the night.

I woke up with a start; I had to pee. Had it been hours or minutes? The streetlight poured in through Stan's bamboo blinds. I could see a blue clock in the corner that Ambrose had donated to our new branch organizer's furnishings: 3:00 AM. It'd been twelve hours since we'd been in the parking lot.

Stan's apartment was two bedrooms, a living room, and a kitchen. One bedroom was the production room, with the mimeo, ditto machines, and paper supply. I crept into the bathroom next to it, the tile floor icy under my feet. Stan's shirt barely covered my ass. I thought about my warm water bed back at my dad's house, and our kitty making her nest in the middle of my quilts.

Stan appeared in the doorway.

"I'm sorry, I didn't mean to wake you up," I whispered from the toilet.

"I'm not asleep," he said. "You say 'sorry' too much. I've been awake the whole time."

"Why?" I grabbed one of his white duck hand towels and wiped my face, getting a glimpse in the medicine cabinet mirror.

He stepped behind me and looked into my reflection. He must have been six feet five. Blue eyes, drooping lids. He braced his arms on the sink's edge, so I was caught in the middle between the sink and his chest. If I moved one inch, I'd be in his arms.

He spoke to me in the looking glass. "You're driving me crazy, you know that."

He said it, he didn't ask. But I still shook my head. I couldn't breathe.

"Yeah, the way you walk around this place, the way you smell . . . "

I could smell myself, too; I could smell him, like gunpowder and Mr. Daniel's—but I couldn't speak. My legs shook a little, my knees still stinging from where the flesh had been scraped off in the parking lot. Stan felt me shiver, too. He put his long hands on my shoulders and turned me around to face him so my bottom was pressed against the sink.

"You know what you're doing to me?" he repeated. He got down on his knees in one motion, parted the shirttail of the chamois I was wearing, and pressed his face right into my cunt. I grabbed the sink to stop from falling over. He steadied my thighs with his hands. His fingers were like soft sandpaper.

He was crazy; it was like he had to get inside me—he had to get his entire head in me. He was going to cannibalize me from the cunt out, put his cock in my pot and stir it until I screamed. The only way to relieve his ache was to take us both right down the rabbit hole. I could feel myself getting bigger and smaller every second.

"He's a great fuck . . . " Wasn't that Temma's advertisement when Stan had first arrived in town? Who was she talking about? Not this man. Not where he was taking me now.

I gasped from holding my breath for so long.

Baby.

I couldn't speak, but he heard me. His tongue was stroking me, and it was all I could hang on to. I doubled over. Stan stood all the way up and lifted me one more time—this man was never going to let my feet touch the floor again.

I hopped onto his waist, hugging my legs and arms around him. He sank into me, like the last piece of a puzzle. My head dropped back. He squeezed my bottom to lift me just an inch off of his cock.

He was going to make me wait.

"I'm going to make sweet belly love to you till you come for me," he said, carrying me across the floor to his bed. His sheets were blue jersey; an *Economist* lay half-read on the floor. I bit into his shoulder.

Who was this man? Xena, Temma—none of them looked desperate when they said his name. Their bellies didn't tremble like mine.

Susie. He called my name over and over.

I pulled all his weight onto me, and he shuddered. The tables turned.

"Are you okay?" I guess that was his big question.

Yeah, I was. Daylight was breaking. He got up to get me another whiskey and a ginger ale. I asked him if I could roll a joint, and he tossed me a baggie from under some Emma Goldman autobiographies on the floor.

"What are you reading her for?" I asked, licking the Zig-Zag.

"I've been reading Emma since I was a draft dodger."

"Yeah, I heard about that. How'd you do it?"

"I wore a dress."

"Like Phil Ochs?" I threw the sheets off. "Or like a Teamster girlfriend singing 'The Draft Dodger Rag'?"

"How can you be old enough to know that song?" he asked.

"I'm not."

I started it, and he caught up to me on the second line:

Yes, I'm only eighteen, I got a ruptured spleen
And I always carry a purse . . .

I reached out for him with my scabbed-up hand. "I'm not eighteen, but I know a lot of things," I said. "You underestimated me—I guess I thought you were an asshole, too."

"Yeah, you got that right," Stan said, and took a drag. "How old are you?" He exhaled. "No, don't tell me."

I wouldn't. I couldn't stand to lie apart from him. I was an infant; I wanted him to cradle me and never let my toes touch the ground.

"How can I go off to Detroit and leave without you? Shit!" I said. I straddled his lap and blew a smoke ring. His blue eyes were framed right in the center. His cock grew hard again underneath me.

Everyone—everyone but Stan and a couple other comrades—was heading to Michigan for the summer camp. This was the first moment I hadn't craved going away. I never wanted another day to break.

"You're going to be fine," he said. "You gotta go." He took the joint from me. "There's not a man alive who's not an asshole—that's all you need to know—but you're gonna be okay." His hard-on started to soften.

Why'd he have to go and say that? *Fuck, Stan.* Didn't he get it? I would have told him I loved him right then, but I knew it wasn't cool.

Instead, I moved his hand between my legs again, and the wet-ness shut him up. *Feel how I feel.* I leaned down to take his mouth in mine and make all the nonsense stop.

GREYHOUND TO DETROIT VIA AMARILLO

This was Motown, this was New France
Where the Chippewa did the firedance
That was long ago
This is here and now
But the memory still remains somehow.

—Sam Roberts

I PREPARED FOR DETROIT TWO WAYS: like I might be back in two weeks, and like I might settle in for good. Tracey promised that if I didn't come back, she would ship my neatly packed boxes to me. I noticed she scrawled, "This is a bad idea" and, "Come back baby come back" on my record crates.

I was taking only a rucksack on the Greyhound. It was like hiking with my dad—"take only the bare minimum." I decided to bring three paperbacks, which Bill and I diligently picked out from my favorite bookstore in Los Angeles, Papa Bach's.

Papa Bach's was the heart of beatnik Venice, an ocean poet's diaspora, even if it was on Santa Monica Boulevard in West L.A. The never-scrubbed floors were laid out like a hoarder's attic, rat-packed shelves ready to teeter over under their own weight. Stream-of-consciousness ruled the store's organization, where sections like Poetry led to Madmen, which led to Charlie Manson's song lyrics.

My dad made a beeline for some of his friend's chapbooks on the poetry shelves. "This is a novel," he said, "but they keep it here anyway," offering me a copy of Charles Bukowski's *Post Office*.

My eyes brightened. "I didn't know he wrote a novel!" I said, and snatched it out of his hands. "About working in a postal office!"

My dad laughed at me. "Yeah, the big time."

"I love stories about what it's like to work somewhere!"

"I know, honey; this is one of the best."

I asked Bill if there were any good Commie writers I hadn't read yet in my IS study group.

"Yeah, lots." He disappeared into the stacks and returned with John Reed's *Ten Days That Shook the World*.

"How about a thriller?" he asked. He had found a copy of *Day of the Jackal* for a dime.

I was set. I made seven peanut butter–and–grape jelly sandwiches. I had granola with chocolate chip cookies. I wore my green STARRY PLOUGH T-shirt, weathered hiking boots, and my mother's old denim sailor's coat.

The L.A. Greyhound Station was in Skid Row, downtown. It smelled like urine and disinfectant. I left before 6:00 AM and was so sleepy I fell into the front row behind the driver and didn't wake up until Barstow, the last of California's desert before you cross the state line. I was starving, and it was my first chance to look around to see who my traveling posse was for the next three days.

I was the only passenger under sixty. Every row was seniors, people who looked like Oxnard's finest—no doubt avid George Putnam listeners. Well, no matter, that was why I had brought my books. I had a lot of diary writing I wanted to do, too—but I had to go to the bathroom first.

"Take care now, little lady," the driver said, when I got up to head to the toilet. "The smoking section's at the back of the bus."

It seemed no matter how tough I tried to dress, everyone treated me like an innocent little lamb—I just had that kind of face. I smiled at him. "I can handle the Marlboros!" The real challenge would be inhaling the toilet-stall air freshener.

The back row of every Greyhound bus has a bathroom on the left and three seats on the right. In those days, the passengers could open their own windows; hence, the smoking section had a vent.

To my great pleasure, I saw that the two smokers in the aisle so far were young, long-haired, and probably smoking something besides Camels. Hallelujah—I was going to move my seat.

It was a boy and a girl, but they weren't related. Lizzie, the hippie girl, was as tiny as an elf, traveling with her skateboard, getting off in Albuquerque to face a felony charge of defacing a McDonald's—she'd sprayed, "Barf, Baby, Barf" on their cement walls one prom night and had been on the lam for six months in Los Angeles. Her parents had told her she had to come in before it got a lot worse.

"How bad could it get?" I asked.

"Oh god, don't ask—but my mom's a tiger," she said. We talked so fast I didn't see half the desert slip by.

The young man propped against the open window was beautiful—like a storybook Jesus with a faint scar on his cheek. Jesus meets Chuck Conners in *The Rifleman*. But he hardly said a word. He asked to borrow my *Day of the Jackal* and looked grateful when I broke out the PB&J sandwiches. I told him I could cut the crusts off for him like my grandma did in Oxnard.

Lizzie and I hugged goodbye in Albuquerque. No new girls got on board. "Jesus" asked me if I wanted to smoke a joint before the driver called us back inside. We walked to the alley behind the station and lit one up. It was quiet next to the trash bins.

"You sure are pretty," he said.

"Me? You're the one who's pretty," I said. The sun was going down, and when he turned to face the last light from the horizon, his eyes were golden.

We returned to the bus, just the two of us in the back, and I asked him if he wanted something else to eat. He reached up to take a cookie out of my hand, but put it back in my lap, his head hanging down.

"What's the matter?" I asked. "What's going on?" I tilted his head up with the tips of my fingers, and his lips parted like a child's. Oh my god. I had to put something there, so I kissed him. A little voice in my head said, *This is not mercy; this will not help*, but the bigger voice said, *Feed him now*, and that's what won.

He sucked on me for the next ten miles. It felt good, and then it felt sweaty—bad sweat, like it was never going to end. I pushed him off. "I like kissing you, but you gotta tell me what's wrong."

He rolled his eyes—the first sign of a sense of humor. "Will you read to me from the *Jackal?*"

"Yeah, of course," I said. I know what it's like to work yourself up to saying something difficult. I picked up the book from where he'd stopped, on page four. Could he not read? I didn't want to ask. I jumped in from where I'd left my bookmark:

> *Col. Rodin: We are not terrorists, you understand. We are patriots. Our duty is to the soldiers who've died fighting in Algeria, and to the three million French citizens who have always lived there.*
> *The Jackal: And so you want to get rid of him.*

Jesus covered my hands with his on the book's open page. "I'm AWOL," he said.

"Oh, shit . . . " I said. "How long, where from?"

Jesus looked around the rest of the seats like he was just noticing that the Ozzie and Harriet brigade surrounded us. He shook his head gravely at me, in a way I recognized from the IS.

"Are you going to keep me on a need-to-know basis?" I asked, trying to get another smile out of him. "I don't even have a name to call you."

"My name's Beau!" he said, like that was one thing he would never deny.

"Well, I thought you were Jesus, 'cause you look so sad and beautiful."

He took my hands in his again and raised them to his lips, kissing them. He slumped to the floor, to his knees, but didn't let go of me—my god, was he having a heart attack?

"I want to ask you," he said haltingly, "I want to ask you . . . to marry me."

"What?" I jumped up, snatched my hands out of his, and banged my head against the luggage racks. "You don't need to marry me; you need a lawyer to keep you out of the brig! I can help you, but you don't even know me!"

He scrambled back up onto his seat and opened his palms to me, as if to show me a stigmata. "When we get to Amarillo," he said, "I will buy you a ring and we can get married. I will get you any ring you want."

Really? How? By robbing a bank? I hadn't been planning to explain my trip to anyone on this bus. And maybe laying it out for a crazy AWOL GI was the worst way to start. But I thought if I could get him to see how different I was from what he imagined, I could help him out of this mess. God knows what had happened to him at Fort Fuckhead or wherever he'd run from. He needed reality and a warm therapist.

"Beau, you and I haven't talked long, but you should know I'm not getting married to anyone," I said, shaking my head. "I'm going to Detroit because I'm a socialist organizer, and we're having a big summer camp to learn how plan our little revolution better—I've been planning on going to this since tenth grade."

"You can go later, after we get married," he said, reaching out and cupping my breast in his hand. Just cupping it, not squeezing or anything. The action was like a Valium for him—the furrows in his brow disappeared.

I had to admit, he didn't flinch about "socialist summer camp." It was like he hadn't heard me at all.

I looked at my watch. An hour more until Amarillo. Maybe we could just sit there with him holding my breast and he'd fall asleep and I could ring the bell or whatever and get the hell off this bus.

"I'll read some more, okay?" I asked. He rested his head on my shoulder and kept that one hand of his in the same spot. Some blue-haired-beehive lady came back to go to the bathroom and shot us a look like she was going to puke.

Well, be my guest.

"Ama-rillah!" the driver called, gliding us over a bump.

I shook Beau-Jesus awake. "Sweetie," I said to him, "I gotta go to the ladies' room real bad, and then we'll go shopping for my ring, okay? Meet me right in front of the ticket counter in five minutes?"

I jumped up ahead of him, before he could even stand up, and barreled down the aisle in front of every aged and disabled passenger, barely catching Beau's cry: "I love you, baby wife of mine!"

The driver waited for each rider at the bottom of the bus steps. I grabbed his arm and dragged him around to the front grille, where the passengers couldn't see us. "You've got to help me—there's a crazy man back there who won't leave me alone. I'm going to hide behind the driver's side back here, and when he gets off, you make sure he walks toward the ticket counter—and then I am getting right back on this bus and hiding under someone's suitcase. Do you hear me?"

He pried my hand off his arm, but he didn't look confused. "I told you to watch out for the smokers," he said. He walked back to the front to help a few more old ladies with canes down from the bus.

I crouched down behind the giant front tire on the driver's side. I could see everyone's shoes walking away from the bus. Beau-Jesus was the very last pair of boots. I could see him pause as the driver pointed him toward the station's ladies' room and the ticket counter. He loped away. What a beautiful creature he was. The driver knocked three times on the steel of the outside door, and I scampered back on board, mouthing, "Thank you." I collected all my shit from the back seat and hid in the Tropical Jasmine bathroom for twenty minutes. When I came out, we were well on our way to Oklahoma City. I looked like a squished sandwich, and I fell asleep for three hundred miles in aisle seat 2B.

THE AORTA

WHEN I MET KIDS MY OWN AGE in Detroit—and I met hundreds, selling *The Red Tide* in front of every public high school in the unified school district—I'd tell them, "I just dropped out of school and moved out here from California."

Their mouths dropped. "You've got it all backward!" they'd say. "Are you crazy?" I had their attention.

"You have something here," I said, "that you will never find in Los Angeles, even if you looked for a million years. Everything is illusion there."

Detroit was the opposite of L.A. However bruised the city was in 1975, it was still based on making things that made America run. If Chicago had big shoulders, Detroit had steel quads. You pushed the pedal to the metal. You meant what you said, and you said what you meant.

When I walked into the IS national offices on Woodward Avenue, across the street from Henry Ford's original shuttered factory, it was a classic case of butt-ugly on the outside and beautiful under the skin. The brick edifice of Ford's plant was abandoned, weeds growing over barbed-wire fences. This was the place that built the first car my grandpa owned, the first time he didn't drive a mule train.

I expected Commie camp would be a great party in the woods, but it would have to compete socially with any weekend night on Livernois and Six Mile. I lived in a brick house in the neighborhood with five other comrades, presided over by a house dad and house mom named Sam and Sheila. They refused my rent money offerings; Sam set me up on a couch that looked like the same model I grew up sleeping on. Sheila made spaghetti carbonara every Thursday night.

Living in a mostly black city meant that, for the first time in my life, there was no racial tension. None. I'd walk down the street and everyone would assume I'd been adopted into an African American family. A biracial family. And I had, in the same fashion of everyone who'd stuck close to old Detroit. Everyone who lived within the town limits was a worker or unemployed; everyone in management had immigrated far out to the suburbs. The segregation took its toll, but the class consciousness was fierce. Of course, the labor unions were corrupt—but people remembered what their grandparents, black and white, had died for. I didn't have to explain the same things I'd had to explain standing in front of a supermarket on Santa Monica Boulevard, trying to convince a real estate broker's husband why people who work should have a stake in what they produce.

Detroit families didn't split apart and move every season, like Malibu sandpipers did. When I met someone new, I'd meet all their cousins, too. The first barbeque we had in Sheila's back yard, there must've been a hundred people there—but Steve P., who'd moved to Detroit from Tacoma, told me, "It's really just three families."

We danced every single night until we dropped. Until the pressure dropped. You didn't go over to someone's house in Detroit *without* dancing.

Legal drinking age was eighteen in 1975, which meant you could get a pass if you were seventeen. My first week in town, my comrades took me to the Aorta, a popular bar down on Six Mile Avenue. I danced with every man, woman, and dog. Who cared that summertime in Detroit was humid, gray, and smelly? Cold beer never tasted so good.

I remember this bar girl, Pepsi, who showed me her moves. She did a slow grind, never taking her eyes off mine. Her feet held fast to the floor as her hips pushed against the beat. Her hands and arms clasped together like she was holding a hammer—bringing it down, slicing it up. A Bunny with a weapon. I took my pen out of my shirt pocket to scribble on a bar napkin: "Dear Tracey Baby: Forget L.A.! Ship me my records and everything!" I drew hearts all around the border. I had to remember to mail this.

Pepsi grabbed me by my waist off the bar stool: "What're you writing, Susie Hollywood?" Those saber-wielding hands of hers were as soft as a puppy's.

I slid off the chair and abandoned my wet postcard.

COMMIE CAMP

CHILI LIKED TO SAY HIS Ford Econoline was "infallible." I loved him, but Chili liked to say everything was the opposite of what it really was—that was his humor. He'd coaxed his "baby" all the way out to Detroit from Oakland, and he had the empty Pennzoil cans to prove it.

When Temma told me we were getting a ride back to town from Chili in his "infallible Ford van," she didn't understand why I sunk my head into my camp pillow.

We were sixty miles outside of Detroit, and I was looking forward to heading home after a week of old-school Bolshevik history lessons, sing-alongs, and labor-organizing tips. I'd been cooking for two-hundred-plus every night. It'd been a blast, but I wanted to fall onto my couch at Sheila's and go to sleep for a week.

"What's your problem?" Temma asked, swatting my bottom. "Chili's leaving camp tomorrow; it's perfect. It's only an hour and a half away." She tucked her long hair behind her ears with their enormous gold hoops.

"Can't you get us one of your 'Cadillac friends' to chauffeur us?" I asked.

Temma screwed up her heart-shaped face. "That's over," she said, and then sang, "It was just one of those things . . . One of those bells that now and then rings . . .

"But it's all over now," she sang, switching lyrics and going flat. "And we have a very nice ride with Chili, if you and Hank Runninghorse can keep your fists off each other."

Runninghorse was Chili's best friend from high school—they did everything together. Runningmouth, as he was often called to his face, was as obnoxious as Chili was kind. But they had built up an Oakland chapter of *The Red Tide* from nothing—I had to hand them that.

"Anyone else coming?" I asked, resigning myself.

"Maybe Joe, maybe Steve P., I don't know. But you have a seat."

Four hours later, Chili found me in the kitchen, stripping the clean dishes out of the Hobart. "Sue, I'm sorry, the Ford is screwed. The transmission only goes in reverse, and that's with a lot of pleading."

I looked around the camp kitchen. We were the only two left. "There's hardly anyone here," I said. "Who's going to take us back to the city?"

Chili said he'd already thought of that. He was a little too enthusiastic—or maybe he was just playing his opposites game.

He told me some autoworker contact named Earl *also* had a Ford van, and he was going to take Hank, Steve P., and me all the way back to the office, door-to-door service. "He lives in Hamtramck!" he added, like that was a plus.

"A new contact, up here?" I was a little startled. The whole point of Commie camp was to better educate yourself so you could be a better recruiter, but you had to be pretty deep into socialism to attend in the first place. It wasn't for newcomers. I'd heard more obscure Trotskyite history in the past week than I'd hear again in a lifetime. Last night Fat Henry had gotten drunk, peeled off his undershirt so that all his fur stuck out, and started bellowing some dirty ballad about a Trot named Max Schachtman and a fat girl.

Really, I had been in the IS for a year and a half now, and I was the closest thing to a "newbie" I'd met in camp.

"This guy Earl's been mostly studying with the UAW caucus in the East Barracks," Chili said, pointing behind him.

I shrugged and told him I'd be ready in an hour. Like young Scout in *To Kill a Mockingbird,* if I could've taken Chili's hand right then, with great prescience, I would have said, "And there started the longest night of our lives."

I WASN'T HAPPY TO BE the only girl in the car. Temma had disappeared into the night with some new beau from the River Rouge plant who wore a silver spoon around his neck and had a Cadillac just for two.

When we gathered at the parking lot at noon, I started to get in the back of the van, not looking at anyone, ready to read my John Reed memoirs in the back seat. Runninghorse grabbed my forearm and said, "No, Sue, you sit up front."

It was impossible to think that Hank was being chivalrous. The best seat in the vehicle? What gives? Hank rejected all niceties of male-female etiquette as counterfeminist, and everyone who knew him understood that he'd let a door slam in his grandmother's puss without a second glance.

I climbed up into the bucket seat, still puzzled, and came face-to-face with Mr. Earl's big yellow grin, and even yellower hair, hopped up in the driver's seat.

"Hey there, jailbait!" the goober cried out. "I'm Earl Van Nuys the Third. God almighty, don't rock the ammunition, darlin'." He reached down into the console between us and came up with an open bottle. He threw his head back and gargled it down—which was saying something, considering the low headroom.

I turned back to the boys in the back seat to accuse somebody of something, but it was too late. They all looked at me with beseeching eyes, communicating one single thought: *Humor him.*

Well, Runninghorse's eyes weren't beseeching; they were more like, *Maintain, bitch.*

Earl finished his gargle and fired the ignition, in a smooth stroke for someone who'd obviously been high for the past several days. He was so gracefully plastered that when his other hand fired up a joint, I realized he was backing up the van with his knees. I checked my seat belt.

Earl was a 'Nam vet—two tours, baby—but they must have gone on forever, because Earl would not shut up about it. He craved our audience, my ears in particular. I had to share his smoke and brimstone—he was a veteran of the U.S. Fucking Army and They. Had. Fucked. Him.

But who was "they"? I mean, he was an IS contact, right? He must mean the army or, at the very least, the VA hospital. But within the first fifteen minutes, he said "fuckin' Charlie" and "fuckin' gook" about a dozen times. There wasn't enough soap in the world to wash his mouth out.

I was cringing and cheated a glance at Runninghorse, who silently shook his head side to side: *Don't do it. Don't say it. Shut up.*

Steve P. looked like a skinny rabbit, his eyes getting pinker and pinker, his forehead a mass of sweating acne. Chili's eyes held my sympathy, and I tried to imagine his meaning: *This, too, shall pass.*

EARL ACTED LIKE THE BOYS weren't there. He didn't pass the joint to them; I did. My heart was beating hard enough to hear it in my head, and I couldn't stop staring at the bottle Earl kept between his knees. It must be nearly empty by now. He might as well have hung a sheet on the side panel: WELCOME, HIGHWAY PATROL, TO OPEN-CONTAINER DRINKING.

If we got stopped, the shock of the booze and pot would soon give way to a full FBI investigation into what was in our backpacks and boxes. We had a full load of incriminating evidence: socialist books, rifles, mailing lists.

Unbelievable. Earl reached behind his seat and pulled out another fifth. I swore under my breath.

Hank moved forward from the bench seat. He grabbed Earl's shoulder. "Hey, man," he said. "Take it easy; we gotta get the youngster home in one piece."

"Hey, *man!*" Earl cackled and shook him off. "I don't take it easy, man; I take it!" he whooped, like a lunatic version of some Wobbly song he'd picked up at camp.

The van swerved, but there was no one in the next lane. Something long and silver flashed out from beneath my seat when Earl corrected the wheel, and I yelped, "What's this?"

It was something in a holster. I picked it up.

Earl shouted again and temporarily forgot to unscrew his next bottle. "Open it up, darlin', and see what's inside!" he urged me. "That's my lady!"

I heard Steve P. whimper, and Chili and Hank moved forward. I was glad for a distraction from the whiskey.

It was a knife. No one would have known what it was at first glance, though, because it looked like a medieval instrument. Earl snatched it from my hand and said, "Isn't she bee-yoo-ti-ful! My lady gutted Charlie many times; oh yes, she did."

I thought I was going to throw up. The blade was a foot long, one side curved like a pirate's sword. On the other side, it was serrated like a saw. The tip formed a hook. I could see why Earl talked about her like she was a person, a she-warrior, a terrorist who could slay all the butter knives and steak cutters in a dishpan army.

Earl liked to talk with his knife in his hand. He gestured and gesticulated through a hundred more soldier stories. My eyes stayed on the western light playing on his blade.

Runninghorse tried to interrupt, wanted to doubt him. Hank had never handled such a knife, and I could tell he wanted to. But Earl wasn't going to let go of it now. I could feel Chili drawing closer to Hank, tempering him quietly. So familiar. If he could soothe Runningmouth, and I could calm Earl, and Steve P. could stop mouth-breathing, then maybe we could get back to the national office on Woodward Avenue in one piece.

We got inside city limits. Earl tipped the hook of his lady at my head and then offered the knife to me; I grabbed it before Hank could make a pass. Earl was loosening his belt—shit, now what?

"Goddamn, girl, I have to take a leak," he yowled, like I was squeezing his tank.

Chili spoke up, his first words: "We're at Six Mile—five more minutes."

Earl took that inspiration to start describing what kind of havoc he and his "gook gutter" could wreak in the same amount of time.

"What's Fleetwood like?" I asked, willing him to leave Saigon. He looked at me like I'd asked him what it was like on Mars.

"Huh?"

"Fleetwood plant?" I began again. "Don't you work there with Zelda and Brent and Henry and—"

"*Work* there?" He choked on his spit. "Well, we'll just see, won't we, if I still work there or not!"

I had no idea what he was talking about. He was still bombing Hanoi. How could someone who gloried in his Vietcong kill count be a contact of a bunch of socialists who, despite our self-defense credo, were more the type to hold hands and sing "Kumbaya"? This guy was a redneck Nazi drug addict. I'd watched my life pass before my eyes for the past ninety minutes, but now I felt something different: fury. Whoever had let this asshole into our cabbage patch, I might have to take Earl's "lady" and cut him into a million pieces.

The neon sign at Larry's Diner came into view, the coffee shop below our office. Steve P. was gasping, but I kept my eyes on Earl's hands, willing them to move to the right, pull to the curb—yes, yes, easy does it.

"We're here," Hank announced, and leaned all the way over me to put his hand on the steering column and yank out the keys. The car shuddered, and we bumped into another parked vehicle in front of us. Runninghorse put his face in Earl's and said over his shoulder, "Sue, open his door." Then to him: "Earl, you're gonna take a piss now."

Chili climbed out the side panel door, yelling back at Hank, "I'll get him, man, I'll get him."

How did Earl drive at all? He couldn't walk. He fell down into the street; I heard him, and the thud, and Chili trying to help him back up. But I was already well down the sidewalk, pushing open the lobby doors and praying the stink would fall behind me.

Steve P. was right at my side—when we got to the foyer, he gave me a bear hug. "You saved us."

I looked at him, shaking my head.

"No, no," Steve heaved. "You're so sweet and nice-looking, and you were so kind to that animal; he's a monster!" He started weeping, and I had to tug at him to get him to continue climbing the stairs with me. We didn't want to get called back for first aid.

"Nice to him? I should've throttled him with both hands."

"You know, you just kept talking like you believed in him, which is the only thing he listens to; he's insatiable."

"He's suicidal," I said, realizing something. I knew it so well. "We should be calling Bellevue—what's 'Bellevue' in Detroit?"

Steve had his keys out for our next set of doors. Our offices were at one end of the second floor of what had once been a small manufacturing firm. There was nothing at the other end except restrooms.

Our new British national secretary, Hugh Fallon, had tightened up our security since he'd arrived with his Manchester ingenuity. Now, instead of one set of glass doors and locks, there were two sets of steel doors, each one so heavy that I routinely had to put my shoulder into them to get them open. The first set required one key that you turned twice clockwise. The second door had a dead bolt that went one way and a knob lock that went the opposite.

It took me five minutes to wrestle through the entrance, but noodle-thin Steve was so quick, we spirited though. The second door groaned when we opened it. Everyone in the office looked up at our grand entrance.

Marty Breyer, our six-foot-tall UMW coal organizer from West Virginia, smiled and said, "Allow me, sweetheart," taking my sweaty backpack off my shoulders. Temma told me he used to be an engineer at MIT—I couldn't imagine it. Marty had this way of listening to everyone in a room as if each person's story went right to his heart.

Secretary Hugh was in the middle of the room, wearing a lavender shirt with French cuffs, scowling at pallets of new books that had just arrived. Our chief copywriter, Ty Burnside, waved at me without even looking up from his typewriter. There was Murray again, his camp chef's toque replaced with a striped printer's cap. I could hear Judith, our bookkeeper who looked like Mona Lisa, talking in the editor's office. Michael, my only Los Angeles comrade in town, sprang up from the back and embraced Steve and me at the same time: "Your timing is perfect!"

I squeezed him back harder. "No, don't even tell me what you need now . . . I'm not going anywhere except into a shower. I've just been through a sewer."

Michael loosened his hug, acknowledging the stench. I wanted the bathroom key; Steve P. went to get it for both of us. But he came back and shook his head. "Sorry." He gestured at the doors where Marty had just passed through on his way to the john. Shit. I hated it when a middle-aged person beat you to the bathroom— you had no idea how long it would be.

"What happened?" Michael asked. I realized he'd shaved his beard off, the one he'd sported since I'd met him my first day at Uni High. Any other day, that would've shocked me. But not today.

Steve and I spoke almost simultaneously: *"Who the fuck is Earl Van Nuys the third?"*

Everyone within earshot looked blank.

"UAW worker?" I continued. "Someone's contact? Supposedly came up to camp from the UAW caucus?"

Steve P. delivered the full picture. "This racist, inbred piece of trash almost killed us driving home from camp, and he says that he just joined the IS yesterday!"

Wow, I hadn't heard that part.

Ty tried to make light. "Hey now, Steve, don't go talking 'bout 'inbred' to your West Virginia comrades."

"You have no idea what we've just been through," Steve spat. He may have sounded like a baby, but he was right. I was freezing, even though it was June; I wanted a blanket and a hot cocoa.

Steve held court about the "lady" knife, and Michael put his hand on my shoulder. Marguerite, the typesetter, came over to me with the purple afghan she always kept on her chair.

THERE WAS A THUD AGAINST the outside doors. Not the inner ones, but the thick outer doors—the ones you had to unlock counterclockwise. I wondered if Runningmouth had lost his keys again—but it wasn't his impatient banging.

No, it was like a big package someone had shoved against a wall.

Christ, I didn't care. Send in the deliveries; send in the clowns. I wrapped Marguerite's blankie all around me and closed my eyes, so tired.

"Marty!" Hugh yelled. "Bloody hell! Ty, Michael!"

Hugh always snapped orders, but I'd never heard him yell like this. I opened my eyes and saw him trying to hold up a much bigger man, failing to push the second doors open. Murray and Michael rushed to help him. The big man collapsed to the floor, and Hugh broke his fall.

It was Marty Breyer. He'd just gone to the bathroom with the key. But now he was lying on the floor, with a huge dark puddle spreading all over his chest. Hugh struggled out from under Marty's body, his lavender shirt soaked scarlet.

My mind went as blank as a stone. A single line entered it, as if in a dialogue balloon: *It looks just like it does in the movies.* The blood looked like it had been crafted for the stage.

Hugh tore off his shirt and pressed it over Marty's chest. It was leaking like a faucet. I heard Marguerite's voice behind me, summoning an ambulance on the phone, her voice breaking up. But that wasn't the only thing cracking. I heard one, two, three rifles behind me, pulling their magazines back.

In the seconds since Marty had hit the ground, every man in the office had reached up, down, or behind shelves and desks to appear holding a firearm. Ty; Murray, our telephone union guy; Chewy—they looked at one another like members of a night patrol. Like something Earl had told us about. They approached the front doors, anticipating an ambush. I realized they thought we were under siege.

"Michael," I whispered, and then realized I was whispering.

Mikey heard me anyway, and held up his hands to the gun guys. "What is it, Sue? Who is it?"

"It's the guy who drove us; it's Earl," I said. "He has that special knife . . . "

The new battalion doubted me. Chewy claimed there must be more men; he and Ty started taking positions to head down the hall to the bathroom and the front gate.

"Secure the front doors!" Judith screamed. She was Chewy's wife, Hugh's current lover. The only woman there besides Marguerite and me.

Hugh excoriated her for calling 911. "You fucking idiot!"

"He's dying, Hugh, you bastard; he's dying!"

Hugh stood bare-chested in the middle of it all, as if Judith's revelation had brought his own self-interest to heart. "I have to get out of here, now," he ordered, and Judith ran up to him, car keys in hand. He turned to Michael. "Give me your shirt."

Michael ripped off his work shirt. Hugh slipped it over his shoulders, stepped over Marty's body, motioned to Judith, and barked, "JFK. Meet me at the airport."

I didn't get it. This supremely selfish man was now leaving town because one of his underlings was drowning in a sea of blood on his fresh-scrubbed floors? I bet Judith had waxed them herself.

Michael saw my disbelief. "Hugh's illegal, Sue. He can't be here when the cops come . . . this is bad."

I could hear thunder coming up the stairs; everything was loud. Michael asked me for my jacket so he wouldn't be half na-ked, so I took off my mom's navy sailor coat and he squeezed into it. His muscles bulged in my skinny sleeves.

He took me by the shoulders again. "Sue, look at me and talk to me now, because the cops are coming through that door in one minute."

Marty was moaning. I could hear his labored cries, and no one else's.

"Sue!" Michael tried once more. "Are you sure it was this guy Earl, this guy with the hunting knife? There's no one else?"

I nodded. "He talked about carving people up the whole ride; he's hysterical about . . . communists . . . he's still fighting in Vietnam."

Michael took it in. His eyes were dotted with red. "I have something very important for you to do, Sue. I want you to leave, now, out the fire exit in the back, and go to the Betsy-Do Laundro-mat, right off Demby—you know where that is?"

Yeah, I knew, but . . .

"Samuel's there; you need to go tell Samuel what's going on and get him over here."

Samuel Jaffe was our national chairman, the one guy above Hugh.

Our national chairman was doing his laundry? I had never seen him do a single practical thing, not even fill a glass of water. I had never even talked to the man; I'd only listened to him expound on the minutia of the "U.S. economy in crisis."

"Is Marty going to live?" I said.

"Just go get Samuel, okay?"

I RAN THERE. I ran past Larry's Diner; past the 1-2-3 Budget Shop, where I'd gotten the tight jeans I was wearing; past the Pretzel Bowl, where Pepsi waitressed and had introduced me to gin and tonics and Bob Marley on the jukebox.

I was amazed I could run this hard and think at the same time. It was as if I couldn't think at all crouching in the office, watching a man with blood pouring out of his chest—but with my legs moving, I could see it all.

Marty was alive; he hadn't passed out. I heard his voice. The IS wouldn't want a murder investigation, because the police would have an excuse to tear the place apart. Everyone was armed to the teeth because of what the FBI did to the Panthers. And look at what happened to Jimmy Hoffa. God knows what revenge the current Teamster president, Frank Fitzsimmons, might exact against our reform efforts.

"Earl Van Nuys the third"—why had he attacked Marty in the bathroom? He didn't even know the man. And Earl had been in such a merry mood when I last saw Hank helping him stumble up the sidewalk. He wanted to take a piss, right? He didn't want to kill anybody, not then. Steve P. said that I had charmed him, that he'd been charmed into drunken bonhomie. I thought he was going to piss all the whiskey away and fall into a dead sleep.

Marty didn't have anything to do with it. Marty was alive.

I walked into the Betsy-Do. Its hot dryer smell, the waves of heat, rendered me stupid for a minute. All my keen powers of sprinting endorphins left me. I was in a hot room with dryers spinning, old ladies folding clothes, some kids playing with Matchbox cars on the floor.

No Samuel in sight, but I kept scanning the machines and rows of orange plastic chairs, like there would be a revelation.

One of the figures in the chairs rustled a newspaper to turn its pages, and I saw it was *The Wall Street Journal*.

"Samuel!" I called, and he lowered his paper, his limpid eyes peering at me as if I were a stranger.

I pushed someone's cart out of my way and got down on my knees in front of him.

"Samuel, it's Sue, Sue B. I'm from the L.A. *Red Tide,* remember? I'm Zelda's friend?"

He used to sleep with Zelda—surely that must register. I could see it was dawning on him that I was there for a reason. He dropped the paper. His skin was yellow in this light.

"Samuel, I'm sorry," I said, my voice sounding strange even to me. "It's Marty, Marty Breyer; he's been stabbed at the office by one of our contacts, in the bathroom."

Samuel and Marty had been very close; they had gone to grad school before Marty had industrialized in the mines. Someone had told me they'd been bar mitzvahed together, but I think that was a joke.

Samuel said, "Would you please say that again?"

I did.

"Is he alive?"

"Yes, yes, I heard his voice; the ambulance is coming—he was alive when I left, and that was five minutes ago."

He looked down at me, the child at his knee.

"Hmm," he said, as if he'd wanted to say something else and stepped on it. "Would you stay here until my clothes are dry and then take them back to my house?"

He reached into his pocket and pulled out a key. "It's 23 Pasadena," he said, "and Fritz won't be there; he's in Philadelphia this week."

Fritz Epstein was another one of our executive committee members, who'd reportedly never been laid. He wouldn't have picked up a gun, either. I wondered if Samuel had.

"Would you do that?" he asked again, sharp, and I realized I hadn't answered him.

"Yeah, sure," I said, looking past him. "Which dryer is it?" I finally asked, but Samuel was gone and had taken his paper with him.

The kids had left, too, and the last old lady was walking out the door, struggling with her cart. I went over to help her and she looked a little jumpy, like she'd rather I didn't.

The door shut behind her. Even though it was so loud in there, with both dryers groaning, it was finally still—no more wash cycles. I could see Samuel's socks flipping in circles through the plate glass of the front loader. I sat down on the orange chair that faced his dryer and watched them spin a few revolutions, like I was watching the most interesting television program that ever aired.

And then I saw that my reflection was part of this program—*Susie and the Flying Socks.* My hair was crazy, falling out of its ponytail, and my glasses were half cocked, like they'd been since I'd mended them with tape. Maybe that old lady had been freaked because, without my jacket, it was obvious I wasn't wearing a bra. My face looked weird, but I couldn't see it well enough in the dryer glass to figure out why.

I rubbed my eyes. I felt something sticky on my face, and I wondered what time it was. It was twilight outside. Michael had my coat, Hugh had Michael's shirt, and I had all these socks— what? To fold?

I found a pillowcase someone had abandoned and piled all Samuel's laundry into it. I pressed it to my chest. It felt wonderful, the most wonderful warmth spreading across my heart. Samuel lived across the street, just a few steps away. I walked out with the hot pillow in my arms, not feeling the cold at all, and crossed Woodward against the light.

RELOCATION

MARTY WAS STILL IN the hospital, but he was stable. Seventeen stab wounds to the chest, and he never lost consciousness. His wife told me that when she got him out of there, she was getting out of the IS for good. I wondered if she'd have any trouble convincing him.

We were supposed to get "back to business." Every morning, we'd begin with a meeting, and after we stopped donating blood, we weren't supposed to talk about Marty anymore. *Move on; don't look back.* I was a malingerer.

The morning meetings began at Larry's Diner downstairs, with the coffee and doughnut order. Red, another comrade from East Oakland, would ask me for money for a doughnut.

"Why are you asking me?"

"You look like a rich white girl."

"You are high."

"Always, always, sugar pie—" Then he'd hit up Hank. And then Chili, and then Steve P. Finally, one of them would give in. I couldn't figure it out, because Red made more money dealing than all of us put together. He just didn't believe in paying for himself.

Michael ignored him. Red never asked Michael for a doughnut. And I don't think I saw Mikey ever eat anything as strong as coffee or doughnuts. He would order a glass of hot milk and a piece of toast. When I asked him about his diet, he just shook his head.

"Ulcers."

"You're nineteen; there's no such thing as ulcers." But maybe Michael did have a special ulcerated intestine that affected only young men who looked like they hadn't had a carefree moment since they were in diapers.

Whatever happened at Larry's Diner set the tone for the group criticism to come. It followed us right up the stairs to our big room overlooking the original Ford plant. In bad weather, you could watch the rain fall right onto the old shop floors. All the factory's windows were knocked out.

"How come they don't open the Ford factory for tours or something?" I once asked. "I mean, it's historic!"

"People here are trying to get out of factories, Sue, not into them," Chewy said. He always had a stern word for me.

Sure, everyone in Detroit was dying to get out of the factories and move to California, except for demented communists like us who were trying to get in.

You didn't count for shit in the IS until you got a shop-floor union job. But none of our comrades could help me get a job, because they were all known "agitators." The last thing a company was going to do was hire another one of their little pinko friends.

Without friends, how did you get work? I showed up in job application queues that circled for a mile around the block and was turned away. I was too young to pull it off against local folks my parents' age.

So far, I had a night shift at McDonald's and a part-time non-union factory job making carburetor parts in Royal Oak. Hot oil and metal filings settled into the pores of my hands, as if I were a caricature of the Incredible Hulk.

"How many newspapers did you sell yesterday?" Chewy held up a clipboard inches from my face. Why did he always volunteer to "supervise" us? He was older than my dad. In Los Angeles, no "grownups" came to our *Red Tide* meetings to manage us.

"Ten."

"Where's the money?"

"I already turned it in to Steve P."

"How many schools did you get to? Did you get to the four we outlined?"

"I got to Mumford, Cooley, and Cass before the third bell."

"You gotta get there before the second bell; where's your contact list?" Chewy's glasses were falling off his nose. His shirt looked like it hadn't been changed in a week.

I pulled out a piece of paper with the names of all the kids I'd met who'd given me their phone number.

At the top was Alicia—she was so cool; she wanted to go to L.A. and become a big star. She had almond eyes with lashes as long as Maybelline's. She asked me if she had the right attitude for making it, and I told her, "Colossal." She had slender, articulate hands that looked like they should be waving from a Rose Parade float.

Alicia told me to come back after school and tell her everything, everything she had to know about Hollywood. I promised her I would.

"Who is *this?*" Runninghorse held up my contact sheet like it was bad evidence. I stared at the button on his beret—FREE GARY TYLER!—instead of his face so I didn't have the urge to smack it.

"I told you," he yelled, "if you can't get the last name of the contact, don't bother doing it at all!"

"I'm not going to interrogate some ninth-grader for her last name, Hank. This isn't the Gestapo; we're supposed to be making friends."

"Yeah, well, Sue, you spend all day 'making friends' while other people are dying, other people who need some discipline among comrades—"

"Shut up, Hank."

"Little Miss Friendship can just take her petit bourgeois ass and have a tea party!" Runningmouth cackled, and he brought his face down to mine to slide out his tongue.

I screamed and dropped my pen, bringing my hand straight up to connect with his cheek.

Chewy grabbed me. "Goddammit, if you two can't behave yourselves, I'll send you home." He looked right at me.

My mouth dropped open. Runningmouth took a piece out of me every morning, and they treated him like he shit gold bricks.

Michael came back through the door with a stack of newspapers for the afternoon shift. He looked so disappointed. He knew me; he knew I'd never hit anyone in my life. What had happened to me? Hank could turn a daisy into a killing machine, he really could.

"Sue, I'm going to need you for this detail," Michael said. "Hank, where do you drive to next?" He gave a long look to Chewy. *Stay out of it.*

It wasn't that Hank Runninghorse couldn't recruit. He could recruit young men looking for a daddy, a serious daddy. He could con young women into his bed—but only the most patient martyrs would stay. Then he'd start beating them.

I wished I could make him pay. He had the whole executive committee snowed. They accused everyone of not "trying" with him, and you wondered just how many of their wives he'd have to fuck, punch up, or insult before they wised up. He was their little bulldog.

I MADE UP MY MIND AT the end of that week. I decided to move to the IS Louisville branch. Chewy, our "nanny," wouldn't have a clue; Hank would be thrilled to think I'd left with my tail between my legs. Michael would understand; Sammy and Sheila encouraged it. All of us who were fed up with the leadership in Detroit were quietly making our move.

Louisville was an alarming destination choice for an organizer—it was hell down there; anyone with the most milquetoast liberal agenda found himself right up against the KKK. But I swore Kentucky would be like Paris in springtime compared with the crew on Woodward Avenue.

I called up the Louisville branch organizer, Luke, to tell him that I'd like to move there in two weeks. He said he'd loan me one of his shotguns.

"What am I supposed to do with that?"

"Well, if I were you, I'd sleep with it."

The comrades in the South didn't care what my motives were—they were so demoralized from the racial onslaught down there. Busing had turned Louisville, like South Boston, into a mini–race war. They couldn't imagine what bureaucratic inferno I was leaving behind. A nice warm gun to cuddle up to at night might just be a tonic.

It was hard for me to keep my moving plans a secret. But I knew I couldn't just leave "of my own accord"—I'd be treated like a traitor.

The worst was coming right up. I had to stage a little farewell plea; I had to get an audience with Hugh. As he reminded everyone in his bulletins, "The national secretary must approve all relocations."

I wasn't a very good actress—you could see everything on my face. But I was counting on Hugh's weaknesses, his famous ego, to let me go—because by his definition, I was already damaged goods. He'd sexually appraised and rejected me a good year ago.

How did the IS ever end up with Hugh? He was our very own British pretender to the throne. He was rumored to have run an OTB office in his past life—not to mention that he'd been a carny, a card player, and a whoremonger. A Brian Clough wannabe. Whatever his resume, he'd created a Queen of Hearts atmosphere where everyone was primed for a kangaroo trial or a casting couch.

The previous Sunday night I'd printed ten thousand red-white-and-blue flyers for him, with the headline "Justice Means 'Just Us,'" atop a caricature of a white foreman holding a black employee in a headlock. The illustration had become my own private insignia.

It was odd to make an "appointment" with Hugh. On our first—and last—occasion to speak in private, he'd been the one to make an appointment. He had called round to be wined and dined and fucked. I had still been in L.A., in the middle of my affair with Stan, and had just dropped out of high school.

Hugh was touring all the U.S. branches, and he was dying to see Malibu. Stan got kind of queasy when I told him Hugh had "called" for me, after Temma wasn't available. But Stan didn't stop it.

I could tell Hugh considered my assignment—being his date, his chaperone—a great honor for me. My curiosity got the better of me. I'd never played geisha before. My lovers were my friends, not men who called long distance with a list of their likes and dislikes.

It all went wrong with Hugh. I took him to Topanga Beach at sunset, and he stared at it like it was nothing but a cold pile of sand. I took him to a spaghetti restaurant that everyone at Uni High thought was fancy, and he pronounced it rotten. I barely had enough money to cover his bar tab.

I hoped that the sex of the evening would save it, but it was not to be. He was barely in my apartment before I accidentally sat on his leather coat and he lost his temper.

"You fucking cunt, you've wrinkled it!" he said.

My eyes watered, and he was quiet for a moment.

Then he asked me if I had any early Rod Stewart. What a face-saver. It was a good thing I had a decent record collection, because we both had to concentrate on something while we screwed each other. The needle thankfully didn't skip. I don't remember his penis inside me at all. "Maggie May" was a tranquilizer.

Now, a year later in Detroit, I had my second appointment with the great man. In Hugh's office, that same blond leather jacket of his was hanging on a wooden hanger on the back of his door.

"So what is today, luv?" He put his feet up on the desk, as if we had cozy chats like this all the time. I don't think I'd ever been alone with Hugh in his office. No electric mandolin to help us out this time.

"I came to talk to you because things haven't been working out for me here," I said. "I'm too old for the high school stuff. I'm eighteen now, and I haven't been able to get a job in auto or Teamsters—"

"Yeah, it hasn't been your year, has it?" he interrupted.

I had to get to the point quickly, before he became too interested in running down my character.

"I'd like to move to Louisville. I talked to the comrades there—you know they're being hammered by the Klan, and they're desperate for some new blood."

That was a stupid way to put it. But if Hugh was the butcher I thought he was, he'd appreciate my meat-related metaphor.

For a second he scanned me up and down. I thought his paranoia might prevail. He'd yell, "You're wearing a wire, you fucking cunt, aren't you? You've come to do me in!"

But I gave him too much credit; I always did. He kicked back off the desk and said, "Yeah, you look like shit. You've been useless here. I'll tell Louisville you're coming; see what you can do for them."

This was the point where I was supposed to say, "Thank you, Mr. Fallon," like a dutiful daughter. I hated him so much.

"You can't leave until you train Marguerite on the press, though," he said, saving me from the impossibility of feigning gratitude. He pointed to some camera-ready copy on the corner of his desk.

"We need six thousand of these by"—he checked his gold watch—"five o'clock, so let's get going, eh?"

He got up to open the door, keys in his hand, ready to lock it behind us. I realized he couldn't wait for this to be over. Some other lucky cunt must be waiting outside.

I left the office to go downstairs to the party store for a Baby Ruth, and called Sammy and Sheila's house from the pay phone. I bet they'd be a little sad to see me go.

"He believed me!" I shouted into the phone. "I just have to scrub a few more floors with my bare hands, and then I can go!"

Sammy laughed like a pleased Santa. I could tell he had a drink his hand. "You did all right; I knew you would. See, this is going to work out." I could hear Sheila yelling in the background that she was going to kiss me all over.

"Yeah, I'll come home as soon as I finish these flyers. Tell Michael when you see him that it went through."

I had to re-ink the mighty AB Dick printing press a half-dozen times. It took forever to print six thousand back-to-back in red ink: No Contract, No Work. I did feel like a traitor now, the ink stains all over my arms, legs, and face. The first time I had ever turned on the machine, six months earlier, Chewy had shown me into the press room, hauled out a mountain of 8.5-by-14-inch goldenrod and said, "Turn straw into gold." That was how he'd left me.

SAMMY AND SHEILA COULDN'T say enough about Louisville when I got home. They were living vicariously through my imminent escape.

"The handsomest men in this whole organization are in Louisville," Sheila said with authority. She was so good-looking herself, with her titian hair, you had to take her at her word. "If it wasn't for Sammy, I'd be on a train myself."

I'd seen the comrades she was talking about at an anti-apartheid conference the previous March, and it was true. All of the Louisville comrades, women and men, were better-looking than average. Maybe they just slept at night.

I'd been entertained in Louisville one weekend. Jimmy J. and Cary R. had taken me to Churchill Downs, not when the horses were running, but on a slow day, to admire the place.

They took me to the Winner's Circle and put a wreath of roses around my neck. We all posed for a picture, the two of them on either side of me, their arms encircling my waist. Jimmy had been an English teacher before he started driving trucks for Rykoff. Cary was a photojournalist, an old ballplayer from the minor leagues, and he posed me in front of his granddaddy's Oldsmobile. I never stopped laughing except to put some barbeque in my mouth. It was a beautiful day.

I told Sheila about our day at the races. "See, I told you so!" she said, petting my hair. She was one of the only ones I could talk to about a day off, who wouldn't look at me like, *What do you mean, you fiddled while Detroit burned?* She knew I needed a pleasant memory to pack my bags and move somewhere where I really didn't know anyone at all.

Sheila snuggled with me under her satin quilt, along with a week's worth of papers she was determined to catch up on. She admitted to me that I was not likely to sleep in a bed of roses every night at my new destination. It might be hard.

Louisville was in the national news all the time in 1975. Sheila read a story aloud from the *Times,* saying how nine out of ten white families had pulled their daughters out of high school because they didn't want them going to school with blacks.

She looked at me apologetically and whispered, "The only white people in Louisville defending busing are communists."

Well, great—I'd fit right in, then. I wasn't nearly as fetching as Sheila, but I had no fear. I was not afraid of any place I could run away to.

THE PERFUME COUNTER

MY FIRST ORDER OF BUSINESS in Louisville was to find a job. I rented a cheap carriage house apartment in St. James Court, where I subsisted on one can of tuna per day.

As before in Detroit, no local comrade could help me find work because they were already known to their employers as "communists" and "nigger lovers." I turned in my applications as a complete stranger. My references were two thousand miles away: Would you like to call them?

No one did. My appearance was deceiving.

The first position I found, I discovered in the *Courier-Journal* classifieds. It was for a stock clerk at the largest department store in town, Byck's. It reminded me of the old I. Magnin in San Francisco. It featured a glove counter. Perfume tables filled the foyer with aroma. The most expensive ladies' garments were on the third level, where Miss Dreycall, the store manager, interviewed me.

She gave me a written exam, of a type I hadn't seen since junior high. It asked the meanings and contexts of words like *ancillary* and *infrequent*. There were some arithmetic questions, and a story problem about a squirrel that went to a party. I had to squirm instead of giggle because Miss Dreycall was sitting ten feet away from me.

The test had nothing to do with fashion. I'd hoped she would ask me, "Who is your favorite designer?" or, "How do you make a Dior Rose?" As long as it was impossible for me to industrialize, I might as well enjoy my other interests. No one ever asked those kinds of questions in the IS.

Or maybe no one asked because of the way I looked these days—not exactly a Dior Rose. White, but no debutante. I appeared before Miss Dreycall in an acrylic striped sweater and denim skirt; ribbed, pilled tights; and scuffed Mary Janes.

Miss Dreycall had me sit in front of her at a tiny desk with a built-in chair, like a Catholic schoolgirl, while she graded my paper.

"You seem to be quite intelligent," she said, peering over her glasses. I wished she would tell Hugh that.

"Are you planning to attend college in the future?" That sounded like a trick question.

"Yes, ma'am, but I need to work right now."

"You will be assisting Miss Love, our couture buyer. She will require your courtesy and attention at all times—she needs a smart girl."

Miss Love! With special sauce, I hoped.

I was put to work in a back room, filing out inventory cards with a group of five other young women, each of whom lived with either her father or her husband. You didn't need to know a thing to do this job, except how to count to twenty.

All the girls who lived with their parents were engaged, except Shelley, who was "almost engaged" and in a panic about her ring. Shannon, the youngest, had been engaged at sixteen and had been pulled from high school when busing started.

"Well, my father put his foot down!" she explained, as everyone else nodded. Of course. "I don't know any girls who haven't left," she added. More vigorous agreement.

I went to an IS meeting that night and asked Katrina, a local girl, to spell it out for me. "Does that mean that their fathers are afraid they'll have a black boyfriend or something?"

"That's not the way they'd put it," she said. "They'd say, 'No nigger is going to rape my little girl.'"

"Oh, c'mon!"

"I'm serious."

"So, if someone's dad doesn't pull his daughter out, that means he wants her to get raped?"

"Yeah, well, it's the end of public schools, as far as they're concerned."

"But this girl I work with didn't even get through tenth grade!"

"Neither did you," Katrina said, and poked me in the side. She had graduated with honors from Oberlin. All these Phi Beta Kappa Teamsters.

"That's different. I went to Pinko U. instead."

It was hard to be ringless at Byck's; I'd never had so much attention paid to my bare hands. I got asked if I had a boyfriend, and I stuttered. They must have thought I was either frigid or a prostitute. Of course, I was a Yankee, and Yankee girls don't have anyone looking after them, which is why they are frigid. Whores.

I could not say to them, "I'm having sex with the branch organizer and the head of the Teamster caucus after our meetings—sometimes with the two of them together—but it's not serious."

I could not say, "You should really go to the West End clubs sometime and see what it's like not getting raped and having a ball instead."

It was funny to me that they thought "not white" men were so sexually aggressive—paralyzingly attractive. As if they weren't just men. No, they thought a black guy just looks at a white girl and her legs fly open. A pulp novel: She screams, but no words come out. She is caught on the flypaper of his cock; it's inescapable. She's ruined afterward, unsatisfied by anything else, unwanted by her own kind.

What a fantasy. Tell it to your vibrator.

Here you are, I'd think to myself in imaginary arguments with my coworkers, *with a grade-school education and nothing to look forward to after your wedding except an endless line of Tupperware products and racist legends.*

The Byck's girls never said anything about the appeal of their men, not even that they were cute. What was appealing was getting out of their mothers' kitchens into one of their own. Plus, those diamonds on their fingers.

I ate my Baby Ruths alone at lunch, uninvited to showers and shopping sprees. They talked around me, as if I were a potted plant.

The day Miss Dreycall hired Byck's first black employee, it was like a bomb went off. The young woman was immaculate, of course. On her first day, she wore white gloves with a mustard-colored melton coat. Her hair looked like a 'do from a 1965 *Ebony* magazine. Her name was Belinda Matthews. She did not use contractions when she spoke.

No one else spoke at all. The stockroom went from a henhouse to a Christian Science reading room. Deirdre had tears in her eyes because her desk was right next to Belinda's. She kept her coffee cup on the farthest corner.

In the cloakroom after hours, I heard Deidre whisper to our veteran inventory clerk, Peggy, "I haven't told my father 'cause I need the money for the wedding—but if he finds out, I'll have to quit. And I just don't know if I can take it."

Belinda was terribly proper. Her posture made the rest of us look like degenerates. I could not share anything with her—my only success in her presence was to be unfailingly polite.

"Would you like the creamer, Miss Matthews?" I'd ask at the coffee table.

"No, thank you, Miss Bright," she'd reply. She never took anything offered from my hands. And no one else offered her anything at all.

The day she was fired, two weeks later, I was called into Miss Dreycall's office again. I wondered if she was going to try to explain Belinda's disappearance. I was livid. I had fourteen bags of ugly sequined prom dresses on my desk that I couldn't care less about. What the fuck did they think they were doing with their pathetic little affirmative action program? Go ahead, give the Yankee a reasonable excuse. Maybe Dreycall understood that, because I was so "intelligent," this would upset me and I needed to know why it hadn't worked out.

Miss D. asked me to sit down in the schoolgirl chair, and then she stood up. My god, was it really that bad?

"It pains me to tell you this, Miss Bright," she said, "but we must pay utmost attention to the personal hygiene of our staff."

Belinda had been fired for hygiene? But she was like a bar of Ivory soap!

"You must bathe and use deodorant every day before you come to work," Miss Dreycall continued. "Miss Love is very upset."

Me? I felt the chair turn into a wasp hive under my bottom. My face and chest flushed as red as the yellow roses on Dreycall's desk. Worst of all, the acrylic sweater under my arms seemed to turn, in one instant, to liquid stink—I could feel the cloud of it overcome me. I smelled so bad I couldn't move.

"I realize you are above average in IQ," Miss Dreycall said, and sniffed. "But there is no position at Byck's that does not demand personal hygiene as the first priority. Do you understand me?"

I tried to open my mouth.

"This is your warning, and there will be no other," she continued.

I thought of the labor meeting I had to get to after work, where we would discuss the telephone contract, and the coalition of black and white workers who were holding together by a slender thread, despite the busing issue. They were trying to keep their maternity leave and overtime hours—but all I wanted was a shower. "Gee, I'm sorry, comrades, but at my job, I'm going to get canned because I smell bad."

I went to the cloakroom by myself and got my navy peacoat. I buried my head in its dark lining and took a deep breath. It smelled like damp wool. The crisp snowflakes from early morning had all melted. I sobbed into it.

Someone touched me softly on the back. I didn't want to know who it was. I was never going to take this coat off my head.

"Miss Bright." It was Peggy. "Don't cry . . . Miss Love can be very, very demanding."

Peggy had been married two months before. Her diamond was yellow, one carat, and she had the honeymoon-special package from Tupperware.

"Why was Belinda fired?" I asked, still not coming out of my peacoat shell.

"Belinda! What?" Peggy pulled her hand away. "Well, she was stealing."

That did it. I pulled my head out, stared right at her, and wiped my snot on my arm. Why not.

"Oh yeah?" I snorted. "Is that what Miss Love says?"

Peggy took a step back. "No, that's what we all say," she said, and turned on her ivory patent-leather flats. "All of us."

EXPULSION

THE DAY THAT LUKE, the Louisville branch daddy, took his shotgun back from me was the day before everyone drove to Cincinnati for the special "expulsion" convention.

The IS was having another faction fight. I'd heard about faction fights in history books, among Bolsheviks, and here I was in the center of one myself. The last one in the IS had been in the early seventies, when I was in eighth grade, innocent in Edmonton.

A special convention was being called to throw the dissidents out. That would include me. There really wasn't any suspense;

Hugh Fallon had the majority votes in his pocket. So why were we even going?

I knew there were big "principles" at stake, but it seemed to me another sort of worm had turned. Working-class solidarity had become a fetish game: Wonderful people were being kicked out like dead wood. There wasn't a vision; there were only snitches and bullies.

A couple years later, I discovered that this very same Luke, Mr. Louisville Autoworker, Our Beloved Branch Leader, was on the payroll of the FBI, infiltrating the IS to plea-bargain down a drug arrest. In 1979, he drunk-dialed his old IS girlfriend from a rehab center to sob out the whole soggy mess. He'd been busted selling coke again.

No wonder Luke had been so eager to lend me his gun. I guess he hoped I'd do something exciting with it, to impress his G-men friends.

But in 1976, I knew only that Luke was on the majority team of a faction fight, a minor captain in our *Lord of the Flies* reenactment.

The day I'd arrived in Louisville, six months before, I'd had no reputation to speak of. But now it was mud. Every Klan member in town knew where I lived. When I was at Byck's one day, they broke into my apartment, left dead rats on the toilet and in my bedsheets, and tacked a little white-supremacy note to the mirror above the headboards: "Niger-Loving Communist Cunt." I guess they dropped out of spelling class, too.

Luke came on the Tuesday before the expulsion convention to get his firearm. He knocked at the door, at the bottom of the stairs, and when I ran down, he could hear my *thump, thump, thump* on the narrow steps.

I probably sounded a little heavier carrying a shotgun. It was still cold, and he was standing outside, hidden behind my glass and wood-frame door, which was covered in a glaze of ice. When I opened the door, I saw his forehead was covered in sweat and his long blond hair was matted. Good lord, he was really worried I might blow him to kingdom come.

I had to suppress a fit of nervous giggles. Before he said a word, I handed him the shotgun and reached into my bathrobe pocket to cup the shells in my hand. I offered them to him like chocolates, five of them. Luke's face relaxed when he realized I'd removed all the ammo. Such a little guy, really. He didn't ask for the sixth shell. I imagine he couldn't think that straight.

IT'S ODD WHAT I REMEMBER about being expelled. I remember the white Indian elephant earrings I chose for the occasion, the denim I wore, and a telegram that I got from Stan. Yes, Stan Holmstrom. He was back with Shari; Hugh had relocated them to Indianapolis. Stan couldn't look me in the eye in Cincinnati, but I bet he watched my ass walk out the door.

Lots of people couldn't look me in the eye in Cincinnati. I had thought of them as friends for life, as family, but I realized I didn't know anything about anybody further back than two years. Who *were* these people before the IS? I had no idea. But I'd taken a bullet for them.

Expulsion was the end of all that.

We'd dodged gunfire and been put in handcuffs and stood up in court together and been told we were "menaces to society." Each of us had an FBI file three inches thick with every other word blacked out for "reasons of national security."

Now we would cross the street and not say hello.

I remember asking my mom once if she would say hello to her own father if she ever saw him in a crowd, and she shook her head no. She meant it. I didn't know if I could be as hard as she was.

I thought about the guy who'd rung up my books at Papa Bach's the day before I left California for Detroit on the Greyhound. He told me he'd gotten thrown out of a Trotskyist sect in 1969. Now he was a yoga guru. Was that how bad it could get? You got expelled and put on leotards?

I liked my Indian elephant earrings because they reminded me of living with my dad. Home. Where was that now?

"E is for *elephants*. E is for *expulsion*." The IS faithful gathered in the Cincinnati Veterans Hall—you always had to wonder who these patriots thought they were renting to. There were American flags hanging over a piano in the corner. Half the IS national leadership were wearing flags on their jackets, too, to better appeal to the "regular" Teamster. A couple hundred people were about to expel a couple hundred other people.

I was told ahead of time that I would be formally expelled for "traitorism." Like Judas. Had I betrayed them all with a kiss? Probably. Everyone had fucked everyone, and now one half was jilting the other.

I had lied to Hugh. I had organized secret meetings to bitch about our wretched decline. I had written letters abroad to sympathetic comrades.

I was accused of joining or leading a cult of personality. Which one? I didn't know what my personality was anymore. The opposition's list of complaints and deceits sounded tinny. I hadn't changed at all except for the innocence bit, which had blown away like dandelion fluff. Did Judas betray in despair; did he kiss in desperation?

I still felt the same way about the world I had the day I'd begged Geri and Ambrose to let me join the IS. I noticed they weren't at this monkey trial.

I wore a tight jean skirt and vest I'd bought with my last check from Byck's. I was sealed up, nothing flimsy showing. I sat on one side of the room, with "our" crowd, the traitors. Michael was the only *Red Tide*r there with me. He was furious, hollowed out.

The little girls from Detroit were crying on the other side of the aisle, all the girls I remembered from Cass, Western, Cooley High. Alicia's face was puffed up. Hank R. gave her a punishing look, but she couldn't stop. Baby-faced Marika, who once stayed up at night with me to ask me what a lesbian was, snuck a peek at me. I was waiting for it. She was fourteen, too young for this crap. I mouthed, "I love you," but Hank jerked her aside.

It was forbidden to whisper "I love you" in this room. Hugh, at the mic, was entertaining a motion to expel.

I counted heads. Under three hundred people. Fewer than three hundred people could afford to split in half? Here we go! We'd moved so many mountains; now we would divide a grain of sand. Ronald Reagan had won.

I don't remember a single word at the mic. Nor did I save the tower of documents that lay in my lap. I dropped them all in a HELP OUR VETS! waste bin on my way out the door.

Stan's telegram in my pocket was the one memento I saved.

He sat across the aisle and voted to expel us like the rest of them. He hadn't returned my letters when I'd written him six months earlier and asked him what he thought was going on. I'd asked him how he felt about the "workerism," which was turning more surreal every day. I reminded him how we used to make fun of sectarians who pledged to use only "powdered garlic" in their kitchens, because the working class wouldn't ever use the raw stuff.

Stan was the Indianapolis organizer now; Shari had gotten a tenure track position at a local campus. He hadn't written me a love letter since my first month in Detroit, and I didn't expect one now. But I thought maybe a faction fight would persuade him to say a few words to me. *Pick me up, Stan; remember who I am.* I didn't hear anything back.

The night before the expulsion, while packing my army trunk in Louisville, I received a delivery from Western Union:

Dear Sue,
You're a sweet kid. Have a nice life. Men are shit.
Stan

It was yellow, one of those old-fashioned telegrams from Western Union that was supposed to say: "I LOVE YOU STOP AM HAVING YOUR BABY STOP ARRIVING TOMORROW STOP"

I didn't know Western Union would let you write *shit*. Stan's last word. I didn't recall characterizing men as shit. Was that his old Amazonian wife, Marie, talking through his memories? Did I remind him of her? Maybe he had gotten us confused.

Stan had taught me how to enjoy a good breakfast; he had read *The Economist* out loud to me while I curled up in his lap; he'd nursed me and brushed my hair when I was sick. We watched *The Treasure of Sierra Madre* together, my first time seeing it. I'd made him a triple-layer cream cake for his thirtieth birthday, embroidered a Dylan lyric on his work shirt, and helped him blow out the candles. No one else was there on his birthday except us. He cried when he took me to the airport. Did I get anything right?

Hugh banged a gavel on the Veterans Hall podium. Michael, all the others, and I stood up in a group. We paraded out of the meeting room with sticks up our asses. I caught a cab to the airport, destination LAX.

My dad had arranged my ticket. He'd called me my last day in Louisville, after Stan's telegram. I told him I was about to get the boot from the IS and I didn't know what to do next.

"You can come home, you know," he said.

"Really?"

"You could apply to one of the state colleges," he said.

He said it so quietly. I knew he remembered my vow not to go to university.

"What would I do there?"

"You don't have to figure that out now; no one else knows what to do, either."

He loved me so much. Why hadn't we talked in so long? There was no way I was going to say, "I can't go to college because all those people who just kicked me to the curb will say it just goes to prove that I'm a wanker."

I couldn't get over it, that my dad wanted to help me. My dad. I'd thought I was surrounded by people who wanted to be with me, help me, share everything we did together. Now we looked like we'd been run over by a six-way split.

I packed up all my stuff; it wasn't much. I decided I could let go of about fifteen Lenin posters. I liked them, but it was like Vladimir was staring at me, doubting me. I didn't have any other belongings besides my clothes and books.

WHEN I ARRIVED IN Los Angeles, it was a beautiful day, a lovely day in paradise. Bill drove us back to the Westside along Lincoln Boulevard so I could smell the ocean. I kept holding his arm, letting him drive with only one hand. I remembered the same feeling I'd had when my mom had shipped me back to California from Canada: I could breathe again. You could always turn to the ocean; you always knew where the sea lay, where the mountains stood.

I had a summer to work in Santa Monica before I started my first semester at Cal State Long Beach. I got a job in a copy shop, printing out parish bulletins, weird amputee pornography, whatever anyone walked in with.

The pressman asked me the first week how I had learned how to run the machines, and I said, "I was a socialist organizer." He didn't know what that meant, but he didn't miss his three-martini lunches, either, so he wobbled away.

The only Teamsters I saw were the UPS guys who delivered at three in the afternoon. I had a quickie with one of them on a Friday when everyone else had left. Afterward, he remarked, "You sure know a lot about my job." I sure did.

Tracey, my best friend from Uni, from the original *Red Tide,* came to collect me, and we went to Venice Beach. She was enrolled in the Feminist Women's Art Studio downtown. She'd shaved her head and looked like a dyke priestess, with jade rings on her fingers. She asked me if I'd heard of the band Castration Squad, and invited me to the Pussycat Theater basement to see them that night. Double bill with the Dils.

Sure, why not. She referred to it as punk rock. I liked that; I felt "punky."

I put on my Boycott Coors T-shirt, the one with swastikas where the double O's fell in the brand name.

"Pin razor blades to it," Tracey said.

"Yeah, right on the nipples," I said. I started dulling some safety razors from the medicine cabinet. I came out of the bathroom with the blades swinging from the apex of my shirt.

"You look great," she said

I smiled for the first time that night.

"You know, I hate to say, 'I told you so,'" she said.

"Well, go ahead and say it while I'm armed to the tits."

She laughed. "Are you ever going to break down and admit the IS was all a big crock?"

"But it wasn't . . . I'll never say that!" I frowned. She sure knew how to wipe the grin off my face. "If that's what you think,

I don't even know where to begin. I can hardly tell myself what went wrong. But it wasn't all that way."

"Well, I can tell you: Your leadership was a bunch of male chauvinist bullies—art-hating, self-loathing, egocentric closet cases who could use a good ten years of radical therapy."

"I wouldn't waste a psychiatrist's time." I took out my pink lipstick and turned to the mirror again.

Tracey wasn't getting my joke. She grabbed the lipstick out of my hand. "You condemned all of us before you left! You never wrote me! You abandoned all your friends and acted like we were all a bunch of nothings, because of what? Because we didn't *industrialize?* What the fuck *industry* are you in now, and what have you got to show for it?"

I pressed the tips of the blades hanging from my T-shirt against my fingers. If I bled a little, I would be able to feel something. But I didn't. "Tracey, look how it all turned out. You all are thriving. Your art is beautiful. I've got a rap sheet and gunpowder burns from fucking Michigan. I'm at your mercy. Are you going to give me another chance?"

"I don't know." She was angry now; her eyes were stinging. Was another expulsion coming?

I felt like I'd been saying "I'm sorry" for a million years, a clothesline of apologies that went 'round and 'round, dripping wet.

I hated saying it anymore. Flawed, yes, I was—you'd never come to the end of my regret. I was a traitor, a slut, a moving target; I was a wanker, a commie dyke nigger lover. I still kept Danny's sixth shell in my jean jacket pocket.

Did she want me to apologize for not joining her milieu? For not staying in high school? For not playing guitar in a punk rock band? What industry was that? I could line my coat with razors, and there'd never be enough sorrys to please everyone.

"Death by a thousand cuts"—that's what Ambrose said when I asked him, "What happened to us?" When the first 999 razors nicked us, we didn't even notice.

I could stand in the shore break at Venice Beach, the tidewater pooling around my ankles, and tell you where I lived. That was real. I could breathe again. That part was good.

But I was cursed by too little faith and too many kisses, like Judas and the rest of his crowd. I couldn't begin to tell you what was going to happen next. Maybe a little bit more suffering. What's one more cut?

I took Tracey's hand and brought it up to my cheek. "Please don't get pissed at me for a while. I love you, and I don't know what else to say right now. I never stopped loving you."

She grabbed me and we held each other, the blades pressed flat between our chests.

"Oh, come on, then," she said. "I like last chances."

We got in her '67 Mustang and headed down Sunset Boulevard.

ALL ALONG THE GIRLTOWER

SCHOOL DAYS

I ENTERED COLLEGE THE WAY some people enter the Witness Protection Program. I was supposed to start my "new life," but I had no idea what that looked like. I was in disguise—I looked like a freckle-faced undergraduate, but I had come out of an underground cell.

I got a campus job pasting up the Cal State Long Beach school newspaper, and it reminded me of my days as a basketball score girl. The merry headlines of *The Forty-Niner* celebrated sports team wins and a new candy machine at the campus bookshop. Everyone on the editorial staff was serious about being a journalist, but their idea of big-time news was covering a fire. My take was that you started your own fire and people covered you. Then you wrote a blistering editorial!

I couldn't help myself. I did a small story unmasking a fraudulent college job agency ("Students! Earn $1,000 a Day in Your Spare Time!"). When the Ginsu Knives big shot called the paper administrators to complain, I was sent to an "appointment" with a faculty adviser whose Harlequin glasses sported rhinestones that matched the sparkles on her cardigan sweater.

"Susannah," she said to me. Why is my full name employed only when I am in trouble? "You are endangering your college career."

"I'm used to all kinds of danger," I told her. I switched my paste-up hours to the graveyard shift, which seemed to employ the stoner faction—none of them were enrolled in the J-school, but many were moonlighting over at the local daily, the Long Beach *Press-Telegram*.

I decided to give up being practical-minded and just sign up for the classes that captured my fancy. The theater department, I discovered, was putting on an alternative-works "festival," and I heard a rumor that there would be a "lesbian collective" script. Before the IS had all but banned the arts from my life, that was the kind of thing *The Red Tide* used to whip up between classes. We used to have fun.

CSULB had a brand-new women's studies department. Just walking by their small office in the sociology building, I could tell they were the most radical professors on campus. Their potluck flyers looked like Marxists'.

I thought all you had to do to be part of an "alternative lesbian play" was show up on time with a labrys around your neck and piles of enthusiasm. I had practically memorized Rita Mae Brown's *Rubyfruit Jungle*:

> *Why does everyone have to put you in a box and nail the lid on it? I don't know what I am—polymorphous and perverse. Shit. I don't even know if I'm white. I'm me. That's all I am and all I want to be. Do I have to be something?*

I was ready!

But my first day in the actors' studio, I didn't see any bare-breasted Amazons. Instead, I met members of a very serious theater department who'd all had formal training. Everyone had to audition to get into the festival. The program director expected us to have a monologue in our back pockets. Many of these young actors were in school only between frantic drives to Hollywood for tryouts. I realized this was the competitive world of the child actors and film-colony castoffs I'd known in my father's old neighborhood. They would all get commercials and soap operas and cop shows—some of them would even end up on Broadway.

I didn't have a memorized piece of anything in my pockets. I ran back to my Long Beach squat to see if my lefty book crates held any monologues I could memorize in an afternoon. I found a big pile of scripts from the San Francisco Mime Troupe, including "Civil Rights in a Cracker Barrel"—but no long solo pieces.

Aha! I discovered a paperback, a black drama anthology, which was sort of an Up Against the Wall Motherfuckers compendium of black theater. There were only a couple pieces for women in it, and one character was an elderly black woman sharecropper contemplating her life. It was five pages; I could do that before 4:00 PM.

Professor Brainen, the festival director, called all the women trying out for the "lesbian collective" onto a small stage. First, we had to "vocalize," open our vowels and lungs. She led us in a chanting exercise that seemed familiar to everyone except me:

> *Lolita, light of my life*
> *Fire of my loins*
> *My sin, my soul, Lo-lee-ta!*

My vowels were disgraceful.

We lined up in alphabetical order to audition. First up was a redhead who did a rendition of a feminist poem by Alta, called "I'm Frigid When I Wear See-thru Negligees."

I didn't realize we could do something like that.

Someone else did a set piece from Ibsen's *A Doll's House*—in costume.

It was my turn. I launched into my version of what seemed to be Miss Jane Pittman's radical cousin. My gold-rimmed glasses slipped up and down my nose. I was still dressed like a Mao-ist bookstore clerk, all in blue. Since I was incapable of any Southern dialect besides imitating the girls at Byck's Department Store, I spoke in my normal voice, prefacing my recitation by saying that that I knew this piece had nothing to do with dykes, but it was about a strong fed-up woman, and I was dying to do this show.

The group flinched when I said *dyke*. But wasn't that why we were all here?

There was complete silence at the end of my five minutes.

"Where did you find this monologue, Miss Bright?" Professor Brainen asked.

"It's a Leroi Jones anthology, I think," I said, "a black drama anthology from the sixties."

"*Leroi Jones?*" Brainen said, apparently aware of the author's black nationalist reputation.

I think that's when it finally dawned on everyone that my character wasn't supposed to be a white teenager. Afterward, in the locker room, I received a ray of hope. Renata, the first theater major to speak a kind word to me, touched my shoulder and said, "I thought it was all right. Black students have to do white monologues all the time," she said, referring to her own satchel of books and scripts.

Later I found out from the well-spoken redhead, Caitlin, that it was gumption that got me into the dyke play, after all. Brainen had taken her aside—Caitlin was the Meryl Streep/Joni Mitchell of our department—and asked her what to do with me.

"Cast her!" Caitlin said. "She has so much *energy.*"

I was still underage. I had never been part of gay bar life or the closeted side of the L.A. entertainment industry. Everyone I knew who was queer was out of the closet and parading down the street with a sign. After all, the first American homosexual civil rights group, the Mattachine Society, was founded by embittered Communist Party members. I took this for granted. I thought if you were "out," you were on the Left and spoke your mind. It floored me that most of my new friends in the theater department were gay in their personal lives but didn't say one public word about it.

Long Beach was thick with drinking clubs of all kinds, including at least a dozen gay bars in the worst parts of town. Some of them were close to the docks and shipyards, like the dives in Wilmington, where you had to know the right code word to get in the door. I made a fake ID on a first-generation color copier we'd just acquired in the *Forty-Niner* newsroom. Now I could finally get into the finest queer establishments.

My first night in a Wilmington club, the Long Beach police made a raid at midnight. Everyone in the bar ran yelling and tripping for the exits. One minute we were dancing to Robert Palmer's "Every Kind of People," and the next it was chaos, even the DJ leaping out of the booth.

"What do they bust you for?" I asked Corinne, the girl I ran down the railroad tracks with, my lungs ready to burst.

"Lewd and lascivious behavior," she said. "And anything else they can cook up. Then they make you a sex offender and you can't get a job for the rest of your life."

Women's Studies was a refuge from bar life. One of my favorite classes was nicknamed Women's Bodies 101. Our teacher, Betty Brooks, lectured that women were so unfamiliar with their own genitals that they might spend their whole life not knowing what their own vulva looked like. Quite a different life experience than a man's. It reminded me of my girlfriends from *The Red Tide* when we'd torn up the sexist health-class textbook.

Brooks had some inspired ideas. She told us to go home, get out crayons and a mirror, and draw our cunts. Brilliant! I went home and called over Corinne; we couldn't wait to get out the paints and paper. "Why didn't we think of this before?" All our vulvas were different, just like faces and thumbprints. Why didn't we see art and anatomy like this all the time?

The next day in class, the students requested open-question time. Betty was like a one-woman hotline, and we hung on her every word. A girl with dark curls and a widow's peak raised her hand, put it down, then raised it again even higher.

She took a huge breath. "I feel fine about . . . masturbation . . . you know, by itself," she said. "I'm really glad . . . I'm lucky I know how to give myself an orgasm." She looked around like someone might take it back from her. Betty gestured with her hands: *Yes, yes, what's bugging you?*

"I have"—the dark-eyed Madonna paused, twisting in her peasant blouse—"rape fantasies." Her voice cracked. "They make me come sometimes. Yeah, sometimes I can't stop them and I feel so bad; I know it's bad. What's wrong with me?" With her dimples, she looked like Shirley Temple.

Betty didn't have a chance to reply. "Shirley's" confession made the whole room explode. Other students rushed to answer her. "It's the patriarchy! We've been fucking brainwashed! It's not your fault! You can change!"

Others pulled back like turtles in their shells. I was one of these. The first thing I thought was, *Well, I have those kinds of fantasies, too. I have all kinds of crazy fantasies.*

I didn't talk about them, but I realized I would like to. If I was alone with that girl right now, I would take her by the shoulders and say, "This is normal."

I doubted she wanted to be raped or assaulted. Duh. No one does. I had been bullied and pushed around and forced to do things I didn't like. It was nothing like my erotic-fantasy world, where everything went exactly according to my arousal and whim. In fantasy, I got only as scared as I wanted to be. I was only as subservient or sadistic as I cared to conjure. It started and ended with my trigger finger. Contrary to my real life, fantasies were . . . *mine.*

Everyone must realize that—why was everyone in class speaking so literally?

Sex education in women's studies was an odd duck. It was fantastic as far as anatomy went:

> *"Where's your clit?"*
> *Here.*
> *"Who has the power to determine our body's fate?"*
> *The individual and no other.*

But when it came to the sexual life of the mind, we entered the realm of the psychological, and the women's studies door clicked shut.

I knew a great deal of "psychology" had done nothing for women except declare them hysterical and aberrant if they didn't behave. There was that stumbling block.

But there had always been a bohemian crossroads of art, mind, and spirit. I knew I wasn't the first feminist to get in the fast car. Some of the most inspiring women we studied were sexually unconventional. Victoria Brownworth stood on a soapbox and demanded "free love." Emma Goldman said if you couldn't dance to it, it wasn't her revolution. I had faced this same thing with the IS. Why did some of our comrades pretend that our ancestors were straitlaced? It was as if Americans had to tie every radical aspiration into a puritanical knot.

In the eighties, when I published *On Our Backs*, "entertainment for the adventurous lesbian," many women's studies departments protested my work. I felt like I was running into my CSULB classroom everywhere, like the clock had been frozen.

In 1989, for example, I went to the University of Minnesota to speak on the history of lesbian eroticism in cinema. I was greeted at the podium by a phalanx of women carrying "blood"-stained banners and demanding to read a protest letter. Everyone is unfailingly polite in Minneapolis, so I moved to the side and crunched on my Baby Ruth while a young woman with a voice like Sarah Bernhardt's read from her script:

> *First, it was the Roman Empire.*
> *Then the Holocaust.*
> *And now, the University of Minnesota has invited*
> *Susie Bright to speak on pornography.*

She was serious.

I gave my lecture, which was well received. People laughed with good humor. I didn't seem like the monster whom "Sarah" had described. I was pregnant with Aretha, and when I went to the bathroom, I asked the event producer to escort me. As if on cue, I was rushed by a student hiding in the toilets, her eyes burning like she's been awake for nights.

"You are responsible for women's genocide!" she said. She was carrying something sharp in her hand. She stopped midspeech and took in my big belly, like it hadn't been on her screen before. In my protestors' minds, I was killing women with my wicked fantasies, not creating new life.

I remembered that girl in Betty Brooks's class. Was there a knife behind her helpless plea? I knew she wanted attention. But what kind?

Even in Betty's class, I sensed that if I had comforted the girl—"There's nothing wrong with you. Call off the witch hunt; let's think about this"—it would not have been welcome. Everyone was talking in rhetoric.

I could have told the girl in the peasant blouse, "Someday your fantasies will change, but it will be because you have more sexual experience, not less."

HOW I GOT INTRODUCED TO
ON OUR BACKS

A LOVE POEM BROUGHT ME to *On Our Backs*. A great swirling erotic gust that picked me up and dropped me down in rich dirt, like Dorothy Gaynor.

I was twenty-two. I had one credit left to graduate from college, my "hard science" requirement. I'd transferred from Long Beach to UC Santa Cruz, where activism and adventure were an easy fit. But UCSC still expected me, a high school dropout, to learn my molecules and formulas.

I procrastinated. I thought I might get rich for a summer, in 1981, by joining my friends who were planning a season of work in Alaskan fisheries. Salmon, salmon, and more salmon. The scheme was, we'd eat doughnuts and fish and fly to Hawaii when the season came to a halt or our fingers went numb.

Young people like my Santa Cruz girlfriends and me poured into the fishing town of Cordova, Alaska, every year with such dreams. But the summer of 1981, there was a catch: The full-time fishery workers went on strike.

Ah, catnip. I got involved with the longshoremen's union like flypaper and sap. Getting rich wasn't on the agenda; I was eating doughnuts exclusively. I lived with six other people in a three-person tent located on a pallet at the top of a mud cliff. Dumpster diving, pallet scavenging, beautiful midnight suns—Alaskan days and nights blurred together, and it was August before I knew it.

I began to hitchhike home, starting with a small plane back to the Yukon. I looked like a boy with a bowl haircut out of *The Grapes of Wrath*, and all my muddy possessions were in my embroidered ("Alaska or Bust") Kelty backpack. I had achieved both.

It was a beautiful road trip; for a time I was happily escorted by other adventurers and no fewer than three Deadhead school-bus conversions. I felt close to home when I stuck my thumb out on Interstate 5 out of Eugene in southern Oregon, with a sign that said SOUTH: HUMBOLDT.

A solitary Datsun driver, bald, with a three-days beard, picked me up and started speed rapping. Guess what? Everybody was against him. Another Earl Van Nuys. I nodded sympathetically and wondered how long before the next gas station stop, where I could make an excuse to get out.

The driver—"Call me C.B."—kept one arm on the wheel at all times. But when we crossed the state line, he reached under the seat with his free hand, pulled out a handgun, and set it in his lap.

"I gotta protect myself, shit; the people I pick up, these fucking faggots, I have to protect myself!" he said. I didn't take my eyes off that gun.

Then I tuned in.

"You know, you could suck me off," C.B. was saying. "Suck me right here; I'm doing you a big favor, and I don't even know who you are. You could be anybody, and I couldn't trust you, but if you sucked me off, it would be like we could trust each other."

I answered as if he'd asked me whether I could spare a moment to make him tea and toast. Nice and slow and really quiet: the eggshell walk.

"Let me tell you, mister, it's like this," I said to him. "My sister Tracey is expecting a baby—a home birth—any hour now, and I have to make it to Arcata, that's fifty more miles, on the double."

A MAN FRIGHTENS YOU WITH a handgun, you counter with childbirth. Something equally terrifying.

C.B. let me off in Trinidad. "This is *fine*," I said, opening the door before he came to a full stop.

I walked the rest of the way to Spinster Hollow, my "sister Tracey's" lesbian commune. Eight women sharing all their income and expenses to live on the land. Tracey was in fine condition and not pregnant in the least—but some of her roommates wanted to be.

I walked into a Spinster Hollow biology lesson being held in the main cabin, where everyone shared common space. One of the other collective members, Marilyn, wanted to get pregnant as soon as possible. She'd "borrowed" a microscope from Humboldt State University to take a closer look at whether her insemination tactics were working.

A nice gay man in town was jacking off for her. I volunteered to go pick up his sperm. I drove a 1967 VW bug into town, collected Mr. Good Sport's semen in a Gerber baby-food jar, and tucked it into my down jacket to keep it warm.

When I got back to Marilyn, the turkey baster was ready. Everyone wanted to squeeze the bulb. There was a burst of comic recognition at our desire to each be "the one" who ejaculated, the thrust that would make it happen. "Let it be me!"

We took turns. Marilyn was supine. She did a shoulder stand. After a few minutes, she wanted to test the sperm's motility. We swabbed her, put the mucus specimen on a glass slide, and looked through the microscope. I had never used a microscope before. Wow. More science in one morning than I'd had in a lifetime.

The sperm were wriggling about madly. Exhilarating!

It was too soon to see whether Marilyn's fertility rite had been successful. I had only a few days to get back to Santa Cruz. I made a forlorn but final decision, with Tracey hugging me for luck: I would waste no more time passing my science class. My turn behind the microscope had given me hope that my attempt at completing college might not be a complete fiasco.

I enrolled in San Francisco City College and chose: astronomy. Who doesn't love a dark sky and beautiful stars? I had a glorious memory of the night in 1969 when Neil Armstrong stepped off the ladder onto the Big Green Cheese—my first time seeing color television. Our next-door neighbor Mrs. Lesley made Jiffy Pop popcorn and crackers and onion dip. Even Mrs. Lesley's miserable teenage son crept into the room for the moon walk. All the miserable vapors from America's culture wars disappeared for one evening, as weightless as space junk.

With that history, I was sure I could master the City College astronomy class. When I arrived the first day of school, I was like a constellation, so white, so fair, so filled with literary references.

The only way I could remember anything the professor handed out was to recall the Greek myths my mother had taught me. It was as good a route as any into my professor's heart.

My last course in college became a treat instead of a burden. I would get a respectable B. My real problem became housing, money. I was crashing in my sleeping bag in a gay commune at 986 Valencia Street. All the bedrooms were full, but there was a generous sill below the window in the storefront. The sun poured down on my Therm-a-Rest. Upstairs, a Rajneesh commune performed their self-titled "chaotic mediations" and fucked their brains out, until we, the pinko queers downstairs, tried to have meetings. They called it their "spiritual practice." We called the police.

I did janitorial gigs, waitressed a few banquets out of Local 2, cleaned sinsemilla from the Spinsters in Humboldt and sold it for $40 an ounce. I just wanted a normal wage job. Tracey had moved to San Francisco, and she pointed out a notice in the newspaper: The Golden Gate Bridge District had been ordered by the courts to hire women, after years of discrimination. They need lane changers, the people who move the traffic cones during rush hour. I could do that! I had the perfect interview gambit: "Yes, I know the bridge weather is cruel. It would scare any normal person, but you have to understand: I've been living on a mud pallet in Alaska and skinning my own squirrels. This is nothing."

Those bridge veterans probably met vigorous and physically able women all day long. I was the only one who was impressed with my heretofore undiscovered physical prowess. I didn't know I had it in me.

My love life and my political interests filled every spare minute I wasn't job scrounging. I was part of a queer-artists collective called Mainstream Exiles that went a lot further than anything I'd experienced quoting Rita Mae Brown. Wasn't she dating tennis players now and raising racehorses?

I had a lot of crushes in our group—there were so many charismatic people: Rhiannon, Max Valerio, Marga Gomez, Tom Ammiano, Tede Matthews, Reno, Lea DeLaria . . . it was the birth of the San Francisco gay-comedy and performance-art scene.

I wanted to do a show, too, my own show. I knew what the title would be: "Girls Gone Bad." I had a treasure trove of old pulp novels from the golden years of early paperbacks, the ones that presented titillating case histories of twilight women—insatiable, fiendish, and horny. These kinds of books didn't get discussed in school, but you'd find them in drawers, tackle boxes, under car seats. I was fascinated with literature that everyone knew about but no one spoke of. I wanted to mash up some of that genre with the catechisms of Catholic virtue I'd been brought up with.

One of my old lovers from Alaska—Terry—came up to crash with me on a holiday weekend. It was Carnival, the holiday that turned the Latin Mission district into a tsunami of samba. Tede, my roommate, found a magenta taffeta ball gown in the streets outside my window and said, "It's you, Cinderella." It felt so good. If he could wear beautiful skirts and corsets, surely I could be just as quixotically femme.

When I made love to Terry that night, I put my whole hand inside her. It just happened. My fist curled like a rose hip inside a place that was so soft. She coiled around me like she was lost, like a kitten who hadn't opened her eyes yet.

The day after our rendezvous, my ball gown came off and I was back in Astronomy 101 in my cutoffs and QUEERS SUPPORT THE SANDINISTAS T-shirt. I didn't pay much attention to anything our dear professor was saying, because I was busy writing a love poem:

1. Rocky outer crust
Icy mantle
liquid nitrogen, a kernel
Hissing at the core.

2. Compare planets with lovers:
As with cosmic evolution,
There are many mysteries

Does life exist on other planets?
Where did we come from?
You bitch, your orbit
Was like a magnetic field
baby
That hurts
I was so attracted too
And now
I cannot touch
Your outer rim
Without remembering a dream

I fucked you round a dance floor
Like a wheelbarrow, your hair mopping the ground
And legs about my waist

The sweat ran down my neck
And trickled on the underside
Of your breasts
They curved like a sulphur plume

The next night, Tede invited me to read at Modern Times Bookstore, just two doors down. A gay Marxist bookshop: yummy.

I READ MY POEMS. I felt like Elizabeth Taylor in Maggie the Cat's nylons. My words gave me a presence that my spectacles and hunched shoulders wouldn't otherwise suggest.

Someone during the show's break told me that Good Vibrations needed a "feminist vibrator clerk"; I thought maybe I'd apply for that, along with the bridge job. Good Vibes had one employee who'd left town suddenly with a broken heart. I wondered who that was.

Vibrators, huh? *That could be more fun than changing traffic cones.* My heart was the opposite of broken—it was bursting with leaps of faith.

Two days after the Modern Times poetry reading, I found in my mailbox a handwritten letter from a stranger.

The message was curlicued, in fountain pen, a beautiful hand, from a young woman named Myrna Elana. She said she was the cofounder of a new magazine in the works, called *On Our Backs (OOB)*. I burst out laughing before she even got to the title's explanation: It was dedicated to tweaking the prudery of puritanical feminist publications like *off our backs*. The conservative feminists believed sexual liberation was playing into the hands of the bestial impulses of male dominance. Ah, science!

The premise of *OOB* was going to be that lesbians were *not* celibates-in-waiting-for-the-revolution, or coldly distant planets. We were alive to sex and adventure and being every kind of queer we could be. I couldn't wait.

Myrna wrote that my writing was "beautiful," that she had been sitting on one of the metal folding chairs at Modern Times. She asked me if they could include my poems in the first issue—or anything else I might have in my desk drawer. She said she'd love to meet me. It was my very first fan letter.

I don't think anyone had told me my writing was wonderful save my parents and a couple grade-school teachers. There'd been a gap. My propaganda efforts for *The Red Tide* were always critiqued for their bourgeois individualism, inappropriate humor, and lack of a socialist imperative summary. I'd become expert at aping other people's writing that could get the seal of approval. It was dreary.

Poetry was the one place where originality—my personal lair—was prized. I didn't feel self-conscious.

I wrote Myrna back with one of my green-ink fountain pens.

"I would love to," I wrote. "I will do anything to help get the first issue out. I know how to do paste-up, sell ads, write copy—anything you need to get it together. You have given me the best laugh in a very long time. Call me."

I told her that I might be working at the women's vibrator store on Twenty-second Street, next to the Catholic school and the barbershop. She could probably find me there.

THE FEMINIST VIBRATOR STORE

MY JOB AT GOOD VIBRATIONS was lonely in 1981. Sometimes I'd have only one customer per day. Even if that customer stayed for an hour or two, I had lots of time to sit there and think about what she had said.

> *"My husband has died and I will never achieve climax again."*

> *"The therapist has told me I am sexually dysfunctional and sent me here."*

One little boy darted in and said to me: "My dad's in prison, and he has a bigger dick than anything you got in here."

I could rock our customers' world with just a little information. One little chat, and they wouldn't think they needed to rely
on someone else for their orgasm. Nor would they remain dis-
traught that an MD had "sentenced" them to a vibrator store.
The kid who taunted me about his dad in prison and ran out
the door—I could say something kind to settle him down. Sex
education was so powerful because even the smallest effort was
enlightening.

I got bored when the store was slow. I read every book on our
shelves. It seemed strange that the catalog of decent sex information was so small that one could read it all in a couple of weeks.
There was only one book for kids about sex that wasn't focused
on pregnancy and disease. One! There was a *single* photo book
about men and masturbation that didn't treat it like a juvenile dis-
order or failure. And all of the contemporary "women-authored"
erotica had been penned by Anaïs Nin, circa the twenties. We had
Nancy Friday's sociological surveys of women's fantasies, but I
would advise customers to read just the fantasies, not the patho-
logical critiques of why these women fantasized in the first place.
It would only have discouraged them!

We had what my boss, Joani Blank, called "the tryout room."
The "world famous tryout room!" I called it, although it was really the world's biggest secret.

It was only a bench adjacent to the bathroom, behind drapes.
There were two basic electric vibrators plugged into the wall, sitting on the bench's flowered seat cover. Customers widened their
eyes when I suggested giving it a whirl.

"You'll understand after you turn on the vibrator," I'd say.
"You'll understand in one second, literally."

You could be wearing fleece-lined snow pants and a parka,
but if you brushed the Hitachi Magic Wand against the outside
of those snow pants, you'd know whether you liked it or not. For

many women, it was the first time they'd experienced what men would call an "instant boner."

People always asked me if the tryout room was "abused." It never really got a chance to be during my tenure. Everyone jumped out of there quickly because they couldn't wait to get their own vibrator home.

The only reason to take an extended interest in the tryout room would've been to impress me, and that happened only twice. Each time the customers were friends of the owner.

A cab driver, David Marshall, who was some kind of sex guru on the side, came in with his girlfriend. "Isn't she gorgeous?" he said, walking in with his trophy girl. "Lana, show Susie your tattoo!"

Lana was wearing a long gown that split open on the side. She had turquoise eyes and Lady Godiva hair. She released her magic snap and the Greek-style dress fell open, revealing a serpent that crept up from her instep, around her hips and breasts, and to her neck.

I was their captive audience. I had a gong under the cash register if they became too obnoxious. But they didn't. I'd never seen anyone with a body-length tattoo before. I didn't want them to stop.

David heralded the wonders of the tryout room to his mistress. I hoped Lana wouldn't be disappointed—I mean, it was barely more than a water closet. They disappeared behind the mauve curtains, and their moaning began a moment later. I suppressed my laughter, since I figured they could hear me as well as I could hear them.

This is what everyone thought my job was like: eavesdropping on ardent lovers in the back room, everyone dripping in sweat. In fact, this was a once-in-my-career performance.

David and his Serpent Girl popped out of the tryout room and turned to me, flushed, their afterglow aflutter.

I could have crushed them with indifference, but that was just too mean. They had pushed me a bit to be the voyeur, but really, was I unwilling? No. I had a flash of how unusual it was to be in a sexual space where the rules are what you make them. In my previous life, when men had exposed themselves, they had always gotten the drop on me before I had a chance to respond. This time I was in the lead.

"You look happy!" I fanned them with my copy of the *Chronicle*.

"Do you want Lana to show you more?" David asked. She stared down her aquiline nose. Ouch.

In *my* fantasies, I was beautiful, too, not the stepsister sleeping in the ashes.

"No, I'm good," I said.

Lana hooked up her toga and they swept off into their chariot. It was the week of vibrating dangerously.

Another customer walked in, right in their wake, with a honey beehive and sensible pumps.

She spoke up loud and clear: "I have *got* to get a Magic Wand; all the other girls at the switchboard have one!" She was an AT&T telephone operator. She didn't share one furtive glance, one troubled whisper.

I felt the click, the chamber turning. Here was someone who wasn't claiming to be sick, troubled, widowed, hopeless . . . just a hip chick who wanted to get what all the other gals were talking about.

She pointed at the stickers on the plastic vibes that said Do Not Use on Unexplained Calf Pain.

"What's that for?"

"It's just as silly as you think. . . . It's a response to a lawsuit from so long ago that even the manufacturers don't remember. No one uses battery vibes on blood clots, let alone on their calves."

"No shit!" she said. "Is there such a thing as 'explainable' calf pain?"

"That's a great question!" I wished the novelty-factory morons could meet women like her. They didn't even understand there was such a thing as a woman who bought sex toys. They didn't get that we wanted toys to be attractive and witty and not like some kind of crutch.

The phone rang. It was Olive Oyl. At least, that was exactly what she sounded like: Olive Oyl after a pack of cigarettes. She said her name was Dori Seda, a cartoonist, and she wanted to come down with photographer Terry Zwigoff and cartoonist Robert Crumb and some other dame, and tie themselves up in vibrator bondage and shoot a "photo-funny"—like the kind you see in Mexican comic novellas.

"Okay, I have to call my boss, Joani, and then I'll call you right back. What's your number?"

Joani was a reliable iconoclast. "Oh, it's for Last Gasp," she said, "the underground-comix publishers. Ron Turner's an old friend of mine." He was going to be publishing Crumb and Dori's mad comic, *Weirdo*.

"Of course," she said. "Give them my love—and *no smoking!*"

I told the *Weirdo* crew to come over when the store closed, so they didn't scare anyone away. I said, "You know, there're no curtains in the windows, so you have to put up with whoever's walking by. We're a block from a Catholic church."

No problem. Dori led her troupe in. She was the only one babbling. I loved her, with her big dark eyes and painted Twiggy eyelashes, as tall and knobby as a Popsicle stick. Robert kept his comments to things like "How exactly is this used?" as he picked up the most unusual object he could find on the shelf and waved it at me. He was already drawing it in his mind. Terry chain-smoked. But I didn't want to kill the mood.

"Could I be your vibrator bondage choreographer or something?" I asked. "Because this will take forever if you don't know the toys."

"Oh, yes!" They were in unison.

Their narrative structure was based on *The Perils of Pauline:* Two innocent girls are trapped by dirty old men in a vibrator store and must fight to escape!

I did draping and artful slipknots with electrical cords. I picked up the rabbit-fur mitt and stroked Dori's cheek with it. "Oh my god, that feels so good," she sighed against my hand.

"Everything in here feels good, but you have to endure a photo shoot instead."

Dori told me she woke up at noon and went to bed at dawn, that she lived right around the corner. She invited me to come over and try on rumba panties and draw and drink with her, draw the new feminist revolution comic book together.

"I can't draw and I can't really drink, but I sure would like to visit you."

I HAD OTHER CUSTOMERS I fell in love with for other reasons.

One day two nuns walked in. I know that sounds like a bar story. They were women who'd left their order five years prior. They had both been novitiates at the same time, as teenagers, and had fallen in love. They'd left the convent to be together openly. The two of them dressed as modestly and primly in my vibrator store as any nunnery would've required.

They wanted a vibrator and "something for vaginal penetration." They conferred with each other patiently. They'd been saving up for this purchase the way someone else would be socking it away for a car. I wanted to give them everything for free.

"How long have you been together?" I asked.

The younger one with blue button eyes cocked her head. "Oh, twenty years, right?"

Her lover concurred. They were delighted at the number. "It's our vibrator anniversary!"

I was single. I had never been with any one person seriously more than, I don't know, six months. I was friends with many of my exes, and loved them as family. But day in and day out, for twenty years? How did they do it?

"What's your secret? Why aren't you grumpy and bored and itchy?" I pulled my hair up into a bun, like Marion the Librarian.

They laughed. The older one—with crow's-feet around her eyes—said, "I think it's just because . . . we love each other so much." She slowed her words down, each one followed by a little pause.

I shook my head, not sure if they were teasing me. I guess I had to humor them. Call "Dear Abby," call the Vatican—we have the answer here: "love." But I was disappointed. I wished they would really figure it all out and tell me.

THE BABY SHOWERS

DEBI SUNDAHL, THE COFOUNDER of *On Our Backs,* threw the first baby shower I ever attended, in 1983. She also invited me to the last one I'd attend, when I got pregnant myself in 1990. I can't believe our lesbian guerrilla operation was bracketed by babies, but maybe many women's adventures are like that.

I hadn't attended feminine rituals like baby showers before. I was twenty-five, and I'd never been to a wedding. My mom didn't go for that sort of thing—I observed only the sitcom versions. I had no idea what to expect.

Debi's showers had silly games, pastel wrapping paper, and little plastic baby shoes as party favors. Plus a houseful of strippers, most of them just coming off their shift. They all worked at a peep show called the Lusty Lady, in North Beach.

The timing in '83 couldn't have been better. I'd been rereading that fan letter about my poetry for weeks, the one that Debi's work wife, Myrna, had sent me. They did girl-on-girl sex shows together, a seven-hour shift, and they'd been planning their magazine for months. Myrna said *On Our Backs* was going to publish its first issue "any minute."

So many minutes and months had passed. What was the holdup?

I didn't have a phone number for either of them, just Myrna's letter, with an address in the Haight-Ashbury neighborhood. I walked there from the 33 Muni bus with a handwritten letter that I planned to slip under the door. The address was on Beulah Street, Beulah and Waller. A pink two-story with a basement window that saw a lot of action, people walking up, filling a short transaction, and walking away—like a pie shop, only with baggies and cash.

I ignored the basement queue, walked up the front stairs to the second-floor flat, and stuck my letter in the mail slot. I wanted to knock; I stood there rubbing my cold nose, but I couldn't do it. Sometimes I'm ready for anything, but this time I wasn't.

I wrote to Myrna in my letter that I could do most anything involving putting a magazine out. It's odd to think that at that time, 1983, I really could, because publishing technology hadn't changed much since Gutenberg. I could ink a press, set the type, write the headlines—whatever you wanted.

My phone rang that night. Debi, Myrna's partner. Of course I couldn't see her over the phone, but I can imagine her now, sitting at the kitchen butcher block, chain-smoking, her long nails tapping on the wood, her blond afro bobbing and weaving as she punctuated every question with her Marlboro. She was so friendly, but businesslike, like a charismatic Avon lady setting up a full encampment in your living room.

"Have you ever sold advertising?"

That was the last thing I expected to hear. Advertising? I'd sold communism to Teamsters and high school students . . . wasn't that practically the same thing?

I wanted to say yes so badly to anything she asked. "Sure, is that where you're at right now?"

"That's it; we have a certain number of preorders, but we need advertisers to meet the printer deposit before Gay Day," she explained.

The idea was to distribute *OOB*'s first issue when a million people descended upon the San Francisco Civic Center for the June Gay Day bash. We'd make so much money in one afternoon, Debi said, that we could pay the printer the balance in cash and leave a tip. Six hours to make $10K. Doable!

I thought about all the sex-toy and book distributors I worked with at Good Vibes. Out of sheer gratitude, I was sure they'd want to take out the equivalent of a high school yearbook ad. "Lesbians are lined up to purchase your goods and services!" That made me laugh. When did lesbians ever do anything but line up for the bus? But Debi would've said treating lesbians like they had money was the whole fucking idea.

"Lesbians have never been treated with respect as consumers; no one's ever come to our community with anything sexual we want," Debi said. I heard her take a big breath and exhale through her nose.

When I went out with my dyke friends, we'd walk through the Castro and see all the gay men's businesses, a vertical column of fag capitalism. I temped at a Castro Street bookshop—and more than half of the books we sold were titles that have seldom, if ever, been seen in a straight bookstore. Every real estate transaction, every ice-cream cup, every T-shirt was in queer vernacular, man to man. Five miles away in the Mission, you'd walk down a littered, dirty street to a feminist bookstore—a sweet academic haven, but as impoverished as a church mouse.

"This is my business plan; we can talk more about it later," Debi said, *tappity-tap-tap*. "We're going to have a baby shower for Goldie this afternoon. Why don't you come over?"

"Who's Goldie?"

"She works with me at the Lusty. She's eight months pregnant—such a sweetheart."

Goldie was a doll; she was like a Creole Kewpie—brown skin, brass-colored sausage curls, tummy out to *here*. She sat on a velvet couch of glory. The house was beautiful in the back, off the street. Debi shared it with her lover, Nan—and Myrna. A sunlit Victorian with ferns hanging in the eaves, the smell of pies and chili in the kitchen—no sign of a drug man downstairs.

Debi, the tallest, was surrounded by other dancers. It was like being in the locker room of a girls' varsity team. Their bodies were incredible—all different shapes but so strong, so . . . conceited. Tight clothes, high heels, muscles. Any of these women could pin me with one hand and do a French manicure with the other.

The question on my lips was, how can you be pregnant and strip? Just as obvious to me was that I couldn't ask anything so stupid without blowing my chances. Goldie was lamenting the day of her maternity leave, her disappointment at leaving the Lusty's daily schedule: "The money's so good, you know, too good!"

I realized that I, too, might pay good money to see Goldie's naked body with her bump. Had I ever seen a pregnant woman naked, talking to me? I didn't think so. Most of the customers at the Lusty Lady had probably not had that opportunity, either.

One of the other dancers—who'd come in with a waist-length red wig but had taken it off to get comfortable in her crew cut—had a whole rap worked out on the value of alternative sex education at the Lusty. She was a college girl from the Art Institute. "They oughta send the whole UCSF medical faculty down here to talk to Goldie," Vanessa said, pointing up the hill from Debi's house to the university campus. "She has schooled these men—they are better papas for it, better men for it. Poorer, but better!" She winked at me, her lashes covered in glitter.

Goldie blushed.

Debi motioned to me to start serving cake. She seemed so experienced at everything. "My son's having his tenth birthday this week, too," she said, licking frosting off her fingertip.

Ten? She had a ten-year-old? Where?

"He's with his father now; it's his turn!" she said. "I did the single-mom thing from the time Kenny was born, but when I met Nan, I had to turn it around. Everything we were reading, all signs, said, 'California.' We had to come out here; we're lesbians. I'm going to bring Kenny out here for the summer, and he's going to love it."

She sounded so normal. I imagined Kenny's father was like some Minnesotan version of Alan Alda—doing his share while Debi got her turn to follow a dream. But my thoughts wavered. I knew it was backward, but I thought women gave up their children only because they went mad, flew out the window, lay sick at death's door.

One of the girls turned up the stereo, Vanity 6's "Nasty Girls." Vanessa drew her arm across her body like Gypsy Rose Lee and stepped in front of Goldie's throne. She began to dance for our momma-to-be, her belly trembling, executing a perfect back bend. The other dancers screamed and ululated. A dance-off for Goldie! How was she ever going to choose who was the best?

I cheered—but cleared plates. I've never moved like that in my life.

"Frannie, I love you!" Goldie shouted over the music, blowing kisses in Debi's direction.

"Who's Frannie?" I asked.

"That's my stage name," Debi told me. "Frannie Fatale. This is so great you're here."

Frannie's "business plan" was one part subscription presales, one part advertising, and a Hefty bag of dollars that she and Myrna were making on their backs and in their high heels, strutting on stages with gold chains around their waists.

The dancers' physical prowess was one thing—but the shocking thing about any stripper gathering, I discovered, was that you have never heard women talk so fast and so explicitly about money in all your life. They make the guys on the trading floor on Wall Street look like a bunch of pansies.

Debi was older than most of the others: twenty-seven. She was all about The Plan. "You can only buy so many pants," she explained to me. "You'll make more money dancing than you could ever spend on shoes and earrings. Your body is only good in this business for a few years. You have to think like you're in the NFL. You gotta buy a house, buy investment property, buy stocks, or be like her"—she pointed at a platinum blond—"and go to med school. Get straight A's."

"But if you fuck up and give it all to your lover"—her eyes shifted back and forth, like there were a few culprits in the room—"you might as well not have bothered!"

"What about her?" I asked, pointing toward a gorgeous girl, visibly tipsy, standing at the lasagna table. She'd had something more than pasta.

"That's bullshit!" Debi's afro, like Medusa's, grew in size every time she tossed her head. "I'll tell you one thing: That girl might piss it all away on coke, but everything she spent tonight getting loaded, she spent ten times that much on some loser who's sucking her dry."

"You mean a guy, her pimp?" I was such a tourist.

"No, her boooyfriend," Debi said, drawing out the word like a sick lollipop. "Or her butchie. Her fucking parasite. Same difference."

Every woman in the room seemed to have a lover. Were they the ones she was talking about? The straight dancers were, come to find, members of that same Rajneesh commune I lived below on Valencia Street—they must be the ones paying the rent, not their orange-sashed boyfriends.

Some of the strippers were butches who worked in drag. They brought their femmes, other working girls. Who made more? I hadn't figured that out yet.

I remembered Debi's financial "seminar" many times as the years went by at *On Our Backs*. She was right: Very few strippers took the fortune they made and protected their interests. The manager of the Lusty, Tamara—she sent her fiancé to law school. He insisted she stop stripping—and she was so proud he cared. Then she caught him racking up charges to whores on her credit card. He cracked her hard across the face when she confronted him. She swallowed a bottle of pills that night, and we sat around her deathbed at the UCSF emergency room until her parents flew in from Idaho to turn the machines off.

I thought they were going to kill us with a look. But we were her family, too. The lawyer "fiancé" was nowhere. Her mother and father thought sex work killed her, we whores. But betrayal killed her, and I don't know when that started—it wasn't on a brass pole.

"That's the story," Debi said. "The girls who wanna work one man—they put all their eggs in that basket. Or they want the perfect butch prince to save them. They give them all their money, they buy them a house, then the jealous prick insists they stop working. When our girl isn't dancing anymore, the prince loses interest. He busts her flat, and she's left with nothing."

I floated around Goldie's shower that day with such cheer. I remember everyone's names, stage and real. Debi was right about the short time many of them had left. Mary Gottschalk would die of breast cancer when she was thirty. Ramona Mast ate a Fentanyl patch and her "lover" tried to make money off her suicide. Laurie Parker, the most talented lover in all of San Francisco, hanged herself when her girlfriend left her. Nicole Symanksi had her kids taken away, lost her teeth, and froze to death on the street. Cindy Ricci disappeared back to Yosemite with nothing but a duffel bag on her back. And another, and another. To quote the old song, "she was a friend of mine." Those girls each made a million dollars in five years of work, and it did not save them.

"I don't do that shit," Debi said. "Don't want a work wife who's into that. I walk on the stage and I say, 'We're going to make a thousand dollars in the next forty minutes.' And you turn over laps like pennies until you hit the mark. I want a million wallets in one night; I don't want one trick's charity."

Debi's partner, Nan, was true blue. She had a "real" job, although it wasn't glamorous in the least. She worked for the gas company, one of the few women at the time. Nan climbed up a fifty-foot telephone pole with only spurs and a butt strap to get that job. She had taught physical education at the University of Minnesota, and when I told her about the Long Beach women's studies department, she had the best belly laugh. It was familiar. The other dancers looked at her—able-bodied, articulate, loyal— and sighed. Debi had someone for the long haul.

"We used to bomb porn shops in Minneapolis, can you believe that?" Debi raised her cigarette like an imitation of a Molotov cocktail. "*'Violence against fucking women.'* The university's whole women's studies department was in on it." She smoothed out the apron around her waist. "That's how Nan and I fell in love, back in the old separatist days. I was organizing a Take Back the Night rally in Minneapolis—"

"No, that was before." Nan interrupted her with a wave of her champagne flute. "You were volunteering at the Harriet Tubman Shelter for Battered Women, and I was teaching street-fighting self-defense courses."

Debi winked and took a sip. "It was love at first sight."

"I can't believe I didn't already meet you at Spinster Hollow," I said, telling them about my insemination adventures.

"We all know where we're coming from," Debi said. "Now we're going to make something erotic for women, that kind of sex *we* want," she said. Her green eyes twinkled at you like a wish coming true. "Our little magazine is going to blow them away."

MODELS CRYING

*Do you think lesbians have a different relationship
to what their genitals look like than a heterosexual
woman would have?*

*Lesbian photographer Tee Corinne: I think they have
a different impetus to learn.*

IN THE SUMMER OF 2010, I was at my friend Eddie's open
art studio in Santa Cruz, eavesdropping on a patron who complimented his photographs' sensitive approach.

"You don't abuse the models, dear, do you?" she asked him.
Ed somehow kept a straight face.

I couldn't resist. "Oh, my ex had a different philosophy," I said, turning to her without introduction. "She was the staff photographer for *On Our Backs*. Honey Lee always claimed to be quoting Helmet Newton, but she'd say, 'The shoot's not over until the model cries.'"

Eddie shook his head at me—and put his arm around his fan. Yes, Ed, protect the audience—they don't wanna know what we go through for this.

I'm glad I can make a joke about it now—I was often that very model crying. I gave Honey Lee Cottrell, Tee Corinne, and every other photographer at our magazine what they needed, no matter what the cost. They taught me everything I know about pictures.

The *On Our Backs* pictorials were the most visible, controversial part of our magazine. But the scandals arising from their debut were never on the mark. The critics who despised us said our photo shoots were sadomasochistic, which seemed to be code for other, unspoken faults.

Our photo shoots *were* masochistic, but not in the way they meant. I froze my ass off getting a shot many, many times.

The doubters asked whether one could *look* at a model and be aroused without knowing her resume; what if she was a racist? What if she was a poor example of a human being?

These critics had never analyzed a single piece of art or advertising with this method before, but the *Crucible* atmosphere in the women's movement of the eighties was contagious. It was like an upperclassman marching into your dorm room, drawing herself up to full height, and saying, "You should be *ashamed* of yourselves."

Why did they make such a fuss? For real? My best answer today is that they were guilty, fearful, competitive, fascinated with power—but utterly thwarted in their own attempts to live large.

Our *On Our Backs* efforts had remarkable success. We distributed our zine all over the world. I still don't know how we persevered. We were pushed down so many times, most forcefully by men with money, but most cruelly by other women, our peers.

Here was the real scandal of *On Our Backs* photography: We were women shooting other women—our names, faces, and bodies on the line—and we all brought our sexual agenda to the lens. Each pictorial was a memoir. That is quite the opposite of a fashion shoot at *Vogue* or *Playboy*, where the talent is a prop.

Most of our readers didn't know that professional photography, particularly at that time, was an overwhelmingly male occupation—as macho as any steel mill, but without the affirmative-action program.

The handful of women who worked as photojournalists were overwhelmingly lesbian—and closeted. Think how long Annie Leibowitz, the famed celebrity photographer, has been quiet about her life. When her lover Susan Sontag died, their relationship was not even mentioned in the *Times* obit. That is how mainstream lesbian photographers live, even to this day.

When we began our magazine, female fashion and portrait models—all of them—were shot the same way kittens and puppies are photographed for holiday calendars: in fetching poses, with no intentions of their own.

"Does this please you?" is the cachet of the entire pre–*On Our Backs* era of cheesecake and feminine glamour. Maybe the model is a "Betty," or maybe she's a "Veronica," but the subject has no sexual motive of her own. Contrast that with a photograph of the Marlboro Man: He's thinking as he smokes; his mind is ticking. Now consider Betty Grable looking over her shoulder at you . . . *Am I cute?*

That's what the male magazines' centerfolds of female models were about: *Am I pretty? Am I darling? What do you think? Do you want me? Could you want me? Rate me! Put me on a leash and walk me around the park!*

The great relief of dyke porn was that all that went out the window. We had an objective on our minds; we didn't need to be reassured that we were "hot." We had a sexual story to tell. We asked each participant, "What's yours?"

The first story was Honey Lee Cottrell's. She and I met because she was the "heartbreak kid" who'd left Good Vibrations. I had inherited her job.

When she came back, we fell in love. I couldn't wait to show her what *On Our Backs* proposed to do. Honey and her previous lover, Tee Corinne, had literally invented the erotic lesbian photographic scene of the seventies, entirely underground. At every turn, their photos had been censored by the small lesbian publications they approached. It wasn't Honey's or Tee's idea to shoot pomegranates and succulents as metaphors—they were simply thwarted with their nudes, left and right.

Honey Lee made an elaborate self-portrait for the first issue of *On Our Backs,* in the manner of a *Playboy* centerfold. It was called the "Bulldagger of the Month."

In her portrait, Honey stands like a gunslinger in front of a window in a ghetto apartment, light pouring in. A white shirt is covering her breasts; her belly is pushing rudely over the elastic of her underwear. Her short hair stands straight up, like a brush; her eyes are like a raccoon's, burning into the focal point. She's got a Sherman burning in one hand. She looks like she could eat you in one bite.

On the Bulldagger Data Sheet across from her photo, we reproduced the iconic *Playboy* silly-girl questions about "turn-ons" and "turn-offs," along with Honey's accurate measurements and weight—numbers never whispered in a fashion magazine before.

The centerfold was Honey Lee's secret valentine to me, because under "Turn-ons" she listed: "Tall, smart, talkative, pretty." That was me, her blushing, chatty bride. Under "Turn-offs," which made me howl, she listed, "Andrea Dworkin's hair, oral sex, the refrigerator with rotten food in it." So rude! Honey wanted to make a point that not all lesbians were cunnilingus fans. She said, "Everyone acts like it's going to be like chocolate syrup, and it isn't." We argued, but I had to love her honesty. The slag on Andrea was bratty, but it was such a relief to be flip. We were so sick of the Queens of Saintly Feminism. They put their pants on one leg at a time, just like us, and they probably fucked just like us, too. The difference was a closet.

Similar to the *Playboy* design, we laid out three childhood photos of Honey Lee under the Bulldagger Questionnaire. I picked those out. They are still so poignant to me. The first one is of Honey Lee propped up on the kitchen table in her dungarees, reading *Little Lulu* comics from the Sunday paper and determinedly ignoring the fact that her mother is curling her hair. The way her little mouth is set—*This is not happening to me. This is not happening to me*—brings tears to my eyes. In the next photo, we see her with the curled hair, radiant on her bicycle, standing on a tree-lined street in Jackson, Michigan. Her parents ran a boardinghouse there; her father was an over-the-road driver. She's in a new dress, but I know the reason she's thrilled is because of her shiny bike.

The last childhood photo was from many years later, when Honey Lee arrived, a baby dyke, in San Francisco in 1969. She looks like Janis Joplin, another lesbian, who, according to Honey, used to cruise at Maud's lesbian bar on Cole Street.

Bulldagger of the Month was our first centerfold and maybe our best. I remember the time I marched into *Playboy's* famous offices in Chicago and brought a copy to the reception desk of the photography department. "We're from *On Our Backs*," I said, "and we've caused a bit of a sensation satirizing your centerfold— we thought you'd like to see it yourself." The secretary turned red.

She called security. A queen with a purple ascot came running in like the White Rabbit and scrutinized Honey's figure: "Oh my!"

Our lesbian readers said more than, "Oh my!" There were three distinct reactions.

One was exemplified by a raunchy fan letter addressed directly to Honey Lee. A woman in Port Arthur, Texas (where Janis was from!), sent Honey a picture of herself masturbating with an enormous dildo while she held Honey's photo in her free hand.

"You nailed it!" I said. My eyes were agog on this piece of flotsam. "This is the first documentation of a lesbian getting off to lesbian-made porn, ever. This should be in the Smithsonian."

Outspoken fans like our Texan were the minority. The other two camps were furious.

Perhaps the biggest camp didn't grok the satire or the sex. "Are you insane?" they wrote. "Pick up a copy of *Penthouse* magazine if you want to see what a good-looking woman looks like! No lesbian in her right mind wants to be portrayed as an ugly butch."

It reminded me of a popular phrase in lesbian personal ads at the time: "No butches, No bis. No fluffs." Geez, that kind of cleared the dating pool out, didn't it?

This sliver of insight into their complaint was that it proved my theory that lesbians had been grazing on male porn leftovers for a long time.

The last reaction *OOB* got was the most bizarre—but it was the feminist currency of the time. We got dozens of reviews and letters that said, "I'm supposed to be aroused by your efforts. But I'm not. I *should* be aroused by women-made erotica. But I'm cold. I worry that this model is a bad person. What if she has done something bad in her life? And even if she is good, what if I am not attracted to her physically? Does that make me shallow? If I secretly wish the model was more feminine, thinner, less hairy, does that make me a bad feminist?"

No, it makes you oblivious and ashamed of your own sexual desires. Welcome to the feminine dilemma. What are the fantasies that wake you up at night?

On and on it went. The hand wringers never confessed whether they ever had simple responses to portraiture, to beauty. Surely they had seen a photograph in their lives that had made them swoon—a portrait of sensuality, nostalgia, or lust, one that shot its arrow clean through their cunts. But no one admitted that. It was as if they had never *looked* at a woman before.

And in a sense, they hadn't. Up until that point, lesbians had not published self-identified portraits of themselves. Period. Gertrude Stein was the exception; that's how far you had to look. Putting one's face in the paper was considered suicide. The police might arrest you; your family might have you institutionalized. So here we were, in the eighties: Gay men already published their own image everywhere, and yet lesbian invisibility was Casper-like, epidemic. *OOB's* photographs caused as much mirror smashing as saber rattling.

It was natural, I suppose, for lesbians to greet our first issue of the magazine looking not so much for arousal as for recognition: *Am I in here? What page am I on?*

Our staff didn't suffer these anxieties because we were *in* all the pictures. We put every creative fantasy we ever had on film. I had a half-dozen different wigs, because we always needed a photo and we didn't always have the model ready to illustrate a story. Every day was like dyke improv theater for us.

We heard complaints from lesbian bank tellers and real estate agents and other carefully closeted professionals. A couple of them were sincere:

> *I appreciate your magazine, but can't you get more models who look like NORMAL women? Everyone*

*in your zine is punk rock or butch/femme and not
like anyone who could walk down the streets of . . .
Sacramento.*

I remember the Sacramento one because I wrote that woman
back. "We would love to have lesbian bank tellers in our magazine," I told her. "But the problem is, the punk rock strippers want
to show *their* lives . . . they don't want to put on panty hose. And
the white-collar gay ladies don't want their faces anywhere . . .
until someone gets the nerve. Is that you? We would love to do a
photo shoot of you in your best pantsuit or sweater set . . . You call
me, and I'll send a photographer!"

Miss Sacramento did that. I swear, she had more balls than 90
percent of our readers, and she didn't even take anything off. She
was simply willing to have her Sacramento face, and a knowing
look, in a lesbian sex magazine.

There had not been a woman-made erotic magazine before
On Our Backs. Not for straight women, not for any kind of woman. In the seventies Bob Guccione, of *Penthouse,* started *Viva,* a
magazine that was supposed to be for women, but the photographers and writers were overwhelmingly male. It was still that sexist tripe: *Will he like me? Am I good enough? Is this cute?*

The kind of models *OOB* attracted were women with little to
lose. They'd already offended their families. They'd left the rules
of school and proper employment. In the case of the strippers and
whores, they combined their financial independence with a sense
that there was no need to lie about their sexual preference any longer. Their johns didn't care. If anything, dykes could charge extra
for their bravado.

None of our dyke whores would have been let into a lesbian
feminist meeting of any mainstream persuasion. But the influence
of *On Our Backs* created a guild of sex workers who embraced

gay liberation on their own terms as fiercely as any Stonewall tranny of 1969.

There were models who were oddballs and con artists, naturally. It's not fair that we remember the crazies, but those are the ones Honey Lee and I laugh about now.

By far the most memorable nut job was Frances—one name only. She surprised us by writing a letter to our magazine's post office box and saying, in her flowery script, that she wanted to model. No one knew her. She sent a Polaroid of herself, and it was breathtaking. She had long red curls, a face like a Sloane Ranger, and a delicate figure. Not a bank teller, but definitely someone's Elizabethan fantasy.

When she showed up at Honey's studio apartment, she brought an enormous can of Parisian talc and a powder puff the size of Milton Berle's TV prop. "You'll need to powder me, everywhere," she said, handing me her makeup tools as if I were in a maid's uniform.

George Washington's wig never took as much powder as Miss Frances demanded. My god, we vacuumed up after that girl for weeks.

The shoot itself was conventional; I was disappointed. This was a young woman who wanted to be gazed upon like a porcelain figurine. In theory, it should have appeased the critics who demanded we show "pretty" girls in conventional portrait settings. But they never wrote us with their approval. We never got a postcard that said, "Oh, thanks, that latest pictorial was just what I was looking for. You've redeemed yourselves. Now I believe in your sincerity."

Too late, I realized the women who "hated" us were fixated on images that offended them. They played this slideshow of atrocities over and over in their minds until you had to ask: What is your obsession? They beat off to our pictures in private and bullied us in public. It was like Dr. Seuss's *Sneetches*—we weren't allowed to their frankfurter parties, and we never would be.

Frances's powder fest didn't end with her debut in print. We never heard from her again, not once, but we got a phone call from some low-voiced butch lawyer who claimed to represent her. She warned us that Frances was running for Miss California in a national beauty pageant and that we had to either burn all the copies of the issue we'd just printed so that we wouldn't soil her reputation or pay her thousands in reparations. Or both.

What happened? That kind of thing put me in a panic. "You lied to us? You're in a straight beauty pageant? Where are your ethics?"

Honey Lee and Debi were more on the same page. Honey Lee wanted to size up the butch lawyer in person—thank god that didn't happen. Debi asked to see Frances's model release so she could find her address and "go slap her face." She said Frances was a whore who thought she was going to rip off the other whores and turn *OOB* into an "opportunity."

"I'm sorry," I said. "Whatever happened to sisterhood, to dykes in arms?"

A year after Honey's Bulldagger centerfold debuted, she wrote in our summer 1985 issue:

> We all know a cute tomboy butch at 25 or even 35 is a little silly in the same outfit when she's 40 or 50. So what's an aging baby butch to do? It seems a natural profession to develop into a bulldagger. Right or wrong, I have it in my head that bulldaggers are old dykes, and I feel like I'm getting there fast. The image has such a fearsome negative meaning I hesitate to cross over the bridge. Like aging people everywhere, bulldaggers dress funny, have transcended their

sexual impulses, and tend to be either very sensible or eccentric.

Bulldaggers embody my worst fears about aging within gay life. Like being bitter over the losses suffered in broken relationships. The one fear that has been my constant loyal companion, "When will I ever be a mature adult woman?" A blatant gay identity has always been considered childish. It's not the position I had hoped to find myself in. So preliminary investigations are under way. Who shall I be for my 40s?

Those who see my picture first and meet me later say, "You don't look so tough in real life." Some sound disappointed.

It's true I don't look so tough in real life. Maybe that makes me a fake bulldagger. Because if I really believe in it, I would pay the price no matter what the cost.

I am still surprised Honey Lee doubted herself. If she, and every woman at *OOB*, didn't pay the price of a very adult confrontation with the infantilists, the hypocrites, and the chauvinists, no one did. She had a vision, and, like the best of *OOB*, that vision changed the female picture forever.

LES BELLES DAMES
SANS MERCI

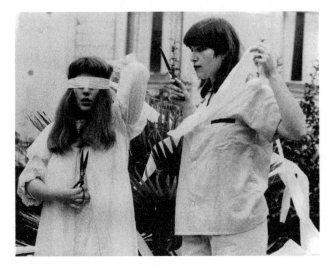

DEBI HANDLED MONEY pressures differently than I did. I always wanted to toss in the towel, give up, throw myself at the mercy of the public.

If we could have hired an ordinary press to print *OOB*, it would have cost us $5,000 in 1980. But because we were women printing sex, there was only one printer who would "take the risk"—they produced gay men's sex magazines, too—and they charged $1 apiece for a forty-eight-page black-and-white magazine. That was before we even got them bundled up and loaded onto trucks. I would call printers, looking for a reasonable quote, and urge them to look at the photographs of Robert Mapplethorpe in *The New York Times* . . . to no avail. *On Our Backs'* taste in photos was more "avant-garde feminist art show" than "Times Square backroom" (though hopefully we found the perfect synthesis), but we were treated like obscene pariahs.

Joani Blank, my old boss at Good Vibrations, had warned me this would happen. She would put together serious sex-education books, like Jack Morin's *Anal Pleasure & Health*—no photos; books that could be used as med school text. Then she would be stopped in her tracks because she couldn't find a bindery to glue them together. "Some Christian at the bindery has objected to anal sex."

We were too obscene to glue together. All of us, the women in erotica and in sex education, ended up paying what amounted to enormous bribes to be printed at all. And the printers' risk? Zero. The U.S. attorney general's office, to this very day, has the same attitude toward women's sexual potential as that held by the Victorians: They really don't believe lesbians have sex.

My FBI file—available upon request, thanks to the Freedom of Information Act!—is concerned entirely with my labor and anti-racism organizing—what the feds considered "the big boys." They weren't going to press charges against a publisher involved in something as ephemeral as "feminist pornography"—they couldn't even imagine it.

But the "boys only" blockade never ended. We couldn't open up a business bank account or get a credit card to process customer orders, because we were considered a "risky business." We couldn't get fire insurance—why? Do lesbian pornographers burn down their cubbyholes often? Everywhere we went, men who bought whores every day turned us down because of "the nature of [our] business."

Debi was pissed, too, but she considered these complications a "tax" for being in business at all—a potentially lucrative business. I never saw the lucre; rather, I feared being marched out of the office at gunpoint because we hadn't paid our rent in three months.

Debi liked to say, "What would Steve Jobs do?" Steve Jobs was her number one favorite man in the whole world. She had me fooled for a year that she knew him personally; she quoted him so extensively that I thought they had met in the Copenhagen Room at the O'Farrell Theatre for a lap dance.

"We're not going to pay for typesetting anymore," Debi announced one day. "It's too expensive, and it's irrelevant. Steve Jobs has a computer for us that's going to change all that; we'll do it right here in the front room." She said this as she pointed at their living room, which had been transformed into our paste-up and layout den.

A computer? I imagined Hal in *2001: A Space Odyssey*. Impossible! I couldn't man a rocket; I knew only how to write, edit, wax down copy, use a proportion wheel.

Debi came home with an enormous, beautiful white box that looked like it belonged on a Milan runway. In it was the 1984 Macintosh desktop computer and a keyboard.

I started sniveling. "I can't do it. You don't understand . . . I barely passed ninth-grade algebra."

She took a cassette tape out of the package and put it in her boom box. "Don't be ridiculous."

Flute music started up on the tape as if we were about to attend a New Age seminar. I felt as though someone had placed either an egg or a bomb over my head, but I couldn't tell which.

A woman's voice came over the speaker. She sounded beatific. "Take the monitor out of the box," she said. She patiently explained how to insert the plug on both ends. Debi rolled her eyes.

The disembodied Apple Goddess said, "Press the power button *on.*" It was like a priest declaring, "Body of Christ." A heavenly tone came out of the computer, as if something were being born. The screen flickered and a smiling little "box face" appeared on-screen. It twinkled at me. It said, *I don't care if you didn't understand ninth-grade algebra.*

I blew my nose in my wet Kleenex one last time, and Debi said, "So, how fast can you type?"

Debi wanted everything Steve Jobs had—like investors. Giant loans. People clamoring for our innovation. I felt she was ignoring political reality. "People don't think Steve Jobs is a pervert," I said. "No one's trying to take him away in leg irons for frightening the horses."

"He *is* frightening the horses," Debi said, cupping her face in her palm like she and Steve had just spent all last night having pillow talk. She was going to be Doris Day to his Rock Hudson.

On Our Backs was embraced, at first, by San Francisco's Commie and anarchist bookstores. They loved us. That had to be good for about a hundred copies in sales. We were a big hit on the emerging Internet, too, circa 800-baud modems. There was no World Wide Web. We picked up devoted *Star Trek* fans on Usenet.

Finally, the gay men's bookstores opened their arms to us—they loved us, too. That meant a few thousand dollars—a glimmer of hope.

In every major city there were large women's bookstores—the heart of feminist publishing—but each one took a different position on us. Mostly "against." Some, like the Toronto Women's Bookstore and A Room of One's Own in Madison, Wisconsin, issued press releases in which they accused us of being virulent racists and anti-Semitists, of practicing female genocide, of endorsing white slavery, of being pimps masquerading as women. When I spoke on the topic of female orgasm in western Massachusetts, I got bomb threats at two different campuses.

There was one rumor that Susie Bright and sex theorist Pat Califia were one and the same, and that this individual was not actually a woman at all, but a pimp hired by an entity composed of the Mitchell Brothers and a Japanese porn syndicate, which was selling women as sex slaves overseas. Yeah, we got "letters to the editor" like that.

This swell of protest against "lesbian pornographers" had two main, charismatic leaders, both of whom were loath to mention our names in public. But we said theirs all the time: Catherine MacKinnon, a legal scholar, and Andrea Dworkin, a poet and writer.

I was fascinated by Dworkin because she was truly radical, a poet who took her manifesto into philosophical deep water. She wasn't content just to whine about porn or "traitors," like *On Our Backs*. No, she questioned the very nature of penis-vagina intercourse itself. It didn't make much physiological or psychological sense—her impression of intercourse was biblical, rather than scientific. But she had flair. Like arguing with Freud but being happy he was taking you for a ride. When I read her novel *Fire and Ice,* I thought, *Look at this: She's re-created de Sade's* Juliette. She was de Sade's most brilliant student. She could write sadistic sex scenes and vicious critiques of the bourgeoisie like few of her peers. If I could have gotten Dworkin to sheath her sword, I would've loved to sit down for a conversation. Unfortunately, she didn't have time for most women's minds—not mine, not anyone's. She was a patriarchal opponent who preferred the company of the most cerebral male scholars.

MacKinnon, on the other hand, was a square, a nonoriginal. She had sterling judicial provenance from her family; her father was a judge and former congressman.

The same year I was editing my first issue of *OOB*, MacKinnon and Dworkin went to work for the Minneapolis city government to draft an antipornography civil rights ordinance that deemed "pornography" a civil rights violation against women. It allowed women who claimed "harm from pornography" to sue the producers and distributors for damages. It specified that "pornography" and "harm" were whatever you said they were. After all, we all know it when we see it, don't we? They pursued the same strategy in Indianapolis. Most influential of all, Andrea and Catherine's activism completely revamped the Canadian customs code for what kind of literature could enter the country.

Let me give you an example of how that worked out in practice: I would submit a story for a feminist erotic publication . . . about two lovers who have a conflict but then make up and live happily ever after.

Snore? Not to the Canadian customs department! Our publication would be stopped and seized at the border because no woman could have an *argument* in an erotic publication—that is "violence against women." No one could have anal sex, because that is "violence against women." No woman could masturbate with a sex toy, because that is "violence against women."

Of course, this was enforced against small presses only. If I wrote or edited a story with the same elements for a major New York publisher, it sailed across the border.

Catherine and Andrea were not naive about the consequences imposed on lesbian, queer, and feminist presses. Their slippery slope was greasier than a leather-boy bathhouse. Both women's efforts in Minnesota and Indiana attracted the support of Christian conservatives, who joined them in their efforts to drive the legislation through. They didn't always win in the courts—but the link between Bible thumpers and porn bashers was made perfect.

As traditional puritans like Jerry Falwell, Pat Robertson, and Phyllis Schlafly adopted "feminist" rhetoric about "the degradation of women," any thought of eviscerating the patriarchy blew away like so much dust. Whatever MacKinnon's plans were for women's liberation, she ended up erecting a chastity belt around the First Amendment.

Of course, I took it personally. How could these leaders and their shock troops think they had more in common with crooked televangelists than they did with me, someone who drew pictures of clits on walls? I started to feel like the "crooked" part was what they had in common. Either that, or grudges so old we couldn't fathom their origin.

In 1997, I got an invitation to speak in Madison, Wisconsin, about a slide show of lesbian photography from *On Our Backs*. It was work featured in *Nothing but the Girl,* a book on which Jill Posener and I had collaborated.

Curiously, our picture show was sponsored by A Room of One's Own, one of the bookshops that had declared a jihad against *OOB* when we debuted in 1984. When I got to meet the bookstore staff, I was curious about them—and they were so happy to see me. Hugs and kisses all around.

"I don't get it," I said to them. "I don't mean to be rude, but you never carried *On Our Backs* before; you led the protest against us. It was like Andrea Dworkin's marching orders. Who died?" I was trying to keep it light.

The five women who'd greeted me looked down at the floor, guilty. My host adjusted her paper-clip necklace and tried to keep her voice steady. "Um, one of our founders died, actually. She'd been fighting cancer for a long time, and . . . "

That's what it was like.

Our dreamed-of investors—the feminist foremothers, with whom we thought we'd be best friends—had made up their minds they were going to die before they let us in the door.

And Main Street America? Well, we were just whores to them; they didn't talk to us during business hours. It didn't matter what the Constitution said, how the Miller test determined nonobscene speech, what Henry Miller or D. H. Lawrence had accomplished in the courts. We didn't have lawyers and civil rights leaders pressing our case. Most of our audience, no matter how sympathetic, was made up of men and women who didn't admit their sexual preferences in public. They dreamed only of being out of the closet. They weren't going to make a phone call.

One day while we were laying out our second issue, Nan was on the office phone with Barbara Grier from Naiad Press. Grier published hundreds of lesbian romances—sapphic Harlequins—and made a handsome living selling to an audience the rest of the world didn't even know existed. Their top title was about lesbian nuns.

Barbara didn't mince words. "I don't have a problem with you," she said. "We've known Honey Lee for years." Translation: *We are old-gay butch/femme—we couldn't give a shit about the feminist sex wars.*

"But," Barbara continued, "everyone we know thinks y'all should be assassinated."

And whom did she know? Their little sisters included all the feminist-bookstore owners, the "wimmin's" music-festival producers, the tarot card printers, the separatist land communes, the moneymakers and key holders of the lesbian womb-ocracy. They were the economic and political capital of lesbian feminism. They'd made a dollar and set a tone.

Nan's eyes flitted over our dildos, latex lingerie, and lube still strewn across the floor from last night's photo shoot: "We don't fit in anymore."

We knew the feminist world; we had created it. How could we be the enemy? How could there be a split?

Barbara's description of "assassinators" wasn't rhetorical; our adversaries never gave us a moment's peace. We got hate mail every day, largely unsigned. The anonymous furies reminded me of the students in Muriel Spark's novel *The Prime of Miss Jean Brodie,* the ones who'd follow their charismatic guru anywhere, even if it meant over a cliff. In Spark's story, a schoolteacher named Miss Brodie whips her little girls into going to fight for Mussolini, which is little more than an exercise in her narcissism. Tragedy and scandal result.

In our case, everything was present except for the swastikas and a railroad wreck. The anonymous antiporn warriors put everything they had on the line to *stop* us. While the "grownups" at the Dworkin-MacKinnon headquarters barely acknowledged us by name, their acolytes, armed with knives, baseball bats, legal threats, and buckets of fake blood came at us in bars, on the street, and at literary conferences. They talked to one another in code. *On Our Backs* supporters were considered the gender equivalent of "race traitors."

The most eloquent among the feminist anticensorship crowd— Ellen Willis, Pat Califia, Gayle Rubin, Nan Hunter, Lisa Duggan, Dorothy Allison, Ann Snitow, Carole Vance—made the case for sexual expression and women's demand to articulate their desire. It was lofty, it was deep—it changed the social sciences and humanities in academia forever. The 1992 book *Caught Looking: Feminism, Pornography & Censorship* was so eloquent and rational it would have made Rousseau swoon. But Rousseau was not active in most women's studies departments.

For all our influence, the *On Our Backs* staff members weren't creatures of academia. We were artists, sex workers, activists, publishers. We were "in the trade."

If I had a gold coin for every one of the "anti-*OOB* feminists" who had a dildo or whip in her closet, I'd be Midas. I couldn't fathom their duplicity. The people who had tried to blacklist or beat me before—during my *Red Tide* years—were white supremacists. Strike breakers. Cops on the take. Mafia goons. Whoever heard of a woman your own size determined to drown you in the bathtub?

In the beginning, I thought our feminist critics needed only a sensitive explanation, a bit of sex ed—much like my old customers in the vibrator store. "The tryout room won't bite you!"

But the bullies weren't our customers or students—they were our competition. We were fighting over scraps, the oldest bitch game in the world.

I ended up in bed—or erotically adjacent to it—with some of my so-called political enemies.

One spring, the first year of *On Our Backs,* I was seeking the attentions of a Teamster bulldagger, a known stone butch who made me weak in the knees. She was a Stonewall decade older than me. I'd look at her well-worn hands, she'd stare at my cunt, and my stomach would start to churn.

I saw her flirting with other women. When she wanted you, you could barely stand on your feet. When she worked security for a queer event, she could drive away straight men, cops, and poseurs with one flinty glance. Between her threatening disposition toward adversaries and her appetite for pretty women was a hair trigger I couldn't wait to tease out.

I found out where she lived in the neighborhood. She had an apartment on Potrero Hill, which sported some of the best graffiti in town: WOMEN'S LIBERATION GONNA GET YOUR MOMMA, GONNA GET YOUR SISTER, GONNA GET YOUR GIRLFRIEND.

One day I passed her apartment building coming from my bus stop. I had such a girlish crush that I dawdled and daydreamed: *What if she's coming home from work? What if we run into each other? What if I said I was selling Girl Scout cookies?*

And then she did come home—just as I was thinking of Thin Mints.

My butch dreamboat hustled across the street holding the arm of a slim blond woman wearing a scarf, neither of them even noticing me. I watched the door slam behind them, heard their quick footsteps ascend the stairs.

I imagined them dropping to the bed, to the floor, my Teamster babe peeling off Miss Veronica Lake's trench coat and scarf. My stomach flopped.

I ran home and phoned Margie, my friend at *OOB*. She was taking a break from packing boxes. I knew she used to drink at Maud's bar with my crush, back in the sixties. Maybe she'd calm me down.

"Margie, what's the matter with me?" I was sweating all over. "I need to get laid instead of mooning around. My dreamboat thinks I'm just a little girl."

"Oh, she put her eye on you—little girls are just her thing. But right now she's fucking Kitty MacKinnon, who's a man-eater. There's no time to fuck anyone else."

What? Veronica Lake was Kitty MacKinnon? And Kitty wanted to get plowed by a stone butch who'd pull her hair and make her moan? *How* could that be true? How could someone as straitlaced as Miss MacKinnon afford to do anything in her bedroom besides keep a goldfish?

Margie had no further time for me: "That's what I heard; I gotta go back."

The rumors continued . . . but they were made up of the stereotypes that enveloped our debate. The "antiporn feminists" were all supposed to be ascetics and celibates. They weren't—they did everything in bed, just like normal kinky people everywhere. The *On Our Backs* staff, by contrast, was supposedly acting out de Sade, page by page. It was all nonsense. When I thought about Kitty or Veronica making bank and getting laid while I was eating government cheese and lying alone with a ratty old pillow, I could just scream. It was easier to go back to work.

I was happiest when working on a new story for the magazine—that was the best part of *On Our Backs*. The stories and pictures we got from our readers "split the world open" with their honesty, as Muriel Rukeyser predicted so well.

How often do you hear women tell the truth about sex? Never! *OOB* was, for me, six years of truth-mongering. It had the flavor of rock 'n' roll.

Madison Avenue took the sizzle of the lesbian feminist sex wars and put it in their own steak. How do you get from Patti Smith to *Girls Gone Wild?* Well, it wasn't our plan. I don't give a shit if anyone *buys* anything for a personal sexual revolution—you can't purchase your way into it.

Straight women never got the power they wanted to come clean about sex. Instead, they got shoe-buying orgies and vibrator tittering on romantic comedies like *Sex and the City*. Their quest was to find romantic and financial fulfillment with the right man.

Sex for the sake of self-knowledge, ecstasy, or communal connection? Nope.

Naiad Press's founders retired to the Gulf Coast a few years after that warning phone call. Good Vibrations was purchased by one of the traditional novelty companies that Joani Blank and I used to laugh about, the dinosaurs. Kitty MacKinnon and Andrea Dworkin formed political and legal coalitions with the Christian Right. The bedsheets really stank. The people who came out on top, materially speaking, were not the pioneers or the innovators. Would you like fries with that?

In 2009, I asked Gayle Rubin to come down to the University of California in Santa Cruz to speak about the legacy of the feminist sex wars. She said, "Oh, Susie, I don't know if I want to go back to this subject. It's been so many years."

"I know what you mean. After all the lynchings, you wonder what the point was. That's why I want you here . . . 'cause we need to do the forensics."

She came down with boxes of books and old documents that no other library possesses—there is very little microfiche on the ephemera of radical feminist history.

Rubin gave a lecture to the young undergrads and showed notable examples of women who, in defending radical sexual liberation, found themselves cast out of Eden. They were decried as Tools of the Man—instead of recognized as the founders of contemporary feminism. Gayle pointed out that the accusations ("Ellen Willis is a sadomasochist!") were absurd. But instead of being laughed at, the censors were taken seriously. People were drummed out for using the wrong word, for being a "sympathizer" with sexual minorities. Being an "SM practitioner" (whatever that meant) was conflated with fascism. One bright white line, over in an instant.

I remember the day I crossed over that line. It was the year before *On Our Backs* debuted. I was at UCLA, attending a founders meeting of a political coalition that was dedicated to answering the Christian-style homophobia of the moral majority. Gay activists from all over the state were there.

I had quite accidentally been assigned to write an amendment to the mission statement, from our San Francisco contingent, in which we said, "As gay people"—cough, cough—"we express our solidarity with all sexual minorities." I named names: prostitutes, transsexuals, the leather community—all those who are singled out and persecuted for their sexual life.

There was a loud hiss on the floor when I read the resolution, then a stampede. Robin Tyler, a stand-up comic who'd become a major producer of women's music festivals, headed up the warpath with her girlfriend, Torie Osborn. They were not going to tolerate perverts ruining their coalition.

I wasn't ready for this. I knew the kind of queerish dive clubs Robin Tyler had come up through. She must've spent more time in stripper dressing rooms than I had! Cross-dressers and hookers surely were part of her extended family. But now the "First Wives Club" was determined to drum us out. They had their eye on me because I was wearing fuchsia lipstick and a studded leather collar around my neck, along with my horn-rimmed eyeglasses.

I was asked point-blank by one of their young acolytes, a girl in a Holly Near T-shirt, if the "leather men" had paid me off to do this.

Yeah, right, guys with black paddles had just given me thousands for a shopping spree.

I told her, "You know, my friends and I brought Holly Near to our high school in 1973, and the boys' dean pulled the plug on her when she sang about Vietnam. But she kept singing and we sang with her, and we wouldn't shut up all afternoon."

Holly Junior glared at me. She didn't believe me.

The debate over "the San Francisco Amendment" raged on in the stuffy empty classrooms we'd rented on the UCLA campus during that spring break. I knew my dad was working in his office over in the linguistics department. I hiked over to Campbell Hall in my "controversial" outfit, feeling more normal with each step. There were kids my age all over campus with ragged kilts, multiple ear piercings, Johnny Rotten undershirts. My lipstick did not distinguish me.

Bill laughed when he saw me. "Your short hair, the lipstick . . . you look so much like your mother." I had been such a hippie girl only a year before, with my long hair and overalls.

Maybe he'd like to tell Robin Tyler about my mom's style. Christ, if my mom saw a butch woman like Tyler, her eyes would turn into slits: "What the hell does she think she's trying to prove?" A good matchup.

I sat on top of Bill's desk. "Look, is there something really, ethically, morally wrong with S/M that I don't know about? Am I naive? What are these people so worked up about? No, don't laugh!"

"Let me see your amendment." He couldn't wait to get his red pen out of his shirt pocket.

"All these people think I'm in a back room, whipping someone to death! I haven't done anything! They won't stop making stuff up!"

Bill took his pen, glanced at my document, and moved my commas inside my quotation marks. "You know, this kind of thing has been going on forever," he said. "Of course, you're right to defend the persecuted. Most people know very little about sex, and you're dealing with that all the time now." He handed my copyedited amendment back. "This stuff you're hearing is the same kind of thing they said about 'homosexuals' when I was in college."

He gestured to a photo propped up behind one of his desks. It was of all the young men in his UC Berkeley dormitory. All queer.

"You remember Jules; I've shown you photos of him in drag before." Bill got out the big white handkerchief he always kept in his pocket. "He was the only one who refused to go into psychoanalysis or try to kill himself. He used the word *gay*—he said it all the time: 'Thank god I'm gay—the straights can kiss my ass.' We would sit around the coffeehouse on Telegraph Avenue and think he was unbelievable. No one else talked like him."

"Daddy, can I blow my nose?" I asked. I loved using his handkerchiefs. I hated to say goodbye. I went back to the conference, and our amendment was trounced in a final vote.

My dominatrix friend Tina once told me, "I'm not spanking Republicans anymore. I've had it."

That's what I wish I'd done. I wouldn't have tried to argue with the Carrie Nation blacklisters—I only titillated them, after all. I provided the red meat.

Have I been guilty of femme-on-femme destruction myself? Why did it blindside me?

The answer to my self-interrogation is hard to spit out. The one young woman to whom I have been unconscionably bitchy, whom I have stuffed in a corner when her voice didn't suit my tune, is my daughter. My baby. My maternal ills in action!

I'd look like a frickin' feminist saint if I hadn't become a mother.

And yet loving my daughter right, delighting in her surpassing me, has been a healing kiss if ever there was one. All the good women I knew, who did love me and mother me, they made a big difference. A huge difference. I have been loved well by most women in my life.

We don't know Snow White's stepmother's name, do we? She, Miss Queenie, was a nobody. She hired the henchmen, spread the ill words. But she had no real power. Just a mad, vestless consort, gazing in a mirror, her pitiful kingdom of shattered glass. Poor you. I know her now, *la belle dame sans merci*. She has cost us so very dearly.

THE DADDIES

THE FEMINIST PURITANS DID succeed in driving *On Our Backs* into the arms of charming pornographers—the very infidelity of which they accused us.

All we did was answer the phone. I picked up the office receiver one day, expecting a weary creditor, and instead heard a fellow who sounded like he had just arranged for a pumpkin coach to come pick us up with a glass slipper.

"My name is John Preston. I'm from *Drummer* magazine, and I think you are absolutely brilliant."

Drummer was a gay men's leather magazine. They were the first to publish photographs by Mapplethorpe, stories by Steven Saylor. They were hardcore as hell, and yet they had aesthetic standards like the Algonquin Room.

I waved my hands frantically at Nan and Debi. It was our first message from a peer, or someone we'd like to be our peer, who could see we weren't just taking off our underwear for the hell of it.

Preston was pointed. "No one else is taking on the status quo like you. I thought the gay liberation movement was fucking dead. You make my secret leather feminist heart go pitter-patter. You are just the Molotov cocktail we've all needed."

In the sex trade, I met many businessmen, peddlers, and film rats who moved product up and down the street. The guys with the gold chains, and the cigars, and the New Age carny versions of Hollywood also-rans. They weren't looking for revolution or sexual transformation. They were looking for you to turn around and show them that fat ass.

Like anyone you'd meet on the non-A-list side of the movie business, porn's entrepreneurs often arrived on the set from "below the line." These were people who'd made industrial films, spaghetti westerns, or B-loops, or had worked in the Army Signal Corps, like Russ Meyer.

Russ was one of the exceptions who loved us. Instead of a hooker with a heart of gold, he was like the dirty old auteur with the same. He'd talk about his own work in great running monologues, then interrupt one of his sagas to look me straight in the eye and say, "You're really doing something, you know that?"

In his dotage, he'd take me out for steak dinners in Pasadena, during which he'd insist I drink whiskey and eat rare steaks—something I wouldn't have ordered anywhere else, with anyone else. He wanted to talk about the war, the beaches of Normandy—from him it sounded like the bloody mud of Normandy. He'd slam his drink down and say over and over, "I'd get down on my knees with this son of a bitch—he's bleeding out on the ground; I'm the last person he sees alive; he's dying—and I'd take his picture, and he'd tell me to call his mother."

"How could you take their pictures at a time like that?"

"How could I not?" Russ waved his arms. "How do you expect them to die, no one seeing them, no one knowing their name? I was their only connection to the living!" And so it was a mitzvah for him. He cried. I've never cried so much over a meal with anyone—besides a lover—as I did with Russ Meyer.

I told him my favorite film of his was *Up!,* which includes a lengthy scene of Adolf Hitler being debased beyond recognition.

"All my movies are about the war," he said.

The Mitchell Brothers, Artie and Jim, who created *Behind the Green Door,* reminded me of Russ, too—if at the opposite end of the political spectrum. Meyer would defend Reagan and Bush to the end. He defended their wars and their cocksmanship. He defended their mistresses.

Jimmie and Artie were the antiwar crusaders, the muckraking Left, but with just as much spirit as the Allies. They were the kind of people you could call in the middle of the night and say, "Let's *do* something and get those bastards," and they'd be right on it, a regular font of creative subversion. Underground comix? Fucking with Walt Disney? Lesbian radicals? AIDS? The Catholic Church? They were game.

One time they called me at an hour when I couldn't make out the clock in the dark. "Come on down," they said. "Everyone's here." That might mean everyone from Ron Turner at Last Gasp to Hunter Thompson to poet Danielle Willis. "We're going to publish a new paper and stop this fucking war in Iraq."

"And of course you can't do it without me?" I asked, rubbing the sand out of my eyes.

"Are you kidding?" Artie roared. He made his trademark *caw* like a crow, blasting through my receiver. Clearly, the White House was doomed.

It's no mistake that Jim and Art, along with Russ, were the most vociferous porn directors about establishing and protecting their American copyright. The reason you see a little blurb on your DVD that says, "Back off, motherfucker, this is protected" is because of their decades-long fight in court to protect their work.

Jim and Art were the ones who said, "Just because you don't respect what we do doesn't mean you can violate our copyright. It doesn't matter if it's horseshit; it's our horseshit, not yours."

Not the Mob's, not the government's. A radical thing to insist in their era.

The pornographic minority—and really, I can count these people on my fingers—were a few bohemians from porn's peepshow origins, the Signal Corps stalwarts, and, most influential, the intelligentsia, epitomized by John Preston, John Rowberry, David Hurles, Boyd McDonald, Michael Constant, Christian Mann, Tony Lovett, Jack Fritscher. They were *On Our Backs* daddies, our Oscar Wildes, our Genets, with address books of printers and video duplicators who wouldn't discriminate against us.

To a fault, they were aesthetically deep. When I was pregnant and considering the pros and cons of circumcision (if I had a boy) John Rowberry would summon his foreskin arguments with quotations from the French. Then he'd make me the most incredible beurre blanc. Jack Fritscher went to seminary school with disgraced cardinal Bernard Law. These men were educated, like my father. They would have found each other to be great company.

My gay comrades from magazines like *Drummer* were very much seminarians, whereas the Mitchell family and Russ's one-man army were the autodidactic infantry.

The queer Jesuits of porn had expansive ideas about beauty, sex, death, transformation. They had zero interest in trying to convince or uplift anyone who didn't already get it. They didn't want to reach out to "mainstream couples," or convince "*Cosmo* readers," or testify in Congress. Their battles were private cuts, not debates on the tabloid pages.

The men's gay publishing and film world was designed as vertically as the rest of the porn empires—they ran and owned their own show from top to bottom. Their audience was devoted, much more discriminating than the straight world, and dedicated to furthering their glory within their own parallel universe. I was green with envy.

Debi, Nan, and I wouldn't have been able to secure the practical means for producing our magazine and videos if our "daddies" hadn't helped us. I was always curious why they made an exception for us, why they loved *On Our Backs*. They had zero interest in us sexually and no possible way of making a dime off their generosity. Nor would their good works ever be advertised.

I think it was a case of mutual inspiration. We needed gods, and they needed a few goddesses. I was a True Believer in the gospel of sexual sacrifice. The eighties were a period of homosexual incandescence that was dying under the brutality of AIDS, "being normal," getting married, joining the army, and being Just Like Everyone Else. The AIDS death march came like thunder, and then everything else was insults that could barely be perceived at the time.

I think the daddies' crazy "Harry" loved our unorthodox "Sally." We cared both about beautiful photography and poetry and about brutal sexual honesty. We were the last of the bohemians, in a nation dying of erotic illiteracy.

I published a few of John Preston's stories at the end of his life, when he was dying from AIDS complications. He was expiring in his apartment in Boston; I was in San Francisco in the back of my kitchen, my toddler, Aretha, drawing furiously on the floor as I typed at my desk to line up all my author contributors. It was 1994, the second year I published my first bestseller: *The Best American Erotica* short-story series.

My stomach churned as I moved to dial John's number. I spent most of the AIDS onslaught like a bowl of Jell-O: *This isn't happening, this isn't happening.* Everybody I looked up to was vanishing, and I could only keep repeating, like a child, "But I don't want you to die."

John had always signed and mailed his contracts to me in good order; it was unprecedented for him to be late.

I let his phone ring five times—no machine picked up. Then a dying man lifted the receiver. I could hear things falling to the floor. His death rattle cursed into the speaker: "Fuck it!"

"John, it's me. It's Susie."

"I know," he croaked. I could hear him sigh and sink down.

"This is awful," I said. "I'm just putting *BAE* to bed, and I know you want to be in it, but I don't have your contract. This is ridiculous! Shall I hang up?" I didn't want to cry while on the phone with him. He must be so sick of people crying. "I love you, John. This isn't why I want to be calling you. . . . " I couldn't stop blithering.

He didn't interrupt me. His breathing was labored. All I could hear was his breath.

"Are you there, John, is anyone with you?" I started to think of who lived close to him and had the presence of mind to batter down the door.

"No, no, M's coming later, it's okay." He hacked a bit. "I don't want to wait, though. I want to fax the contract to you, but . . . if you saw all the tubes in me, and these cords—it just takes some time."

I could hear him trying to get up again. Everything was a bump or a small crash.

"John, *stop it*—this is messed up; it doesn't matter. I'm not going to be the person who offed you getting your signature. I'll forge it, we'll do something; just forget it!"

John stopped his snail's-pace demolition and regained some of his deep voice. "No, this is the only thing that *does* matter, the only fucking thing."

I heard his fax machine whirring on the other end. The one-page agreement was coming through on my end. His signature—he had such beautiful handwriting, remember?—was half of a scrawl.

"Is it all right?" he asked. "Is it all right?"

"It's perfect," I said. "Your story is perfect; everyone is going to be blown away. You're going to make grown straight men cry."

You know, like Russ Meyer.

I have Preston's contracts in my drawers and all his beautiful books on my shelves. His *Flesh and the Word* collections were my inspirations for *Best American Erotica*. The truth was, gay writers, every year through the nineties, wrote "the best" erotic fiction in America, and everyone else was only struggling in the back of the heat.

Why were they better? Because their audience was not sitting around wondering whether it was okay to be sexual, to be a man, to have a sexual, literate mind. They demanded it.

Women, our intended audience, were just crawling out of their eggs. Was it okay to be a mature woman? Was a whore's integrity something to cherish? Did our education, our power, add up to something that wasn't only maternal?

Straight men, or "ostensibly straight men," as John would have said, were so guilty. Drowning in the muck of it. Loathing themselves, hiding, unable to see the beauty in themselves or any other man.

Most of the businessmen I met in the sex trade were like that: *not okay* about sex. Deluded by the material payoff. As sexist as . . . Archie Bunker. Their question to me was the same question as square America's: What's a nice girl like you doing in a place like this?

In the late eighties, I made a movie show-and-tell called *All Girl Action: The History of Lesbian Eroticism in Hollywood*. I put all of my most thought-provoking film clips inside it. Russ let me have a print of *Vixen,* the first American feature to include a lesbian sex scene—and perhaps the most amusing one produced to this day.

We premiered my show at the art deco Castro Theatre in San Francisco at the annual gay film festival. One of the festival veterans, Bob Hawke, was instrumental in making sure I could show each clip in its original medium: 16 mm, 35 mm, Beta-max, whatever. We had four different projectors set up for every movie format.

After the festival, I wanted to settle in with Bob for a long, pot-filled evening of queer-film gossip, but I couldn't find him. His number was disconnected. A volunteer at the festival interrupted my search, grim-faced—"Bob's gone, Susie," she said. "He said he just couldn't live anymore."

What was this treachery? I didn't know anything about his personal life. What had happened? I couldn't process the losses anymore.

In 1999, I was invited to speak at a Los Angeles film conference. I walked into our panel's auditorium and directly into the black polo shirt–covered chest of Bob Hawke. I was all made up for the cameras, but it was for naught—my mascara streamed down my cheeks in tears.

"I thought you were dead!" I cried—the first time I've ever greeted anyone with those words. I hit his chest with my fists.

Bob held me tight but struggled with an explanation: "No, no," he said. "I just . . . I just dropped out for a while. I should have told you—a lot of people. I should have . . . "

He asked me if I had seen a new movie he'd produced, *Chasing Amy.*

One of the event producers passed me a handful of Kleenex. "Uh-uh, I haven't," I said. "It's supposed to be about lesbians, right? When did you start producing movies?"

This was the opposite of suicide, right?

Bob got a strange look on his face. "Well, lesbians, not really. It's more about . . . *you!*" Then he flinched, as if I might punch him again. "Actually, you should see it. You really should."

I came home and wondered why *Chasing Amy* was about me. I had not been chased lately. Why had no one said anything to me? Were all my friends too snobby to see a Hollywood film about lesbians? Probably. I rented the video.

Chasing Amy turned out to be a story about a slacker who falls for a bisexual dyke. She's blond, femme, tough. He's a square guy—not a dyke daddy—and not at all sure if it's okay to be with someone as "open" as Amy.

Every word that comes out of the heroine's mouth blows the young man's puritanical mind. But he likes it. There's a scene where Amy's on a swing at a playground and she starts talking to him about sex:

> *ALYSSA*
> *"Fucking" is not limited to*
> *penetration . . .*

> *HOLDEN*
> *Well, where's the penetration in*
> *lesbian sex?*

Alyssa holds up her hand.

HOLDEN
A finger? Come on. I've had my
finger in my ass, but I wouldn't say
I've had anal sex.

ALYSSA
Did I hold up a finger?
[Waves her hand.]

HOLDEN
[Beat; then he gets it.]
You're kidding?!
[She nods.]
How . . . ?!?

ALYSSA
Our bodies are built to pass a child,
for Christ's sake.

It was so strange to hear a conversation of mine coming out of her mouth on my television set.

The two characters proceed to have an affair. The boy rejects Alyssa *not* for being a dyke, but for having fucked around too much . . . she has been the high school "slut." Ah, that was familiar, too.

I wrote to Bob that I had published a new book, a little further afield than *Amy*. It was called *Nothing but the Girl,* a book of lesbian erotic photography. The book had a dedication, which I copied for him:

This book is dedicated to all the lesbian artists who would not, could not, and cannot imagine being in this collection:

because you fear for your job
because you fear abandonment
because your lover is a closet case
because your family is ashamed of you
because someone threatened to take your kids away
because the academy didn't like it
because the gallery disdained it
because your estate does not wish to cooperate
because it's politically incorrect
because it's politically inopportune
because you don't approve of the word "lesbian"
because you don't approve of the word "dyke"
because you don't approve of "porn"
because you think sex should really be private
because it was different when you grew up
because you don't see the point in bringing this out
into the open
because you don't feel like living anymore
because you didn't mean it that way
because you're locked up
because you're doped up
because what did lesbians ever do for you, anyway
because it hurts to be criticized and cut down
because people are cruel
because you're not a hero
because
the first cut
thank you
is the deepest

MOTHERHOOD

You can house their bodies but not their thoughts.
They have their own thoughts.
You can house their bodies but not their souls,
For their souls live in a place called tomorrow,
Which you can't visit, not even in your dreams.

—Kahlil Gibran

I GOT PREGNANT IN 1989, when I was thirty-two, the same age as my mother when she had me. I was due in early June, which inspired a flood of Gemini good wishes from my *On Our Backs* readers, who were as surprised and curious as everyone else.

"Did you inseminate or did you party?" asked Marika at our Christmas party. I laughed so hard, she said, "Oh! You partied."

I did party. But I also was falling in love. And then out of it. My bisexual heart was in a bit of torment.

It was the eve of a baby boom—I didn't know any other women my age who were taking the plunge. They'd all done it a lot earlier or had forsworn the whole racket—that would've included me.

My daughter-to-be, Aretha Elizabeth Bright, surprised me in every way—including her late-June Cancerian arrival. She had eyes like dark moons, and when the midwife put her in my arms, she looked into me like no one has ever looked at me before.

When Aretha was six months old, an old neighbor of mine saw us walking home from the grocery store, baby tucked into her stroller, a loaf of bread sticking out between her curly head and the diaper bag.

"Look at you!" he exclaimed, as if a figure of the Madonna and child had sprung to life. Well, I didn't mind if he wanted to make a fuss. The oxytocin was flowing through my veins.

This old codger, Mr. Hera, had always taken a dim view of what he knew about me from the newspapers—he'd make a chauvinistic, what's-the-world-coming-to? remark whenever we ran into each other on garbage night.

He leaned over to admire Aretha's little face, then looked up at me with a smile: "Now, isn't this the very best thing you've ever done with your life?"

I covered my eyes with my hands and laughed. "Oh no, Mr. Hera, please, don't ruin it." Then I straightened up and touched his shoulder. I'm a few inches taller than he. "You know, Mr. Hera, you're right, you're right—more than you even know."

My pregnancy and my daughter's life worked on me like true north. I had to Protect the Baby, but I ended up Protecting Me. My maternal certainty was a tonic. I knew whom I had to defend. Malingerers, fakers, and self-destructive impulses were red-tagged and booted. I had a magnet in me for doing the right thing.

How could someone like me, who got pregnant by accident, unpartnered, uncertain of her future, find motherhood such a gift? Is there really a time to every purpose under heaven?

When I was pregnant and staring at my enormous navel, I wondered if this was my comeuppance. All the time I spent as a child fuming, crying, hiding, swearing I would never put another human being through such cruelties as were visited upon me . . . would I now be humbled?

I did get pregnant unexpectedly. I spent the first thirty-one years of my life being either a lesbian or a complete martinet about birth control, and all of a sudden, I got sloppy. It was out of character. So was my pregnancy test . . . I burst into tears when I got a (false) negative. "It can't be true; it can't be true!" I sobbed in the car next to my friend who drove me home from my doctor's appointment. She was bewildered at my rage and tears. "But you never wanted to have children!" she said.

That was true. I could convince anyone about zero population growth; I would rant about the narcissism of parental conceits. I'd written articles on why a woman's worth is not the sum of her womb. I'd write them all over again, too.

But the real reason I couldn't imagine having a baby was that I was afraid of my temper, afraid of doing those things for which you can't ever fully apologize. I knew that my mom had been "sorry" that she had hit me (after all, it wasn't as badly as she'd been hit). She didn't remember threatening me (after all, we did survive). Maybe it was my fault sometimes; isn't that what kids think? *Mommy, I'm sorry, I'm so sorry.* It changed nothing for her. But then, her actions had very little to do with me.

If I stayed pregnant, if I had the baby, I had to take a vow. But a real vow entails keeping your promise . . . could I keep a pact that had been broken to me, however much in sorrow? Could I say to my daughter, "I will never hit you, I will never lose you, I will never hide the truth from you, I will never try to extinguish you"?

It's not like anyone "planned" to do differently with me.

My conception appeared madcap to many of my friends. Yet I think I had a much better idea of what I was getting into than my mom did when she was thirty-two.

I had a soft spot for the man I conceived with, but we knew we weren't destined for longevity, nor he for any kind of parenting. We talked about it frankly. I told him, "I'll never ask you for anything, but I know, wherever you are, you'll be proud of her." He asked me to take care of his family belongings before he went on the road again—I knew he trusted me. He was the High Plains Drifter, shimmering into disappearance in the heat.

ROTATION

I MET JON SHORTLY before I got pregnant; we became lovers and friends and stayed that way for the next twenty-some years.

I met him because my tires needed to be balanced. He will tell you that I arrived at the mechanic's garage in a black catsuit, like Emma Peel, and that I tried to lure him away to a beach down the coast where everyone strips off their clothes and huddles, making love in driftwood caves that other nudists erected to protect themselves from the wind.

It's true, I flirted with him; but it was because he was a really good talker, handsome, and completely alone in a run-down tire shop in the Outer Sunset. It was such a sweet escape to have a moment of screwball comedy in the Ocean Beach fog.

He didn't come away with me the first time. My only remembrance from the tire shop is that we kissed goodbye, my low-profile tires beckoning. I don't think I'd ever kissed my mechanic before.

He kept my number, which I'd scrawled down on the credit card receipt, and six months after our meeting, he left a message at my office: "Do your tires need rotating?"

My whole life needed rotating.

We both had other lovers, we'd both had messy breakups, we both had recently ended relationships with "older women" whom we cared for dearly. We also had a talent for putting ourselves in peril by climbing into bed with some scary characters. I remember once when *my* current shady character and *his* scary girl sought each other out and took each other to bed. It was two con artists sizing each other up. They wanted to see what the other one was capable of. Maybe they wanted to compare notes on the thrills of fucking Raggedy Ann and Andy. The bandits competed to see who was the most deadly. It was a draw.

During my thirtieth year I had started seeing a therapist, and even though she barely said a word, there is something about sitting in a room, talking to yourself, a kind face across from you nodding at your every word, that is bound to reveal a few things.

I made a joke to her one day: "Well, I have to say, at least my new friend Jon isn't trying to kill me or himself or anybody else." He was . . . in favor of living, so to speak. He took great care. Everyone enjoys those qualities in a lover. But at my low ebb, distressed at breaking up with Honey Lee and embarrassed by my leaps into the abyss, Jon was like a hand that unexpectedly reached out to me. It wasn't a matter of whether I was attracted or not—I just had to grab it. I grabbed—and my attraction grew exponentially.

Jon has a good story from when he worked as a marine rescue guard in the oceans of the Northern California coast. He saved people from drowning and retrieved corpses from the water. One day, his crew got a message that there was a woman, fully clothed, ranting and raving and dog-paddling, out beyond the city wharf. The fire department directed one of its swimmers, Logan, to jump in with Jon and swim out to the victim with a raft. Logan approached the woman, his red lifeguard float in front of him, and called out, "Grab on to this!"

The vic yelled back, "Get that away from me; it's just an extension of your penis!"

The woman was a strong swimmer, albeit intoxicated, and not yet fatigued by the cold. Jon swam a little closer to her. He complimented her great swimming; he suggested that they could swim together, that he'd follow her. He was counting on her not being in a condition to last out there too much longer. Her fantastic gender lecture notes grew quieter, less frequent. All three of them started paddling down the surf line; as she tired, they harnessed her with the rescue float.

I think I wore out, too, though perhaps not as gracefully. Pregnancy gave me such a new kind of appetite. I was hungry for someone whose patience preceded him.

My first trimester was biblical. Each promise, made in great sincerity, came to pass. The family members who drew close to me at that time were in love with Aretha from the time she was an unnamed twinkle. Jon, who is her dad in every sense of devotion. Godmother Honey Lee, her second home. Aunt Temma and Tracey. Auntie Shar. My dad, his wife and family. And my mom, too. For an only child without a ring on my finger, I was loved, and Aretha was cherished, in one abundant circle after another.

My mom's the one who sealed the deal on picking her name. I'd been reading baby-name books until my eyes crossed. I sent Elizabeth a list of a few that I liked, including Aretha.

My mother wrote back the next day with great excitement. "Oh, Susie, *Aretha* is Greek for 'the very best,' the most outstanding and virtuous. That is the perfect name for the perfect baby." She wrote the Greek letters out in cursive.

Neither of my parents knew one thing about R&B, or about most popular music. The day after I got my mother's message, my father sent me a color travel postcard of the stone ruins of Goddess Aretha's Grecian temple, which lies in what is now Turkey.

Only Bill and Elizabeth, of all the people in the world, would respond to the name Aretha with the enthusiasm of the antiquities.

I knew family ghosts don't go away. I've enjoyed the beneficial ones. But I knew that abuse loves reruns. Penance and exorcisms don't work. I still needed a plan to keep my promise to be "a good mom," something stronger than good intentions.

I would probably lose my equilibrium—or come close to it. I confided to Jon, "If I fuck up, I have to tell another adult what happened, right away, and get some help picking up the pieces."

It made Jon cry; he knew how hard this was. He had been raised with the same "discipline methods" and tempers as I had. We were sitting on my bed; I was folding my Grandma Bright's pillowcases.

"Plus, if I lose my temper, I have to tell her that I was wrong— and that there's no excuse for it. . . . " I looked up at him. "You know, I think you can tell your kids those things no matter how old they are. They know what's going on."

And it came to pass. I remember calling Jon from the pink bathroom in our apartment when Aretha was three. I had yelled at her and pinched her arm hard. I was a dragon. It was over nothing, of course. I had done the full Halloran Vicious Intimidation. It was like falling off a log.

I can't see the truth when I'm losing my marbles—but five minutes after the explosion, I can. You imagine you're going to feel so great when you unload on someone—and instead you despise yourself.

Jon came over. He stayed and stayed and stayed, and I realized that, wow, proximity to another grownup was 90 percent of the battle. If there's more than one of you in the room, one can go crack up and take a cold shower while the other steps in.

People talk all the time about the benefits of a "couple" taking turns parenting—but let's face it, there were lots of times we could have used a third, and a fourth.

I broke the physical-abuse regime in my family tree. That gives me awestruck pause. But I didn't stop using my mean mouth with my loved ones. I could take a time machine back two centuries and there would probably be waiting for me a redheaded woman with her freckles practically popping off her face when she lost her temper.

When Aretha was eleven, she'd reached that age when we could start to have deeper talks about stuff. One day we drove to the drugstore for shampoo and lemonade. I parked the car in the shade and said, "You know, I realize things are usually fine—we work things out when we have a problem. But there're times when I go off on a tear, and you probably know by now, there's a tone to my voice when I'm not being rational."

She nodded, wary that I was considering a demonstration.

I wanted to continue without crying. I felt like I was handing her a secret weapon. "I know you can tell from one word when I'm messed up." I exhaled. "And I want to tell you now—'cause I can't tell you when I'm angry—that you should just *turn your back* and *walk away from me.*"

Aretha's brown eyes got just a little bit bigger. "But you won't . . . "

"Yeah, I know," I said. "I won't like it. I'll try to get you to stay and argue with me. It won't be cute."

She nodded her head, like, *Duh.*

"But don't worry about me; I'll be fine. As soon as I'm standing alone in a room with no one to hear my bullshit, it's like a pail of cold water—I sober up fast. I don't want you to stand there and take it, like I used to; it's poisonous."

Aretha winced. She didn't like hearing about my mom and me, like we had a hereditary bad seed.

"Honey, seriously, if you stand up to bullies, sometimes all it takes is turning your back on their nonsense. Let 'em try talking to your dust."

"But what if you get mad?"

"I'm already crazy, totally crazy, when I'm in that zone. But when I can't lash out at you, I come to my senses sooner, and I will always be so sorry. I'll be so proud of you for not putting up with it."

"I don't know, Mom. Why do you have to go there in the first place?"

I could see her point. She had that prepubescent wisdom. I think today she would possess more understanding of where an irrational outburst comes from, and more sympathy for it. But children's innocence is correct. Why would I need to tell my loved ones to take cover and spray me with Mace if I could just control myself?

People ask me all the time about how I've parented my daughter, hoping for some sex education tips. *When should I say 'X'? When should I tell them 'Y'?* They want their kids to be confident, sexually savvy, not neurotic like their own generation.

What you *tell* your kids is so . . . secondary. It's what you *do*, what you do every day, that they'll learn from.

My daughter is capable and caring—I bask in her virtuous light quite unfairly. She is her own doing.

But if I had to answer parenting questions, how new parents might have a fighting chance to raise a sexually mature and wise young adult, here's what I'd say:

> *Don't hit them.*
> *Don't lie to them.*
> *Respect their privacy and your own.*

Good food would also be nice—and birthday cakes, and warm coats and mittens, all of that—but I'd say those three actions are the most important.

Since I first started giving sexual "advice," I've been hearing people's confessions. What causes the most damage, the biggest problems in people's sex lives, is when they have been abused within their own family or church.

Following on the heels of that crime is the sin of growing up with terrible lies about who you are, where you came from, what's happening right in front of your nose. Violence is always part of that original lie: "We're punishing you because you were bad. Everything is fine, but you better not tell anyone else, because it's all your fault."

Finally, privacy, that pearl of quiet and self-awareness. That's the most nuanced rule to explain. Kids need time to be on their own, to read, to play, to talk to themselves and their stuffed animals, to masturbate, to write, to daydream, to kick a can. And we, their parents, need the same. People who don't know how to have private moments of clarity are in a difficult spot to grow up.

When Aretha was fourteen, she came home from basketball practice with another girl, Lorraine, who was a year older than she. Lorraine looked so different from Aretha—physically mature, a head taller. But she followed behind my daughter like a younger sister.

Aretha took Lorraine's hand. "L's worried that she might be pregnant—and she can't tell her parents; they'll throw her out."

Lorraine pulled her hand back.

"I told her to come home with me, that you could help her." She turned back to Lorraine and took her arm again. "Really, it's going to be okay."

I looked at the two of them. I had not taken a girl to the free clinic for a pregnancy exam in nearly thirty years, since I was in *The Red Tide.*

I offered Lorraine a chair. "I'll help you; we both will," I said. "There's a clinic just down the street that will give you a checkup for free, totally private, and all the birth control or medical help you need. That's their main thing, helping teenagers and people who don't have their parents to turn to, or a lot of money."

Lorraine looked at me through her long blond hair. She had perfect eye makeup. I couldn't read her.

"Sweetie, we can do this right now, or tomorrow if you like." I wanted to bite my nails, but I didn't want to do that in front of her. "But I have to ask you . . . are you sure you can't tell your mom?" Because even if I wasn't getting along with Aretha, when it comes to something like this, I would want to be the first person on her side."

Lorraine shook her head vigorously.

"Your mom loves you—" I started.

"I don't know," she said. "Yeah, but not this. She couldn't handle it."

I said, "You know, we'll do this, and you'll get whatever you need, and next time you'll know how to do it on your own or with your lover. . . . But you will probably not get to know me—and I'll never get to know your parents—because I couldn't stand to get close to your mom and keep a secret like this.

"You might even be embarrassed to see me later on. . . . " I traced a pattern on her chair with my finger. "But maybe if you ever tell your mommy, like when you're thirty, you can call and tell me it's over, so I can exhale."

She laughed, the first time. "I'll *never* tell her!" As if, *And you and she would never be friends.*

We took Lorraine to the Planned Parenthood clinic. She turned out not to be pregnant, but she had pelvic inflammatory disease and anemia—along with four or five other things. The doctors weren't surprised. I was.

Aretha and Lorraine giggled over an enormous bag of condoms they were given at the end of the appointment. I looked inside the bag: "God, who's going to live long enough to use all these?"

My activism was always maternal, and I never knew it before Aretha. I knew the fight in me was creative, erotic, intellectual, historic—but I never knew it had a nurturing engine.

Motherhood is not for all. I wanted to be parented, very much—and I thought I wouldn't be good at parenting anyone else. It turned out to be the opposite: I could mother someone, even more than one—and it was like the balm that makes the burn go away. I turned out to have a thing for wearing aprons, and kissing tears away, and holding on tight.

AGING BADLY

I WASN'T READY FOR DEBI'S reaction the day she got cut from the Mitchell Brothers' club dancer schedule. After seven years of continuous stripping service for the most elite club in town, she did not see it coming—I don't think any veteran does.

I knew something bad had happened. She picked me up in her Saab and started gunning down Divisadero Street, through the Castro, barreling along Twenty-fourth, barely missing babies in strollers.

"What *is it?*" I asked. I wanted to grab her hand, but I was afraid to touch her.

"It's what I always told you; it's what I told *everyone:* They call you in, and you're telling them you don't want to work Wednesdays next month, and all of a sudden, they're like, 'Why don't you take a break; we don't have anything open right now.'"

"What does *that* mean?"

"Yeah, right! *What does it mean?* That's the temptation, to ask, like it's not dawning on you? And Vince is like, 'Maybe it's time for a change,' and then you're sitting there—"

"I don't understand, you've been making the same money you always have; you look exactly the same!" My attempt at comfort.

"That doesn't matter. They have a new lineup of eighteen-year-olds, and so it's snip, snip, snip at the other end." Debi rolled down all the windows. The wind was fierce.

"Red light!" I yelled at Folsom Street. I wondered if she had control of the door-locking mechanism as well.

We were waiting at the light. Some *vato*, his baseball cap low over his eyes, walked up to the car, leaned in on Debi's windowsill, and made a play:

"Where you goin' tonight, beautiful ladies?"

Debi didn't say one word to him. She took her cigarette out of her mouth, exhaled, and with one sweep of her hand crushed out the butt—on our visitor's forearm. He yanked his arm off the door just as the embers reached his short-and-curlies.

"Fuckin' bitch!" He stumbled onto the asphalt.

Deb flicked the fag on the ground and just sat there. The light turned green. "This is a setback," she said.

And that was the last rational word we had on the subject.

Debi set about marrying one of her customers from the O'Farrell. She was in love with the idea of pulling a fairytale ending out of a bag full of shit.

I could not follow her thinking. First of all, *marrying* some guy whom none of us knew meant breaking up with Nan, her real wife of the past decade, still her best friend, our business partner, the woman whom she relied upon every day. Nan was our rock.

This fellow had a contracting business and piles of money. Plus two "crazy" ex-wives who "didn't understand him sexually." Really? I know this is what the sex business is based on, but why do people marry other people whom they are sexually disgusted by? Why do people turn their lives upside down just to have an orgasm in peace, without humiliation? Does it have to cost so much?

The "groom" was offering to dig *OOB* out of its considerable hole. The magazine never made any money, our lesbian strip show benefits had their ups and downs, and the video money relied on keeping production going all the time, without a break. Our creative back was being broken, not to mention our credit and grocery bills.

And here, like a well-curried lamb, was a prince who was grateful that Debi let him enjoy a fetish or two in her arms. Welcome to the world of high finance.

I'm sure she was ready for anything. She'd read every business article and every issue of *Fortune,* and had watched as the flimsiest and most absurd ideas were funded with millions. But we were "girls." We were "whores." Making a sex magazine for "lesbians," whoever they were. When we stopped to look at the numbers, it was dismal. Nan came over to my desk one morning and whispered, "We are in dire financial straits. Debi is going off the deep end and my hands are sweating every night."

Debi's groom was supposed to be our knight in shining venture capital. But it didn't feel like good times. Debi hid in her room with her Marlboros and the wallpaper samples for her new Eichler-retro home remodel in Marin County. We needed her to go to press, and her response was, "If someone interrupts my wallpaper decision one more time, I'm shooting them."

I'd look at Nan, like, *How can we go on?* and she'd shake her head. We couldn't stop the train.

Debi asked me to be her maid of honor. She was agonizing about our dresses. I hadn't been to a wedding before; now I felt like I was stuck in the gum of a *Brides* magazine special issue.

We were lesbians, for goodness' sake. We didn't do this. We were feminists. We counseled, "Don't let the state be your pimp." Who gave a shit about a wedding to a goddamn john? I didn't say it out loud, but I talked to my own pillow in frank terms.

Aretha wasn't one year old yet when Debi was planning her wedding. I talked to my little one many nights, to calm her crying. I cranked her mechanical swing after it wound down, every fifteen minutes, and said, "There is a limit to how long this can go on."

Maybe the O'Farrell Theatre was giving Debi a bigger break than she realized. Art Mitchell had become so dangerously drunk and high by 1991 that he was carrying a pistol to all occasions and had just recently fired it at Mayes Oyster House on Polk Street, a block from the club.

It was a case of Dr. Jekyll and Mr. Hyde, to be sure. When I had first been pregnant, Artie and Jim had hugged me like a favorite niece. Art had told me with great earnestness how he'd chosen each of his children's names, and all his hopes and dreams for them. He cried easily. He brought cushions for my sore back and wanted to be reassured that I was going to have the best prenatal care in the city.

Now he was a terror. There wasn't a day that went by that he didn't threaten someone, quite convincingly, with bodily harm. He attacked our dear dancer Tamara on the staircase, called her a whore, and ripped her costume—and that was only *her* five minutes of his all-day rage.

Within a week, Tamara had made her successful suicide attempt—yes, the same Tamara with the faithless boyfriend. Her Plan B had fallen to pieces. She would never get old.

Tamara had been let down by her family, her fiancé, her insane boss—what was going to happen to Debi? None of this had been conceivable a month before.

Debi invited me over for supper, something we always liked to do. I could see how a meat loaf and two bottles of wine might loosen the lumps in our throats. I wanted to talk. But when I'd start, Debi would say, "Oh, you have to see where we're going to stay on the Russian River this summer." She'd get out the brochures and photos, talking as if we were taking a retreat from Condé Nast.

If my eyes brimmed with tears, if I tried to say one name, one note of what we'd witnessed over the past months, her mouth tensed. Her jaw flexed back and forth as if she were tasting the toad I'd turn into if I uttered One. More. Word.

I knew that warning strike all too well. *Oh, Debi, please don't lose it—come back, come back, wherever you are.* I bit my tongue and hoped for one little break, just one little something, that would save us.

The phone rang in the middle of the night on Wednesday, February 27. I was up anyway, with the baby and her tick-tock swing set. I kissed Aretha. "Please don't tell me another of our girls is in the ER."

It was a friend, Cherrie, from the O'Farrell. "Susie, Jim's shot Art."

"*What?* What do you mean? You mean Art's shot Jim? Where are you?"

"No, Jim has shot his brother. Artie's dead. . . . " Cherrie broke down in sobs.

Am I my brother's keeper?

The first thing that crossed my mind was *Jim will kill himself now.* I did not know, standing there in the dark, how such a thing could have happened. Self-defense? Planned attack? The most fucked-up Okie intervention ever gone awry? At 5:00 AM I knew only that these two men were Irish twins, and I couldn't imagine one living without the other.

The fratricide filled every news headline in the morning. Every prig in town expounded upon pornography's wages of sin. One brother killing his other half, his soul mate, was sensational enough—but add "hardcore" to it, and it was as if everyone in the sexual counterculture were on trial.

Reporters called me: "Did you see it coming? Were you pressured? Were you afraid? Did you get high with them, take it up the ass before the guns came out?"

Their questions were crazy because they all assumed that sex had led to violence. Not despair, not religion, not the empty bottle of abandonment. It was the unraveling of a family knot that should have been all too familiar to those who have watched one half of their kin destroy the other and will never be able to put it all back together again.

I remembered the look on my mother's face when she admitted her sister Frannie had died. Her fingers fretted over and over on our kitchen table, as if on piano keys. She was too afraid to tell me Frannie's death was by a rope. I could see that old photograph of her sister, torn to pieces, then tearfully patched with yellow tape. But the tape didn't save Frannie. The threats and Band-Aids didn't save Art. It was so late in the game. The casualties just kept coming.

Debi called me at 10:00 AM. I didn't try to hide my crying this time. "I can't hear you—bad connection," she said. "I'm calling because you'd better be on time for the fitting."

"*What* fitting?" I looked at the receiver like I'd been slapped.

"We are fitting the bridesmaids' dresses today in Sausalito, as I told you last week three times, and if you can't pull yourself together—*tappity tap tap*—I'm just going to have to call my sister in Minneapolis and see if she can do this without being a complete idiot."

There we were—our revolutionary dreams crushed by prejudice; our friends losing their jobs, their identity, and their lives, strung out, crazy. Comrades whom we thought were immortal were shooting each other, and Debi was going to ream me if I didn't get a dress zipped up.

I caved in. I moved through her fittings, her wedding, in a trance. Margie didn't go. She told me, "Don't go to weddings on boats. You can't get off a boat."

Debi left for her honeymoon the day after her bridal party. I took four loads of laundry down the street to the Giant Wash-O-Mat. I was like a baby about to get the natal veil lifted from her eyes.

Maybe it came from lifting my own infant every day. It was a pleasure to wake with Aretha, to join her in the evenings, but I felt like I was going to crack, like I couldn't do the fifty hours at *OOB* and pick Aretha up from childcare downtown and then go home—the two of us—and just *maintain*. I was so tired. I could cry at the shake of a diaper pail.

I'd sit there, without any dinner for myself, nursing in the rocker, hypnotized by *Star Trek: The Next Generation*—the high point of my day.

I had one real baby. I could not carry on with another surrogate baby, the magazine. It was too much. *OOB* was insecure, and Aretha needed to be secure. It was plain. I remember going to the kitchen one night and deliberately lighting a candle on both ends to take a photo of what I was doing to myself. The metaphor was on target. My fingertips started to singe.

WHEN I CAME BACK FROM MY HONEYMOON

WHEN DEBI WENT ON HER honeymoon, I could finally think. The *OOB* workload was still enormous, the bills daunting, my postpartum health shitty—but the great relief of not humoring Bridezilla was a tonic. No tiptoeing around, no fragile egg that might turn into a grenade. My lungs filled with air.

I still felt guilty—shitty that I was in thrall to such a beautiful woman, but that I couldn't stand her requirements any longer. With Debi out of town, I could at least say it out loud. Did she know we were saying goodbye? I still had her little notes to me on my old *OOB* production binders: *"I love you—D."* I couldn't look at them.

Walking home from the subway one day, I got a slice of almond cake at Dianda's Italian bakery. I wanted cake and a carton of cold milk—that sticky almond paste, raspberry jam, and milky swallow. It must have had a magic bean inside.

I licked the last of the powdered sugar off my fingers and thought, *This reminds me of when my dad picked me up at the airport in Vancouver and everything was going to change.* Reality could look very, very different.

I called Nan that night from bed. I said, "You know, this thing of getting up at dawn to get Aretha to childcare and then picking her up after the sun goes down just isn't working. And I can't be the 'part-time' editor of *On Our Backs.* The rubber band has snapped."

"I know, it's been pretty tough. . . . " I could hear Nan's sympathetic cluck.

"I want to find a successor. I want to know that within a year, someone else will be doing this—you know, all these dreamers who write us saying they want to be 'guest editor,' let's put one of them behind the wheel."

"How long have you been thinking this?" Nan asked. She wasn't chuckling at my joke. "Have you told Debi? I don't know!"

"I just had this moment when I realized I've been wanting to 'say the unsayable,' but it seemed like I couldn't add to the dog pile . . . and now it's finally quiet. For a week. I want to tell Debi as soon as she comes back. But I want to tell you *now.* You're not crazy; you're my partner. I feel like I'm bursting. I want to hire a new editor. I want to find someone wonderful."

"What is Debi going to say?"

"Well, what do *you* say? I mean, I have no idea; she's always the one who says at any moment she could retire and devote herself to ballet. It's like listening to Zelda Fitzgerald."

I could hear Nan's fingers rubbing something. "I just don't know . . . I just don't know." Her tongue clicked against the roof of her mouth.

I told Nan not to worry and to let me know as soon as Debi got home, and we'd meet up.

I talked to Jon later in bed, the blanket over my head. "Nan's scared of her—the way I'm always intimidated by her—but we can't go on like this, with Debi the scariest part of the whole enterprise."

Later that night, I woke up when Aretha woke up. I looked at her long lashes and blew on them until they shut. She was my True North, and she didn't even know it. If I just did the right thing for her, then I would end up doing the thing I should have been doing in the first place.

I never got my chance to deliver my Almond Cake Realization to Debi. I didn't see her the night she flew in. I came home from work, nursed Aretha, and conked out in a coma myself, half dressed. Jon let himself in after dark, just off his cab-driving shift. I could feel him pulling off my jeans and rolling me over like a jelly doughnut under the flannel sheets. "Humph." I never opened my eyes.

My door didn't have a bell; it had a loud brass knocker. People who knew me just rattled their knuckles on the wood. But at 3:00 AM, *bam bam bam* went the knocker, like the Devil himself was paying a visit. I stumbled over a squeaky toy; Jon was right behind me.

I opened the door and there was a young man in a suit coat, a blue tie, and purple trousers.

"Are you Susannah Bright?"

Shades of Mrs. MacKenzie and Garneau Junior High. "Yeah?" I said.

"You've been served," he said, chucking a sheaf of papers at me and turning to skip down the stairs.

I looked at the document and saw only a few phrases I understood: "Debi Sundahl . . . on behalf of Blush Entertainment . . . suing Susannah Bright . . . fiduciary duty."

What time was it, exactly? Well, if it was going to be an all-night party, I was going to start waking people up, too.

I called Nan. "Debi has just served me with papers . . . it says you're suing me. Is this you, too? What the fuck!"

Nan could barely talk. I could hear her wringing her hands; it was like a Pontius Pilate sound effect. "She made me tell her; she doesn't understand," she kept saying. "I'm sure we can work something out." She sounded worse than I did.

Debi's position demanded that I never write again and said that whatever I did do for a living, I would have to pay her 20 percent of my earnings because I had abandoned my "corporate" duties. Given that all three of us had done everything except give blood to *On Our Backs* for the past seven years, it was hard to imagine what the rhetoric referred to.

The next week was my last one in our editorial offices. Debi took down all my artwork from the office and disappeared with it. My old Mac disappeared from my desk.

On Friday, she confronted me with a box that had arrived in the office mail from the Mitchell Brothers O'Farrell Theatre with my name on it.

"What is this *bullshit?*" she asked. "You're going to open this in front of me, right now."

I had no idea what it was. In my mind, I was thinking, *Something from someone who's died.* It looked like a brick. I didn't touch it. I didn't know what she might do.

She tore off the thick cardboard flap. Two small framed photographs fell to the floor, with a note from Jeff at the O'Farrell Theatre: "Jim thought you would want these." We'd taken the photos years before, when the Anti-Porn-Feminist-Whomever had accused *On Our Backs* of running a white-slavery ring out of the Mitchell Brothers dungeon. I'd been in Artie and Jim's poolroom one day, opening some hate mail, and had said, "Why don't we make a parody of this? Let's do a tableau where I'm some horrified prisoner of your evil empire." Our staff photographer Jill Posener grabbed her camera. I posed Jim to look as if he were going to putt a golf ball into my vagina as I lay spread-eagled on the floor, in leather fetish wear, while I asked Artie to hold up my head by my ponytail so I could shoot a look of open-mouthed horror into the camera's eye.

On top of the photo, we wrote a caption in black Sharpie: *"Contrary to the rumors!"*

Debi stared at the photos she'd dropped on the rug.

"You know what I remember most about that photo shoot?" I asked. "Artie was worried that he was pulling my hair."

"*Anything* that comes into this office belongs to the corporation," Debi said, and walked into her office and slammed the door. Her wallpaper samples were strewn all over the shipping tables.

I didn't know what to do next. I wasn't leaving *OOB* for another job. I didn't have one. Of course, I had the same freelance stuff I'd been doing all along. I was the only one of the three of us who worked outside of *OOB* to pay my bills. But there was no sudden call to fame; no one had asked me to sell my Rolodex and become a lesbian superstar. There *were* no lesbian superstars. At that time, Ellen DeGeneres was inconceivable.

My reason for quitting—motherhood—was a truthful reckoning except for one thing: my anxiety about Debi. I didn't want to work with her, this new apparition. I couldn't keep "painting the roses red" every day.

Yet for all Debi's delusions, I could blame only myself—because I never said, "Enough!" There was always some part of me that believed her, that believed we really would run away and become ballerinas, and her husband would pay everyone's bills, and Steve Jobs was going to be our best friend, and there was big money in being lesbian pornographers, and . . . I just kept playing through.

If she could have sued me for being a gutless, codependent, naive nail-biter, she would have had ample cause.

I needed a lawyer. Of all people, my male-chauvinist neighbor, Mr. Hera, counseled me. "Anyone can sue you for anything, no matter how preposterous, and if you don't sue back, they win." He gave me the name of his lawyer, Ron Murri, who worked in one of those Montgomery Street skyscrapers that I hadn't seen since I worked as a temp my first year in San Francisco.

I rode the elevator up to the top floor with three men who looked like John Gotti. I was probably leaking milk in my lavender wifebeater. I had never been to an attorney's office before; my only context was television, and Murri's suite lived up to the celluloid dream. Everything was massive, mahogany; gorgeous, quiet women dashed around getting things for talkative men in suits.

My new attorney listened to my tale of woe and handed me a Kleenex box. He was very experienced. As I talked and cried, he looked through my copies of *On Our Backs* that I'd brought him and burst out laughing. In delight.

I knew that laugh—it was one of the reasons I loved doing *On Our Backs:* because people who'd never seen it before had their minds blown. I knew that my magazine was the most interesting forty-eight pages of anything in his entire multimillion-dollar office.

It took Ron a while to realize the state of our assets: minus zero. The cash flow: nonexistent. Everything was based on potential. Our second distributor had just gone out of business, writing off five figures in debt to us. We hadn't paid the rent in months, and the printer was holding our film hostage. I was one fewer mouth to feed. I would never get back the money I had put into the business.

I didn't care; I just didn't want this psychotic tin can attached to my tail for the rest of my life. *Never write again?* No way.

Debi had sent a message through her lawyer that perhaps my writing "fiction" would be allowed—with attendant extortion, of course. I'd had no idea she thought of me as such a cash cow. I certainly hadn't done anything to warrant it.

Ron moved the tissue box off the desk between us and folded his hands on the table. "Ms. Bright, I'm going to take care of this for you."

"I haven't even asked you what this is going to cost. I just have to—"

"No, not at all. I am going to take care of this myself. Don't think another thing about it."

"But what—"

He just shook his head and waved his hand at me, as if a small child had tried to pick up a bar tab. "It's going to be fine. Forget about it."

"How can you be so sure?" I wanted to believe him so badly. But that was what had gotten me into trouble with Debi in the first place.

"I will tell you why," Mr. Murri said, glancing at his watch and then looking straight into my eyes. "Because one day your adversary will have a bigger problem than you—and when that day comes, she won't be able to get rid of you fast enough."

IT WAS TIME TO DO the laundry again. I had five loads and a giant bag of quarters that I was going to let Aretha play with while I cleaned every last rag. It was a foggy day in the Mission, and I was walking around the corner for a candy bar when I ran into Spain Rodriguez, my neighbor and *Zap Comix* cartoonist friend from down the block.

"Hey, baby," he said, giving me a big hug. He didn't know about *On Our Backs*. He had some flyers in his hand. "Do you know anyone who wants to swap pads and live in southern France for a few months?"

I had to burst out laughing. "Yeah, me! I don't have a job anymore, and I don't know what I'm doing next."

I called Spain's French American friend, Maureen, who was part of a minuscule American expat community in France that consisted of retirees from COYOTE, the first prostitutes' rights organization, and other *Zap* artists, like Robert Crumb and Gilbert Shelton. It turned out that Maureen knew Honey Lee from waitressing back in the day. Now she needed a house swap so she could care for her American parents and finish a novel. Her home in Languedoc was part of a tenth-century stone fort, alone among miles and miles of farmland and vineyards. I felt a little guilty that all she got in exchange was my freeway-adjacent cottage across the street from a twenty-four-hour gas station.

Maureen's fort was quiet for an American like me with a little baby. On those rare occasions when I met people who spoke English, I knew they must've hailed from North Beach in the sixties.

I worked on a book. I charmed my neighbors with "pancakes" and my little angel, Aretha. I'd draw coal up from the "cave" under the fort to heat a stove every night, and the Mistral blew through and chilled the fort's stone walls until they were like blocks of ice. Eventually, I got pneumonia. The French midwives in our village came to my bed and gave me shots in the butt. I got better. If there was ever a case of the kindness of strangers . . . I was deeply grateful to the many new friends I made. Little Romper grew up fast. I loved her so much.

One day, I got a long-distance phone call from my attorney's exquisite assistant in San Francisco. "They're settling today. Ron just went to court to sign the papers; you're all done," she said.

"What happened?" I asked. "What's going on?"

"Ms. Sundahl is apparently in Marin County jail, booked on assault charges."

I faxed a friend, Sukie, who had sold red-haired bud to Debi's dear husband back in their courtship days. Debi never touched the stuff.

Sukie faxed me back: "OMG! Yeah, he cheated on her, all the time . . . and when she found out, she beat the living shit out of him. I heard her mother is driving from Minnesota to come get her and take her home."

Take Debi home? It had been so long since I had thought of her Minnesota origins. What had happened to her son, whom she had spoken of the first day we'd met? He must be a teenager now. Where was he? She loved him so much.

I rocked Aretha and watched a *Star Trek* rerun. My phone rang, but I didn't pick it up. I could hear the cassette tape taking the message: "Yeah, Susie, this is Gina's girlfriend. Listen, I don't know what you heard, but Debi and her old man got in a big fight. He left the house but he came back and found her in the pool about to slit her wrists with razors and he took her to Marin General and they put her in the psych ward and wouldn't let her out until someone took responsibility for her; then her mom—"

The tape cut off. There was no dress for it, no fitting end. I could see Debi's mother, her car wheels spinning on the highway, cigarettes in her purse, taking her curly-haired woman-child away from all of this, back to where she came from, back to all that snow—and something else, something I'd never figure out.

SANTA CRUZ

Stupendous and unheard-of splendors await me below, and I shall seek them soon.

—H. P. Lovecraft

WHEN I CAME BACK TO the States, I got an interesting offer. My old faculty adviser from UC Santa Cruz, Carter Wilson, called me and said, "We're so proud of you. The community studies department wants to know if you'd like to come teach a class for summer session. What would you like to do?"

Wow. I thought about it. I loved the road show I'd been touring, "How to Read a Dirty Movie," which was inspired by Vito Russo's *Celluloid Closet*. I decided I'd love to do an extended version of erotic forensics.

"Ten weeks is a session, right?" I asked. "I want to do something like . . . the "Politics of Sexual Representation." Yeah! I don't want to use cheap code words anymore, like *erotic* or *pornographic*. I want to make students figure out what we're really saying when we look at sex."

Carter loved the idea. The department loved it. I called Jon and started talking up Santa Cruz in glowing terms. "I was bored silly when I was an undergrad there," I told him, "because I didn't want to jump in the waves or hug a tree; I just wanted to run to another all-night meeting in San Francisco."

Jon laughed, and I could hear him flop down on his bed. "Yeah, I bet you just can't wait to get your arms around a tree now."

What mother of a four-year-old wouldn't agree? I didn't want to stay up late anymore; I wanted to sit in the sun and watch Aretha chase seagulls. I could write a syllabus for a class I'd always dreamed of while I basked in the sun and sand.

Jon and I started packing. We decided to live together for real—no more keeping barely separate households. We kept whispering to each other, "It's ten degrees warmer down there." I could feel the sun on my shoulders already.

Two days before the moving trucks came, I got another phone call from Carter.

"Susie, something awful has happened. The dean of our division, Murray Sabre, has just written the department a memo, saying"—I could hear Carter shuffling papers—"'Susie Bright will only teach at the University of California *over my dead body.*'"

What did the dean of the social sciences division have against me? I recalled he was an antiwar leftie back in the day, the kind of guy I had met a million times in the IS. Was he just like Kitty and Andrea, a leftie George Putnam, enraged by "the dirtiest thing" he could imagine me presenting in a classroom? Would I perhaps hold up a picture of "a woman's private parts"?

I couldn't bear to tell Jon or any of my San Francisco friends. The moving-van wheels were in motion. We'd already broken our backs carrying a 1905 upright piano down two flights of stairs. We had to go forward.

I drove down to Santa Cruz on my own, along the scenic coastline of Highway 1, always a meditation on California enchantment. Dark blue waves, deep ravines, wildflowers everywhere, rocky cliffs like castles. My dad knew the history of every Indian creek and mountain name from here to the coast of Mexico.

It's a road made for singing, and I was belting out "Always True to You in My Fashion," when an enormous tan buck jumped in front of me just north of La Honda Road. I saw the white of his deer eye; he saw the white of my human eye. I hit the brakes hard, and everything in the van came crashing toward my head. *Don't swerve, don't swerve*—that's what they always tell you—*take the beast head-on.*

The buck, floating in the air, came down, glanced off the right side of my bumper, and kept bounding. He was alive! I was alive! The front seat was buried under every fragment of loose belongings we'd stuffed in the back. My head was wet, I hoped with sweat.

No one was behind me—the luckiest bit of enchantment yet. I put my foot back on the gas, accelerated to twenty, twenty-five, thirty miles per hour. Maybe that was the way to do it, slow and easy, counting each artichoke in the fields as I passed.

When I got to the Santa Cruz apartment we were subletting, there was a crayon note on the door, from one of the assistants in the community studies department:

Sad News/Glad News! Murray S. has had a heart attack and will NOT be returning to campus anytime soon. Class is ON. See you next Monday—bring everything.

Aretha came running out of the apartment with Jon, who'd arrived earlier in a separate truck. She had a red plastic bottle of soap bubbles in her hands, shouting, "Look at this, Mommy. Look!" She blew a bubble the size of my head. A pair of lungs to be proud of.

It really was ten degrees warmer in Santa Cruz. I looked up at Jon. "You would not believe what happened on the way down here—twice. You're going to forget all about carrying that piano."

"Even the water's softer here," he said, holding up a pile of sheets. "And there's a surfboard in the garage."

"Do you have to drive back the city tonight?" I asked. I felt like I could sit on this stoop for a while, maybe until "Porno 101" began on Monday.

A white goose, don't ask me from where, waddled across the front lawn ten feet in front of me. Every animal familiar was greeting me. I was Saint Francis, and they were all paying me a little hello.

"Yeah, I'm working tonight," he said, standing in a flurry of Aretha's bubble making. "I'll drive back tomorrow. And then—"

"Yes, *then!*" I said, opening my arms wide to the sky for a mountain lion appearance, a bear, some coyote scat.

Jon said, "Yes, then, I think, we can start the rest of our lives."

One of Aretha's iridescent soap bubbles floated toward my face. I stuck my finger in it. The surface tension was just strong enough that it went all the way around my finger and never popped.

NOTES

THE RED TIDE and *On Our Backs* were significant publications with hundreds of people involved over many years, dozens of whom were my close friends and colleagues.

For my narrative purposes, I have changed the names of many people who never became public figures. I also made composite characters out of individuals who each deserve their own special edition. Time was greatly compressed in this story, and snapshots have been taken of long campaigns. I hope many of the figures I remember from these years will add their own memoirs and biographies to our history.

The histories of *The Red Tide* and *On Our Backs* are not well documented.

For research purposes, the best place to look at *The Red Tide* is an Internet archive of all the back issues and relevant documents, which Michael Letwin has curated. You will find it at http:// theredtide.wordpress.com.

For *On Our Backs,* there are university libraries, such as Brown University's, that have a complete collection of back issues. There is the book *Nothing but the Girl,* the photographic homage to *OOB* photographers that Jill Posener and I edited. Jill's and my notes and audiotape interviews with all the *OOB* photographers are archived at the San Francisco Lesbian and Gay History Project. Debi Sundahl and Nan Kinney's video company, Fatale Video, made several erotic videos in the eighties and nineties that document the *On Our Backs* heyday, including live documentaries of the first lesbian burlesque shows: www.fatalemedia.com.

PHOTO CREDITS

THE TIME HAS COME, THE WALRUS SAID: Girl Scout. Sierra Madre, CA, 1968.

THE BUNNY TRIP: Cover of the *University High School Warrior* newspaper. Los Angeles, CA, 1973.

THE CHURNING MIST: Front and back cover of first issue of *The Red Tide*. Los Angeles, CA, 1970.

SWIM BANQUET: *Red Tide* "List of Demands." Los Angeles, CA, 1973.

GEORGE PUTNAM'S SHOW: Susie and Michael Letwin speaking to press at L.A. Board of Ed at a rally to "Protest Police Sweeps, Get Cops Off Campus." Los Angeles, CA, 1974. Photo by Joel Levine.

SEX EDUCATION: Susie and Danielle on first acid trip, Cal Jam 1 rock concert. Ontario, CA, 1974.

YOU ARE NOW A CADRE: Nixon impeachment demo. MacArthur Park, Los Angeles, CA, 1974. Photo by Joel Levine.

PATTY HEARST: Bullet-hole at the scene of the LAPD SWAT squad shootout with the Symbionese Liberation Army in Compton, CA. The surrounding quiet working class neighborhood was turned into a battle zone. *The Red Tide* covered the story from the neighbors' point of view. Photo by Joel Levine.

DAGO ARMOUR'S APARTMENT: Misty's corral, the informal gathering place for Beverly Glen teenagers in the early 1970s, Los Angeles, CA.

NEW BRANCH ORGANIZER: *Red Tide*-inspired Graffiti, "Don't Fergit to S.C.O.R.E.," (Student Crazies Rapidly Organizing Everywhere), University High School, Los Angeles, CA, 1971. Photo by Joel Levine.

THE MASTER FREIGHT AGREEMENT: Tattered flag, Lynwood, CA, 1975.

GREYHOUND TO DETROIT VIA AMARILLO: Susie asleep on bus to Delano, CA, 1974. Photo by Joel Levine.

THE AORTA: *Red Tide* march to support Angola's seventeen-year-old prisoner, Gary Tyler. Detroit, MI, 1975.

COMMIE CAMP: At work in IS newspaper production office. Detroit, MI, 1975.

RELOCATION: Taking a spin in John Everett's Grand-dad's car, Louisville, KY, 1976. Photo by John Everett.

THE PERFUME COUNTER: Taking a drive. Louisville, KY, 1976. Photo by John Everett.

EXPULSION: Susie the night before IS expulsion convention, at Christina Bergmark's apartment, Louisville, KY, 1976. Photo by John Everett.

SCHOOL DAYS: University of California, Santa Cruz. 1979.

HOW I GOT INTRODUCED TO *ON OUR BACKS*: *On Our Backs* office. San Francisco, CA, 1986. Photo by Jill Posener.

THE FEMINIST VIBRATOR STORE: Women in Print conference. Berkeley, CA, 1985. Photo by Cookie Hunt.

THE BABY SHOWERS: Laurie "Raven" Parker and Mary "Cassie" Gottschalk, modeling for *On Our Backs*. San Francisco, CA, 1985. Photo by Honey Lee Cottrell.

MODELS CRYING: Susie in front of graffiti at Van Ness Boulevard and Fifteenth Street. San Francisco, CA, 1984. Photo by Honey Lee Cottrell.

LES BELLES DAMES SANS MERCI: Susie and Caitlin Morgan in promotional still from their play *Knife Paper Scissors*. San Francisco, CA, 1983. Photo by Honey Lee Cottrell.

THE DADDIES: Susie, Scott Worley, and Tede Matthews, Castro Theatre gay film festival. San Francisco, CA, 1983. Photo by Greg Day.

MOTHERHOOD: Aretha and Susie. San Francisco, CA, 1991. Photo by Honey Lee Cottrell.

ROTATION: Jon Bailiff and Susie. San Francisco, CA, 1993. Photo by Jill Posener.

AGING BADLY: *OOB* satire for our fifth-anniversary issue, "A Day in the Life of *On Our Backs.*" San Francisco, CA, 1989. Photo by Phyllis Christopher.

WHEN I CAME BACK FROM MY HONEYMOON: Susie at Golden Gate Park, San Francisco, CA. Photo by Honey Lee Cottrell.

SANTA CRUZ: Aretha's lunch bag illustration. Santa Cruz, CA, 1995. Illustration by Jon Bailiff.

ACKNOWLEDGMENTS

I'd like to thank the following family members, friends, and colleagues who contributed so much to this book with their insight, memories, and support: Kim Anno, Jon Bailiff, Larry Blood, Larry Bradshaw, Aretha Bright, Honey Lee Cottrell, Greta Christina, Donna Galassi, Ariel Gore, Judy Grahn, Andy Griffin and Julia Wiley, Rebecca Hall, Steve Harsin, Nan Kinney, Michael Letwin and family, Joel Levine, Jessica Lockhart, Chris Mark, Lise Menn and family, Caitlin Morgan, Jill Posener, Shar Rednour, Nora Reichard, Gayle Rubin, Cory Silverberg, Jane Slaughter, Brooke Warner, Barbara Winslow, Jill Wolfson, and my agents, Jo-Lynne Worley and Joanie Shoemaker.

ABOUT THE AUTHOR

© Shmuel Thaler

SUSIE BRIGHT is the author of national bestsellers, *Full Exposure* and *The Sexual State of the Union*—as well as *The Best American Erotica* and *Herotica* series, which ushered in women's erotic publishing. She the host of Audible's *In Bed With Susie Bright*, the beloved and longest-running sex-ed show in the history of broadcasting. She was co-founder and editor of *On Our Backs* magazine, and was the first journalist to cover erotic cinema and the porn business in the mainstream press. A progenitor of the sex-positive movement, Bright taught the first university course on pornography, and brought lasting sexual influence to her role in films like *Bound* and *The Celluloid Closet*.

SELECTED TITLES FROM SEAL PRESS

For more than thirty years, Seal Press has published
groundbreaking books. By women. For women.

NO EXCUSES: 9 WAYS WOMEN CAN CHANGE HOW WE THINK ABOUT POWER, BY GLORIA FELDT. $24.95, 978-1-58005-328-0. From the board-room to the bedroom, public office to personal relationships, feminist icon Gloria Feldt offers women the tools they need to walk through the doors of opportunity and achieve parity with men.

AFFECTION: AN EROTIC MEMOIR, BY KRISSY KNEEN. $16.95, 978-1-58005-342-6. A powerful, explicit, and sexy account of an extraordinarily sensual woman's experiences with sex, from adolescence to adulthood, and an examination of how her sense of self shapes and is shaped by those experiences.

FULL FRONTAL FEMINISM: A YOUNG WOMAN'S GUIDE TO WHY FEMINISM MATTERS, BY JESSICA VALENTI. $15.95, 978-1-58005-201-6. A sassy and in-your-face look at contemporary feminism for women of all ages.

MARRYING GEORGE CLOONEY: CONFESSIONS FROM A MIDLIFE CRISIS, BY AMY FERRIS. $16.95, 978-1-58005-297-9. In this candid look at menopause, Amy Ferris chronicles every one of her funny, sad, hysterical, down and dirty, and raw to the bones insomnia-fueled stories.

THE CHELSEA WHISTLE: A MEMOIR, BY MICHELLE TEA. $15.95, 978-1-58005-239-9. In this gritty, confessional memoir, Michelle Tea takes the reader back to the city of her childhood: Chelsea, Massachusetts—Boston's ugly, scrappy little sister and a place where time and hope are spent on things not getting any worse.

CUNT: A DECLARATION OF INDEPENDENCE, BY INGA MUSCIO. $14.95, 978-1-58005-075-3. "An insightful, sisterly, and entertaining exploration of the word and the part of the body it so bluntly defines. Ms. Muscio muses, reminisces, pokes into history and emerges with suggestions for the understanding of—and reconciliation with—what it means to have a cunt."—Roberta Gregory, author of *Naughty Bitch*

Find Seal Press Online
www.SealPress.com
www.Facebook.com/SealPress
Twitter: @SealPress